THE KEYNESIAN REVOLUTION AND ITS CRITICS

By the same author

THE DISCOUNT HOUSES IN LONDON: Principles, Operations and Change

The Keynesian Revolution and its Critics

Issues of Theory and Policy for the Monetary Production Economy

Gordon A. Fletcher
Lecturer in Economics
The University of Liverpool

Palgrave Macmillan

ISBN 978-1-349-08738-9 ISBN 978-1-349-08736-5 (eBook)
DOI 10.1007/978-1-349-08736-5

Softcover reprint of the hardcover 1st edition 1987

 For information, write:
Scholarly & Reference Division,
St. Martin's Press Inc., 175 Fifth Avenue, New York, NY 10010

First published in the United States of America in 1987

ISBN 978-0-312-45260-5

Library of Congress Cataloging-in-Publication Data
Fletcher, Gordon A., 1942–
The Keynesian revolution and its critics.
Bibliography: p.
Includes index.
1. Keynesian economics. 2. Chicago school of economics. 3. Austrian school of economists.
I. Title.
HB99.7.F57 1986 330.15′6 86–13741
ISBN 978-0-312-45260-5

For Laurence and Richard

Contents

Preface

Economist, statesman, Cambridge don, author and journalist, patron of the arts; John Maynard Keynes (1883–1946) was a man of many parts and one of the foremost Englishmen of his generation. The revolution he produced in economic theory transformed our understanding of the working of a modern economy and offered the hope of prosperity in a free society.

It is fitting that a book which seeks to explain and justify the Keynesian Revolution and to defend Keynes against his critics should appear on this the fiftieth anniversary of the publication of the work that brought Keynesian economics into being, *The General Theory of Employment, Interest and Money*.

That it has been possible for my book to make its timely appearance owes much to the willing co-operation and assistance I have received from others, and I wish to record my grateful thanks to the following: Mr T. M. Farmiloe, my editor, for his patience during somewhat extended period of writing the book; Vivienne Oakes, who cheerfully typed successive drafts of a lengthy manuscript amid a daily round of other commitments; Mr Keith Povey, for his editorial skills in preparing the manuscript for publication; The Royal Economic Society, for kindly allowing me to quote extensively from *The Collected Writings of John Maynard Keynes*; my family, for their understanding and support throughout. I reserve to myself responsibility for the conclusions reached, views expressed and errors that remain.

The University of Liverpool GORDON A. FLETCHER

Introduction

It is just fifty years since the publication of what is arguably the single most influential work of economics of the twentieth century, John Maynard Keynes's *The General Theory of Employment, Interest and Money*.[1] In this book Keynes set out his revolutionary new theory of the macroeconomy in which the equilibrium level of output and employment was made a function of the level of effective demand, which was itself determined at the point of equilibrium between aggregate supply and aggregate demand. Because there could be no presumption that in a *laissez-faire* economy effective demand would be at a level consistent with the full employment of resources, economic theory now recognised a legitimate place for state intervention to supply any deficiency.

The contrast with the orthodox 'classical' economics, which provided a theory of the market economy founded ultimately upon Say's Law, was complete. Classical economics envisaged only a unique, full employment, equilibrium, and as against Keynes's 'general' theory was relegated to serving as a theory of this special case.

But in addition to providing an explanation of why economies might experience marked fluctuations in employment, Keynes's analysis also raised a terrifying longer-term prospect – that of chronic stagnation. Because Keynes postulated that the return from new investment would fall as the capital stock grew in size, its inability to fall beyond some low level determined by a 'sticky' rate of interest would bring investment to a halt. If in such circumstances the desire to save remained positive, the level of income would have to fall to give saving–investment equilibrium at a low level of output and employment. Therefore, because all economies which became capital-rich stood to 'suffer the fate of Midas' it was, again, to the state that they must look for their salvation.

The practical effect of Keynes's new theory was to provide a rationale for the policy measures to relieve unemployment which were then being advocated among economists of all persuasions (with isolated but notable exceptions) but which could not be justified on the basis of the orthodox theory to which the generality of economists subscribed.

The significance of this in contemporary terms was immense. For the danger was that *ad hoc* policies of moderate intervention would, in the absence of a proper theoretical underpinning, be overtaken by the extremist solutions of left and right to which much of Europe had already succumbed.

But the *General Theory* had longer-term significance. Confounding its critics the book rapidly conquered professional opinion and established Keynesian economics as the orthodoxy of the following four decades. It also provided the main inspiration for policy-makers, who were able to preside over an era of such outstanding economic achievement, in employment, growth and relative stability of the price level, that it appears in retrospect as a Golden Age.

At last, however, the 'Great Prosperity', the boom years as sceptics have seen them, came to an end, and as the national economy sank into the 'stagflationary' quagmire of the 1970s, so the economics profession became increasingly divided – between the shrinking band of defenders of the Keynesian Revolution on the one hand and the growing multitude of its critics, both monetarist and Austrian, on the other.

What went wrong? Critics of the Keynesian Revolution have in general based their case on arguments which can be summarised in one or both of the following propositions: (i) that Keynes's theoretical analysis is fundamentally in error and so cannot yield the policy inferences commonly drawn from it; (ii) that a policy prescription that accords to government a major role in the conduct of economic affairs is ultimately unworkable in a democratic society and so cannot constitute a viable policy option.

In the following chapters we shall critically examine these propositions in the light of Keynes's own work in order both (i) to explain what the Keynesian Revolution was, why it took place and what it achieved, and (ii) to assess the extent to which Keynesian principles remain valid and, therefore, despite the problems of the 1970s, relevant to our current condition.

The exegetical and critical literature relating to Keynesian economics is vast and no attempt will be made to provide a comprehensive survey. Instead, the case against Keynes will be judged by reference to the specific arguments of his principal critics, whom we identify as: (i) Sir Dennis Robertson, the leading loanable funds theorist and Keynes's colleague and former collaborator at Cambridge; (ii) Professor Milton Friedman, the founder of modern monetarism and leader of the 'counter-revolution' in monetary theory; (iii) Professor

F. A. Hayek, leader of the modern Austrian school and an opponent of Keynesianism since the 1930s, whose views were eclipsed by the Keynesian Revolution but who returned to prominence in the 1970s; (iv) (vicariously) Georg Simmel, the nineteenth-century German sociologist whose views on money and individual liberty have been made the centrepiece of an attack on the public morality and destructive potential of Keynesian monetary policy. By adopting this approach we obviate criticism that Keynes was only attacking a classical 'straw man', for the critics can be seen as the embodiment of the (neo-) classical ideas and assumptions from which Keynes struggled to escape.

As for references to Keynes's own work we shall, because of the fundamental change of direction his thought underwent in the 1930s, reply to the critics and make the case for Keynes on the basis of the text of the *General Theory* and the body of articles, letters and notes which marked the controversy to which its publication gave rise.[2]

The question of the continuing relevance of the Keynesian Revolution is given added point by the events of recent years. For the apparent failure of Keynesianism and the disenchantment with the interventionist economic policy which was its central feature, provoked a political reaction which swept to power a government resolutely committed to the re-establishment of the 'enterprise culture' and the market economy, with the activities of government strictly contained by the observance of rules of monetary discipline. From 1979 economic policy was based on monetarist/Austrian principles and saw as its primary objective the defeat of inflation, in the belief that monetary certainty would provide the framework within which 'real' forces would generate inflation-free (voluntary-unemployment) full employment.

In the result, the problem of inflation has been reduced to relatively modest proportions, but the age of monetary discipline has also seen unemployment rise inexorably to levels historically high in absolute terms and the highest since the 1930s as a proportion of the labour force.

While economic performance is often, like the curate's egg, good and bad in parts, and while it was expected that the cost of reducing inflation would involve a transition period marked by (possibly heavy) unemployment, the most obvious feature of our present condition is that the 'real' economy has shown no concerted tendency to behave in the predicted manner by moving towards equilibrium at full employment.

There may, of course, be many explanations for this outcome but it does at least raise the question of whether the economy is capable, unaided, of achieving anything approaching full employment. For underlying current economic policy is a theoretical model which is based upon what are essentially the same assumptions as those which sustained the classical orthodoxy of the 1930s, against which Keynes delivered his attack.

Therefore, the question which must be asked is, if the full-employment objective is to have a high ranking in the order of economic priorities, will its achievement require the substantial intervention of the state, in the conscious management and purposive direction of key aspects of economic activity?

Lest, however, it be thought that we are posing here a simple choice between collectivism and individual liberty, we must be absolutely clear that Keynes believed that in the face of prolonged heavy unemployment Keynesian principles were not an alternative to but a *necessary condition for* the survival of capitalism and the personal freedom and democratic system of government which are its concomitants. Keynes did not wish to dispose of the 'Manchester System' but to assure the conditions within which it could survive.

We shall find that the overall conclusion on the Keynesian Revolution must be that its central principles hold good and that to dismiss Keynesian economics at the present juncture would be premature. The problems of poor economic performance which increasingly showed themselves in the late 1960s and the 1970s were partly a consequence of the way in which Keynesian economics was interpreted and translated into policy terms. They also reflect the inherent difficulties and disadvantages of Keynesianism, the overall efficacy of which can only be judged when set against the inherent difficulties and disadvantages of *laissez-faire*.

More specifically, they can be seen as the economic symptoms of the outcome of a much broader movement towards collectivism – of which the socialisation of economic life was but an aspect – which was both engendered and given impetus by the circumstances of the inter-war depression and the period of total war which followed it. Keynes detected this movement and the *General Theory* was his response to it. But because the Keynesian Revolution was overtaken by the broader movement, it is easy to confuse the consequences of the one for the consequences of the other.

The argument of the book is divided into three parts, as follows. Part I is largely introductory. The Keynesian Revolution was a revolution of theory rather than of policy and was centrally concerned with the theoretical treatment of money. Accordingly we first examine the reasons for and consequences of the introduction of the institution of money into some hypothetical barter economy and account for the characteristics and functions of the monetary asset. The question which must then be asked is why the introduction of money into a barter economy, which should have the effect of *facilitating* the process of exchange between commodities, is often held to be responsible for the prevalence of 'unemployment and disequilibria'. The answer to this question lies by way of the distinction between a monetary economy and a barter economy, which, we argue, meant for Keynes the distinction between the theory of money under uncertainty and full information. Because money is only accorded asset status (substantive form) under uncertainty, the 'monetary economy' is the uncertainty world of reality; it is only in the full-information world of pure theory, in which money plays the role of *numéraire* and has no substantive form, that we are *in effect* in a world of barter. Two conclusions follow: (i) classical economics in the form of Say's Identity can be dismissed as irrelevant to the explanation of real world problems; (ii) the explanation of 'unemployment and disequilibria' given by the more 'realistic' form of classical economics, Say's Equality, as being due to the disco-ordination of investment and saving, must be reinterpreted. The reinterpretation has four main elements: the principle of effective demand and the key role of investment; the nature of saving and its relationship to investment; the finance of investment; the rate of interest. These topics form the basis of the discussion in Part II.

In Part II we begin by describing the *General Theory* as a picture of the Keynesian Revolution in progress and discuss the effectiveness of Keynes's strategy as a revolutionist. D. H. Robertson is identified as Keynes's most important critic, and his case against the Keynesian Revolution, based upon his loanable funds theory and doctrine of forced saving, is examined. We find that the weakness in Robertson's case stems from his attempt to develop and adapt classical economics, a policy which causes him to incorporate untenable ideas relating to saving in his analysis. The reply to Robertson, by way of an exposition of Keynes's own theory of investment and saving and his monetary theory of finance and interest, leads on to an analysis of the Keynesian economic problem and Keynes's preferred solution.

Part III begins with an outline account of the 'Great Prosperity' of the Keynesian era and of the circumstances of its passing. With mounting economic problems Keynesianism fell into discredit, and rival schools of thought, monetarist and Austrian, moved to the fore.

Friedman's counter-revolution in monetary theory, by reducing matters at issue to the single question of the empirical stability of the demand for money, attempted to reinstate (neo-)classical economics and its implied commitment to *laissez-faire* as the invisible accompaniment to the quantity theory *narrowly defined*. Left out of account, therefore, are the crucial questions surrounding the investment–saving nexus which features so largely in Part II. In general, we find that empirical conclusions, thought to lend support to monetarist ideas, pose a greater threat to post-war 'Keynesian' economics than to the Keynes of the *General Theory*.

Prospects of success for the monetarist *putsch* were threatened by the perceived disparity between the importance accorded to the defeat of inflation as the main objective of policy – an emphasis which distinguished monetarism from Keynesianism – and the lack of justification for this position provided in monetarist theory. The problem was exacerbated when monetarism was reconstituted in rational-expectations form.

The principal difficulty lay in the theoretical treatment of money as a private durable good – a difficulty not shared by the Austrian approach, which regarded money as a social institution. Austrian economics thus posed a potentially greater threat to the Keynesian Revolution, but was in its turn handicapped by (a) Hayek's failure to justify his attack on Keynes with an adequate critique of the *General Theory*, and (b) the practical limitations of the Austrian *a priori* approach as exemplified by Hayek's work on capital theory, which is largely an exercise in pure logic.

The failure of the Austrian case against Keynes on economic grounds is complemented by its failure on political grounds, to demonstrate that the introduction of Keynesian economics will *directly* result in the diminution of individual liberty.

In turn, the allegation that Keynes's employment policy threatened monetary stability and, therefore, individual liberty by its creation of money illusion in the labour market – an allegation based upon Georg Simmel's philosophy of money – fails due to misinterpretation of (a) Keynes's theoretical treatment of money and, therefore, of the meaning of his distinction between a monetary economy and a barter economy, and (b) the Keynesian theory of employment.

Keynesian employment theory is examined and we show that the level of employment is a function of the level of effective demand

and not of changes in the real wage. This explains why the chapter dealing explicitly with employment appears so late on in the book. The classical model begins in the labour market, with the determination of the real wage and the level of employment. Keynes's treatment in the *General Theory* also follows this sequence, in order to refute the classical view first before arguing towards his own position. Keynes's employment theory begins with effective demand and regards changes in the real wage only as a necessary consequence of a change in employment. In the *General Theory* Keynes struggled to reconcile the classical idea that the real wage should vary inversely with employment, with his own preference for stability of the money wage. Only afterwards did empirical work show that Keynes's solution, of a fall in the real wage occasioned by a rise in the price level, was unnecessary, leaving Keynes's theory more purely Keynesian.

Finally, we put the Keynesian Revolution in context, by depicting it as a necessary and timely contribution to a broader movement. But, as a consequence, Keynesian economic policy became inextricably bound up with, and the creature of, political developments. The inherent vulnerability of the Keynesian political economy was fully revealed by cultural changes taking place in British society in the 1960s, the consequences of which brought a revolt against socialisation and an apparent desire for purification through exposure to the elemental forces of *laissez-faire*. The Keynesian era had come, at least temporarily, to an end.

In conclusion, we argue that the problems of the post-war Keynesian political economy must be distinguished from the core of Keynes's theory. The principles, that is, remain. This implies that Keynesian economics is not a simple question of academic fashion, to be chosen or rejected as a matter of preference, but an ever-present consideration. Similarly, it implies that greater attention be given to the stagnation thesis. Finally, if heavy and rising unemployment proves an intractable problem, renewed pressure for socialisation may force a reorientation of policy. If the form of state intervention is not to be such as will quench enterprise and individual liberty it will have to be ordered along lines suggested by Keynes.

Part I
Money in the Economy

1 The Institution of Money: An Introduction

INTRODUCTION

By examining the reasons for the introduction of money into a non-money-using or 'barter' economy, we shall come to appreciate the nature of money, the functions it performs and the economic significance of its use. This exercise will also provide the necessary background for an examination of the characteristics of a monetary economy and a starting-point for subsequent discussion of the Keynesian Revolution and the attacks made upon it by its principal critics. Ultimately it will provide the basis for an understanding of money's role in a broader social and political context.

THE MONEY-USING ECONOMY

Money is an institution the existence of which facilitates the process of exchange between commodities. In so doing it increases the efficiency of markets to an extent that makes possible the development of an economy distinguished by a high degree of specialisation in the production process and a concomitant degree of interdependence of economic function.Such an economy provides the possibility of a relatively high material standard of living. By the same token, however, the monetary economy is made liable to disruption and even breakdown through the activities of money creators and money users. It is by seeking to regulate these activities that monetary policy makes its contribution to overall economic policy.

UNORGANISED BARTER

We begin by assuming that in some hypothetical[1] primitive economy without money, individual producers of the necessaries of life will be motivated to raise their standard of living by way of specialisation in the production of a commodity for which they enjoy a comparative advantage; and by the exchange of the surplus above their own requirements for the output of a variety of other individual producers. However, the process of exchange under barter will originally be difficult and costly. Producers will be subject to uncertainty as to the future demand for their product: that is, where and when exchange will take place and the exchange ratios (the terms of the exchange) that will be established. Under unorganised barter, the necessity of establishing a 'double coincidence of wants' – that is, of seeking out someone who not only has a product which a trader requires but who is also willing to part with it in exchange for the trader's own product – will therefore be an expensive process, in terms of the time and effort consumed; so much so, in fact, that it will provide a serious disincentive to trade taking place at all.

ORGANISED BARTER

Nevertheless, in order to be able to enjoy the benefits of specialisation and exchange, producers will be further motivated to seek ways of making trade more efficient. In the original, unorganised, state of barter, for example, individuals could in principle calculate the number of trading expeditions per time-period which would minimise the total cost of trading a given volume of product. They would do this by observing that whereas costs of search and bargaining would *decline* the fewer trading expeditions were undertaken per time-period, the costs of abstention from trade (storage costs plus subjective costs of having to consume only one's own product) would *rise*. Consequently, choice of the optimal frequency of trading expeditions, at which marginal costs of search and bargaining would be equal to marginal costs of abstention from trade, would minimise total costs.[2]

Thereafter, the process of making trade more efficient under barter would involve the introduction of improved arrangements for enabling traders to establish a double coincidence of wants. For example, as a way of reducing the enormous costs associated with random search, specific trading-grounds ('market places') could be designated to which all who wished to trade could resort, possibly at pre-arranged intervals ('market days'). Direct barter, the direct exchange of ultimately desired goods and services, would take its most efficient and lowest cost form when each trading-ground was divided into a number of separate trading-posts ('stalls') at each of which a specified pair of commodities could be directly traded. Such a system, though logically possible, would be extremely unwieldy, with, for example, forty-five separate posts being required for the direct, pairwise, trading of only ten commodities.[3] Instead, 'a more convenient way to allow for *ultimate* (indirect) pairwise trading of all commodities would be to establish trading posts for all commodities *except* one, the exceptional commodity being distinguished from all others by being tradeable at all posts'.[4]

THE INTRODUCTION OF MONEY

This fundamental change of principle in trading behaviour, with the introduction of a commonly acceptable intermediary commodity, marks the creation of the institution of money and the advent of the system of monetary exchange. The benefits stemming from the introduction of money are immediately obvious, for the real resources previously devoted to barter trading under uncertainty may now be devoted to increasing consumption, in terms either of commodities or of increased leisure. And while it cannot be shown formally that a monetary exchange system *will* actually be introduced in a given situation, it seems reasonable 'to suppose, albeit arbitrarily, that a "quantum jump" in trading costs separates monetary from other systems of trade so that the mere existence of organised markets for monetary exchange effectively ensures that other possible modes are never utilised'.[5]

MONEY, THE OUTCOME OF INDIRECT BARTER

However, the extreme difficulty of establishing the double-coincidence of wants of *direct* barter, even with the aid of elaborate market facilities, means that this mode would be of strictly limited use. Instead, barter would tend to be *indirect* rather than direct and the giant leap in the argument that is implied by the transition from 'direct pairwise trading' to 'monetary exchange' omits this crucial step. We may infer that the desire to build up trade and so improve the standard of living would make transactors willing to accept in exchange for a sale of own-product some commodity which, though not ultimately desired, would provide an intermediate stage in the process and consequently a necessary but temporary abode for purchasing power.

To increase the probability that this commodity would prove acceptable in exchange for the purchase of ultimately desired commodities, transactors would favour commodities which were in common use in their society. Usage would then establish one or more commodities as commonly acceptable, intermediary assets. Once the practice of accepting intermediary assets became general, trading in the economy would change imperceptibly from indirect barter to monetary exchange.[6]

Although it would be utilised in isolated acts of exchange, the widespread use of the technique of indirect barter and its refinement into monetary exchange would be greatly encouraged by the development of market facilities. These would have the effect of establishing and disseminating information about trading practices which would then become the norm for non-market-place transactions. In this way monetary exchange would become generalised to trading encounters remote from the organised market.[7]

CHARACTERISTICS OF THE MONETARY ASSET

The monetary asset chosen by traders could be any commodity deemed to be *acceptable* in exchange. This, as noted earlier, would tend to be some item in common use for which a continuing demand could be observed. Choice would be further narrowed by reference to criteria of convenience: namely, homogeneity (of certain content), portability (easily carried about), divisibility (able to be broken down into small units), durability (not perishable),[8] limited in supply (scarce in relation to demand).

Thus the monetary asset is a commodity money, having an intrinsic use[9] value independent of its monetary role. The most obvious and well-known examples of commodity money were the precious metals, gold and silver, which, being malleable, could be readily worked into pieces of desired size and shape. When these pieces were cut and stamped by weight we have the basis of the metallic currency.[10] It would always be open to the prudent trader to check these details with his balance, but with the growth in power and influence of the civil authority this would become less necessary, for the government itself would begin to mint and issue coin of certified weight and fineness of metal.[11] At this stage the authority of the state would begin to substitute for intrinsic commodity value as the factor ensuring the acceptability of money in exchange.[12]

The problems associated with the use of precious-metal commodity money are well known. Apart from the fraudulent practices of 'clipping' and 'sweating',[13] governments came only reluctantly to accept that if the value of coin in terms of the precious metal was to remain stable then there must always remain the possibility that coin would disappear from circulation as private citizens melted it down to take advantage of a favourable margin between the commodity and face values, as a consequence of the fact that commodity money has both a value-in-use and a value-in-exchange.[14] In addition there remained the temptation for a financially hard-pressed government to add a proportion of base metal to the coinage and to enjoy the profit or 'seigniorage' represented by the difference between the debased and face values.[15]

FROM VALUE BY CONTENT TO VALUE BY AUTHORITY

Notwithstanding the economic gains deriving from the monetary mode of exchange it would be possible to make further savings of resources by substituting for the expensive commodity money a form of currency with no intrinsic value. At first this could take the form of paper notes which could be exchanged on demand for the face value in precious-metal money.[16] Later, however, the substitution of a base-metal coinage would render void the 'promise to pay' printed on the note, and confidence in the money, and therefore its continued use in exchange, could derive only from the 'fiat' (decree) of the issuing authority.[17] For this purpose the authority would specify in law the conditions under which 'fiat money' should be acceptable in the settlement of debts. When so used it would become 'legal tender'.

Consequently, the apparent miracle of persuading traders to part with commodities in exchange for intrinsically worthless notes and coin is wrought by the relatively simple device of deeming contracts settled by a payment in specified form to be legally discharged.[18] In other words, the power of the state, expressed in its legal-tender laws, is what replaces commodity value as the factor compelling acceptability of money in exchange for commodities. Confidence in the currency is therefore a function of confidence in the government, or, more particularly, in the will of the government to maintain reasonable price stability and therefore the value-in-exchange of fiat money for commodities.

THE FUNCTIONS OF MONEY

In the sequence outlined above, money appeared as the end product of a process of refinement of the technique of indirect barter. Indirect barter itself was introduced as a method of taking advantage of a favourable opportunity for commodity sale, in a situation which did not present the corresponding opportunity for a purchase of the ultimately desired commodity. In other words, the institution of monetary exchange was introduced as a way of overcoming the problems of direct barter: that is, of establishing a double-coincidence of wants in a state of uncertainty.

Therefore, because it mediates the process of exchange between commodities, the basic function of money is to act as a *medium of exchange*. But because the indirect (monetary) mode of exchange involves a separation in time between sale and purchase of desired commodities, the exchange medium must in some sense carry forward the value of the sale proceeds until an appropriate purchase can be arranged. In other words, money must also function as a *store of value*. But because the separation in time of sale and purchase implies the need for two separate decisions, the second of which can be changed several times before a purchase is actually made, money can also be said to function as a *repository of general purchasing power*.[19]

But in order to ensure that money will indeed serve as a store of value and repository of general purchasing power, there is a further important and uniquely distinguishing function that the monetary asset must perform in an uncertainty economy: namely, to act as a *means of payment*.[20] Because transactions will very often take place between persons who are entirely unknown to each other and who will expect never to meet again, it will be necessary for the transactor parting with commodities to ensure that he has received value at the time of sale. That is, the absence of information about the *creditworthiness* of a purchaser will compel the seller to ensure that the transaction is concluded at the time of exchange: that is, that payment is final. Where, on the other hand, the seller has personal knowledge of the purchaser's circumstances, so that he feels reasonably certain that payment can safely be deferred, he may be willing to part with commodities for credit. In this case the exchange may be for a promise to pay, or money substitute which, though it is functioning as a medium of exchange, does not provide a means of payment.

MONEY AND CREDIT

In the absence of adequate information about the purchaser's creditworthiness *the seller will look for reassurance to the form of payment offered*. He must be persuaded that what he accepts in exchange will be sure to carry forward the value agreed. Under barter, of course, and exchange mediated by commodity money, payment was always received in commodities retaining an intrinsic value. With the advent of state or fiat money, however, the situation changed. Now it was the power and authority of the state expressed in its laws of legal tender that defined the means of payment.

In casual acts of purchase and sale, attention thus concentrates on the form of payment offered in exchange for commodities, while the individual circumstances of the purchaser cease to be of any importance. So long as he possesses means of payment the purchaser remains anonymous. It is only when payment is not final and a credit element enters that personal and financial information about the purchaser are demanded. This is the real truth behind the credit-card advertisement which states that 'the American Express card says more about you than cash ever can'. What it says, of course, is that the person using it wishes to delay payment when making purchases – that is, he desires credit, – and that the issuer of the card that acts as guarantee to the seller has taken steps to enquire into the creditworthiness of the holder.

On the other hand, only money as so far defined (that is, notes and coin) is anonymous in use, final in effect, and completely impartial as between individual transactors. Instead of providing guarantees which are specific to the transaction in question, the legal-tender rules apply to all classes of transactions and provide means of payment to the amounts specified.

MONEY AND THE MEANS OF PAYMENT

Means-of-payment functions are provided by utility commodity money, by government-authorised commodity money and by fiat legal-tender money. Strictly speaking there are no other forms, though the financial development of the economy has produced many substitutes. These substitutes are financial claims, which provide alternative means of financing transactions and holding wealth, and their use in place of the means of payment will be encouraged by considerations of convenience or reward. When being so used, the claims will correspond, respectively, to money's functions as a medium of exchange and a store of wealth.

By definition, financial claims are a claim on a money balance and *ultimately* that will mean conversion into the means of payment. This is so even when, as in the modern context, the quantity of money would be seen to consist largely of bank deposits, on account of the widespread use of the payments mechanism provided by the banks in the settlement of debts. But the important point of principle to notice here is that, even so, transactions are only completed by a transfer of the means of payment. For the bankers' practice of offsetting cheques drawn by their customers against cheques drawn in their favour and of settling only *net* inter-bank indebtedness by making transfers of the equivalent of legal-tender notes and coin, inadvertently serves to disguise this fact.

IN CONCLUSION

The introduction of the institution of money produces enormous savings of scarce resources (time and effort) which would otherwise have to be devoted to search and bargaining activity and to obtaining information about prospective purchasers and their proffered mediums of exchange. It thus provides the necessary information system – a universal system of valuation and exchange – around which the economy can grow and develop. It is to an examination of the characteristics of a monetary economy that we now turn.

2 The Monetary Economy

INTRODUCTION

In the previous chapter we introduced an economy in which: commodities are produced for exchange; production and trading plans have to be made on the basis of incomplete information; a system of monetary exchange is employed as a means of overcoming the problems of trade under uncertainty. Further, the use of money makes possible the development of a decentralised advanced economy in which commodity prices are largely market-determined, for economic development and expansion without the operation of the price mechanism would imply the rigid regimentation and loss of individual freedom that is associated with a centrally directed, fully planned economy. That is, while a 'monetary information system' is vital to the working of a free economy, it would in principle be possible to dispense with money in a completely planned economy.[1]

THE ECONOMICS OF MONETARY AND NON-MONETARY EXCHANGE

Given that we are dealing with a decentralised monetary economy, the question that must next arise for the economist and policy-maker concerns the precise economic significance of the monetary mode of exchange. That is, does a monetary economy differ in any fundamental sense from a barter economy? In one respect this question can be regarded as the beginning of enlightenment in macroeconomic thinking but, in asking it, it is very necessary to ensure that there is no confusion between the following: (a) the contrast between a monetary economy and a barter economy; *as against* (b) the contrast between an uncertainty economy and a 'full information' system. This is, of course, because in the 'real world' both monetary *and* barter economies are subject to uncertainty; only in the totally abstract world of the theoretical model does economic activity proceed untrammelled by ignorance.

It follows that the distinctions which can properly be drawn are those between the uncertainty world of reality as against the purely theoretical world of certainty, and the uncertainty monetary economy as against the uncertainty non-monetary economy.

MONETARY AND BARTER ECONOMIES UNDER UNCERTAINTY

The latter distinction is the one that Dr Goodhart seems to have in mind when he argues that 'it would surely seem to follow that, if unemployment (and disequilibria) is caused by information failures while the monetary system works essentially as an information enhancing system, then the *existence* of money should lead to a reduction in the prevalence of unemployment and disequilibria'.[2] He points out that nevertheless there are two views as to the effects of the introduction of the institution of money:

> the first that the existence of money, by breaking the link between the demand and supply of goods and services inherent in a barter system, allows the development of disequilibria, and the second that money provides essential information services, which should serve to lessen disequilibria and inefficiencies within a complex economy. My own opinion is that, whereas the monetary system *can* be mismanaged so as to exacerbate disequilibria, the existence of money actually reduces disequilibria and inefficiencies, and allows the development and expansion of a much more complex and decentralised economy.[3]

However, the key point which doesn't quite emerge in Goodhart's argument is that if we are comparing an uncertainty non-monetary economy with an uncertainty monetary economy, then we are almost *by definition* comparing a relatively simple economy with a (potentially) modern, highly complex economy. Furthermore, if the latter is a market economy rather than a fully planned, centrally directed economy it could only have come into existence by producing systems of money, credit and finance as part of the development of its mechanisms of exchange. It is surely not possible to use, as Goodhart does, the example of the difficulties of planning volume car production under uncertainty, as a problem applying to a barter economy. Only a *monetary* market economy could have developed to the extent necessary to produce such complex consumer-goods and the requisite capital-goods for market sale.

Indeed, this point is implicit in Dr Goodhart's own argument, for he writes:

> As the economy expands from a small tribal group, in which everyone knows everyone else, to a vast *impersonal* industrial system, the increase in uncertainty is inevitable. In truth, the uncertainties in a modern, decentralised system are *so* great, that it could not function unless institutions had developed to provide the additional information-flows necessary...A monetary system is, therefore, a necessary adjunct for the development and expansion of a decentralised economy.[4]

Therefore, what is *at issue* is not that the introduction of money makes possible 'the development and expansion of a much more complex and decentralised economy'; this sort of economy will in any case freely develop – it is not a policy choice. Rather, that we are presented with the fact that it will not unaided realise its full-employment potential. The development of the modern economy, that is, will have the effect both of raising hopes and of dashing them.

The complete effect of the introduction of money into a barter economy is not immediately obvious. In addition to providing an information system around which the economy can develop and expand, the use of money both increases the freedom of action of individuals in their economic and social relationships and, at the same time, increases their *interdependence* with other individuals as the division of labour increases. The one element linking all parts of a vast decentralised economy in all its economic and financial aspects is the use of money, which is tradeable on all markets. This is why the conditions relating to the demand for and supply of money are so much more important than those relating to any other single good. In addition, the institution of money itself in the political economy can take on an importance over and above that which is encapsulated in the merely technical 'functions' of money. Money can be seen as one of the institutions contributing to the maintenance of trust, stability and order in a free society.

Ultimately, we shall come to see that, although the question raised by Goodhart is '*not* whether mismanagement of monetary policy within an already functioning monetary system can lead to disequilibria, but [rather] whether the very existence of a monetary system will result in *additional* disequilibria';[5] the crux of the matter does relate to the question of monetary management. The answer to the prior question of what we believe to be the economic importance and social significance of the institution of money will, in turn, determine what the role of monetary policy is to be.

We can now turn to an examination of the other proper distinction we drew: that between the uncertainty world of reality and the purely theoretical world of certainty.

MONEY UNDER UNCERTAINTY AND FULL INFORMATION

Money is introduced into a barter economy as a way of overcoming the problems created by uncertainty so that the presence of uncertainty and the use of a substantive (means-of-payment) money represent two aspects of the same phenomenon in a money-using economy. On the other hand, in a theoretical-construct, full-information economy, the absence of uncertainty ensures that money is a mere *numéraire* acting as a unit of account in calculating exchange ratios.[6] This is precisely because, in a 'certainty' economy, production, consumption and trading plans can be costlessly co-ordinated on the basis of perfect knowledge of the relevant supply and demand functions. The information necessary to make consistent the trading plans of a given set of individuals is assumed to derive, for example, from the activities of an all-seeing unpaid 'auctioneer' whose function is to receive trading 'bids' until such time as a market-clearing set of relative commodity prices is established. Because trade only proceeds on the basis of the correct set of prices, the presence of the auctioneer will ensure that production, consumption and trading plans will always be perfectly co-ordinated, and that equilibrium will always be maintained.[7]

It is because exchange in this curious world can be accomplished without the use of means-of-payment money that it is in effect a world of barter.

This conclusion can be explained and illustrated as follows.[8] By Say's Law of markets there can be no general overproduction in a barter economy because every act of supplying commodities in exchange necessarily involves a corresponding demand.[9] General overproduction implies that there must be something relative to which commodities can be in excess supply, namely money.[10] That is, there would have to be an excess demand for money. Consequently if Say's Law is to apply to a monetary economy, in equilibrium there must be a *zero* excess demand for money.

In a full-information system money exists only as a unit of account. Therefore, by Walras's Law, the over-supply of all commodities in this barter-type economy is *logically* impossible:

$$\sum_{i=1}^{n} P_iD_i \equiv \sum_{i=1}^{n} P_iS_i$$

In an uncertainty economy money assumes a substantive form with a store of value function. Now we have n goods, comprising $n-1$ commodities plus money. Therefore the total value of $n-1$ commodities demanded will be equal to the total value of the $n-1$ commodities supplied *only* if the demand for money is equal to the supply of money. That is:

$$\sum_{i=1}^{n-1} P_iD_i = \sum_{i=1}^{n-1} P_iS_i$$

but only on condition that $D_n=S_n$. This implies that any difference between the demand for and supply of commodities will be shown in a positive or negative excess demand for money. Consequently, an increased demand for money to hold can only be achieved by demanding fewer commodities than are being supplied.

Therefore, for it to be logically impossible for there to be general over-production in a monetary economy, the money market must always be in equilibrium: that is, $ED_n \equiv 0$. That is, money is only demanded for the purpose of immediate expenditure on commodities. This condition has been described as Say's Identity and it ensures that the total supply of commodities is necessarily identical with the total demand for commodities, so that:

$$\sum_{i=1}^{n-1} P_iD_i \equiv \sum_{i=1}^{n-1} P_iS_i$$

Say's Identity leads directly to the 'homogeneity postulate' by which demands and supplies of commodities are affected only by relative prices and not by the absolute level of prices. The money market will be in equilibrium at all levels of the general price level – so that the value of money ($1/P$) is indeterminate. In other words, in order to guarantee the *impossibility* of overproduction in a monetary economy it is necessary to impose the conditions of barter.[11]

It is in *this* sense that the contrast between a monetary economy and a barter economy can usefully be drawn. Thus, to say that the two types of economy are different is merely to affirm that a money-using economy – that is, the real world of everyday experience – will be an economy subject to uncertainty.

The implications of this conclusion are important and far-reaching, as we shall see.

3 Money, Investment and Saving

KEYNES'S CRUCIAL DISTINCTION

The distinction between the uncertainty world of reality and the purely theoretical world of perfect knowledge is the real meaning behind J. M. Keynes's proposition that a monetary economy is different from a barter economy. It is a distinction fundamental to his whole approach and central to his assault on 'classical' macroeconomics. The 'monetary economy' is the real, money-using world of uncertainty. The 'barter economy' is the purely abstract world of classical theory in which perfect information ensures that money has no substantive form, so that exchange is in effect direct and the economy is of barter-type. Keynes argued that:

> The whole object of the accumulation of Wealth is to produce results, or potential results, at a comparatively distant, and sometimes at an *indefinitely* distant, date. Thus the fact that our knowledge of the future is fluctuating, vague and uncertain, renders Wealth a peculiarly unsuitable subject for the methods of classical economic theory.[1]

Keynes explained that our knowledge of the future is uncertain in the same way as, for example, 'the prospect of a European war is uncertain, or the price of copper and the rate of interest twenty years hence ... About these matters there is no scientific basis on which to form any calculable probability whatever. We simply do not know'[2].

THE CERTAINTY WORLD OF CLASSICAL THEORY

Therefore, the term 'uncertainty economy' describes, as we have seen, an environment in which economic initiatives have to be made without access to the information necessary to ensure their successful outcome. Keynes accused the classical theory, on the other hand, of trying to deal with the present 'by abstracting from the fact that we know very little about the future'.[3] The *certainty* world of classical *theory* offered comfort and reassurance regarding the possibility of income fluctuations and the unemployment of resources in the *uncertainty* world of *reality*: 'from the time of Smith and Ricardo the classical economists have taught that supply creates its own demand ... that the whole of the costs of production must necessarily be spent in the aggregate, directly or indirectly, on purchasing the product'.[4] Furthermore:

> As a corollary of the same doctrine, it has been supposed that any individual act of abstaining from consumption necessarily leads to, and amounts to the same thing as, causing the labour and commodities thus released from supplying consumption to be invested in the production of capital wealth.[5]

Though by the 1930s the doctrine was never stated in its crude form, it nevertheless still underlay the whole classical theory which would, argued Keynes, 'collapse without it'.

THE ECONOMIC CONSEQUENCES OF UNCERTAINTY

It was a corollary of Keynes's view of the economy, however, that due to the presence of uncertainty there could be no automatic tendency for saving and investment to be in full-employment equilibrium. It was a further corollary that, because in a monetary economy exchange is indirect and money itself has an asset value (it functions as a store of value), it is possible for changes in the *demand for money* to have important economic consequences.

Taken together, and indeed they are concomitants, uncertainty and the asset demand for money provide the key to answering the question raised in the last chapter. That is, how is it that the introduction of the institution of money into an uncertainty non-monetary economy, despite the inestimable benefits it confers by providing the information services necessary for the development of a complex, decentralised, industrial economy, can nevertheless be held responsible for what Dr Goodhart referred to as the 'prevalence of unemployment and disequilibria'?

We shall see that Keynes's insights into the working of a monetary production economy lead to the prediction that the unregulated economy will be subject to periodic fluctuations of employment and output around a relatively stable average level which will typically be below the full-employment level. Full employment is to be regarded as an optimal but unlikely outcome. Moreover, what in neo-classical or general equilibrium models would be regarded as 'disequilibria' would on Keynes's analysis be defined as equilibrium states. Furthermore, although monetary management is considered to be capable of providing a stimulus to economic activity, the dangers of miscalculation in monetary policy leading to adverse effects are sufficiently likely for this solution to be neglected in favour of direct intervention by the state in the management of investment. Goodhart notes that 'the main argument of those who claim that the institution of money is responsible for disequilibria is, I think, that its existence facilitates the separation of *the decision to save from the decision to invest*';[6] but he also recognises that this cannot be the whole story, as the separation can occur even in a barter economy – given the development of suitable financial instruments – as we shall see.

THE MECHANISM OF EXCHANGE AND THE INVESTMENT–SAVING RELATION

Nevertheless, the answer must be bound up with the timing relationship between investment and saving: that is, whether it is possible to make investment plans without taking account of saving behaviour, or whether investment must wait upon prior saving. In turn this will depend upon the mechanism of exchange employed in an economy. Whereas in a barter economy there can be no demand without an offer of supply (prior accumulation), in a monetary economy exchange is indirect so that while demand cannot be effective without the prior acquisition of a money balance (for example, by the sale of a non-monetary commodity), it is conversely possible to exercise demand for goods and services by the creation of a money balance, either exogenously (for example, by the monetary authority to finance government expenditure) or through financial arrangements which mobilise – and indeed create – money balances to finance planned increases in economic activity.

In a monetary economy, therefore, it is possible to initiate investment demand without any prior real accumulation, so that our attention is concentrated on the activities of entrepreneurs in making *investment* plans in conditions of uncertainty.

The corollary of this is that importance now attaches to the form in which saving is made. If savings accrue in a form – money – which has unique characteristics and an all-pervasive influence in economic life, then again we are right to focus our attention on the investment–saving relationship in a monetary economy. All, therefore, depends upon the view we take of the functions and characteristics of money. The important point to bear in mind in what follows is that if savings take the form of substantive money then at that moment demand – potential expenditure – has come to a dead stop, with no imperative presumption that it should be realised at some certain future time. The money balances which contain the power to exercise demand and finance expenditure must then be enticed from their position as safe and certain stores of liquidity by the offered inducement of interest by those whose expenditure plans are running ahead of their own holdings of liquidity.

INVESTMENT AND SAVING IN A BARTER ECONOMY

In a barter market economy, which will by definition be of relatively simple and undeveloped form, there should in principle be no general deficiency of demand, for each individual act of supplying output of goods and services to the market would necessarily create a demand for the output of others. Similarly, acts of saving and investment will be specific rather than general in effect. If we assume a strict division of labour, so that, for example, makers of wooden furniture must trade in order to eat and to supply other necessaries, then to abstain from consumption is in effect to trade less (to supply less and so demand less), and either to accumulate stocks of own-product or enjoy more leisure. This, note, is a circumstance we dealt with in Chapter 1, above, in terms of subjective and objective costs of abstaining from trade. It arises due to the implication of Say's Law that there can be no demand without a prior supply, so that when saving takes place in a barter economy – which must involve a reduction in demand – there must also be a reduction in the supply of product to the market.

Suppose, now, that the supplies of timber previously devoted to furniture production were to be lent by way of a financial instrument to a contractor who would use them for the construction of a bridge. The return from the venture for the contractor or his patron would have to repay costs of production of the bridge and provide a profit as incentive, and would presumably derive from the payment of tolls in kind.

For the furniture-maker, repayment of the loan, together with payment of interest, would probably be in the form of timber – though this is not at all essential. In fact, in order to provide an incentive for the furniture-maker to save at all, an offer of the right to use the new bridge might be a more suitable inducement. In a barter economy each commodity traded acts as its own means of payment, so that there is no universal form in which loans will be made and repayment demanded. According to preference, loans could be made in one form, repayment of principal in another, and interest paid in a third. Only in a monetary economy, in which exchange is mediated and debts are settled in the form of money, will observance of the trading rule require that loan, repayment and interest should all be in money form. That interest in the modern economy is essentially a monetary phenomenon will be shown below (Chapters 11–13) to be a matter of the greatest significance.

Notice that in the above example of saving and investment in a barter economy the loan which is made possible by the diminution of consumption *will be in a form which will be used directly for investment*. It shows how accurate was Keynes's view that saving is always equal to investment. Only the direction of causation was wrong for a monetary economy: 'the old-fashioned view that saving always involves investment, though incomplete and misleading, is formally sounder than the new-fangled [loanable funds] view that there can be saving without investment or investment without "genuine" saving'.[7]

This example also shows that saving and investment do not invalidate Say's Law. A decision to trade less and to take increased leisure is always compatible with (voluntary-unemployment) full employment; but in the case we are considering the economy continues at an unchanged level of output, with a rate of interest inducing a change in preferences between present and future consumption and a switch of resources into investment for a specific instance of saving and investment.

Finally, we must notice the limited nature of the concept of a pure barter economy. For example, the bridge-builder or his patron would no doubt find it more convenient to receive tolls in the form of commodities in common use whose characteristics were known and which would prove of most use in subsequent trades – so we quickly slip into discussion first of an economy with indirect barter and then of one with the institution of money.

SAY'S LAW IN A MONETARY ECONOMY

With the establishment of the institution of money it becomes possible to save in a form which is distinct from the commodities which are traded in the economy. To maintain the validity of Say's Law in this economy it is necessary to ensure that withdrawals from the income–expenditure stream (voluntary saving) would be matched by a corresponding level of injections (investment). This result could be assured if two conditions were satisfied: that a financial mechanism – however crude – existed which would channel savings through into investment; that saving does not involve any change in the demand for money (to hold) – that is, money received as income will be passed on immediately either by expenditure on consumption goods or by the purchase of interest-bearing securities (financial instruments). Money-holding at any time will thus be confined to 'transactions balances' required to bridge the gap between receipts and disbursements over the pay period. In this view the role of money is strictly limited, in a neutral-money, barter-type, economy.[8] Saving and investment are still, strictly, 'real' phenomena, with monetary transactions only *representing* real transactions.

THE CLASSICAL CAPITAL MARKET

If investment is to take place in this economy, then with a given level of output it will be necessary for investors to utilise resources otherwise devoted to consumption. Because individuals' preferences are assumed to be for present rather than deferred consumption, the loss of satisfaction implied by the decision to abstain from consumption would require the payment of compensation. Consequently, the supply of savings out of income is made an increasing function of the rate of interest, which thus becomes *the reward for not spending*.

On the demand side of the capital market, entrepreneurs are assumed to take up more funds for investment purposes the lower the cost of borrowing, so that the rate of investment undertaken is made a decreasing function of the rate of interest (see Figure 3.1).

The equilibrium rate of interest is determined by the intersection of the two flow schedules, with savings equal to investment expenditure. The important implication of this model is that an increased propensity to save – an increase in thrift – will not only lead to an increased flow of funds onto the market but will also produce a fall in the rate of interest, which will in turn give rise to increased investment expenditure just sufficient to offset the increased saving. The change in the relative shares of saving and consumption out of income will be reflected, therefore, in a change in the composition of output in favour of investment goods.

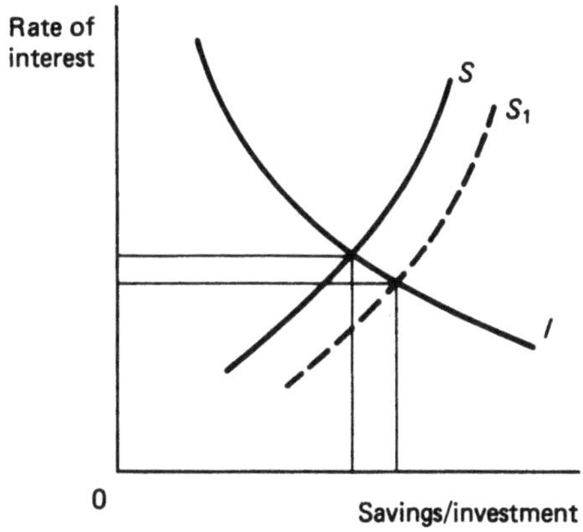

Figure 3.1

KEYNES'S CRITICISM

For Keynes, this approach could not provide an adequate theory either of saving and investment or of the rate of interest. Although it correctly saw saving as being equal to investment, it failed to take account of the effect of income changes on the level of saving and of the effect of investment expenditure on the level of income.[9] Consequently it was able to imply that an act of saving would give rise to new investment and that new investment would have to wait upon prior saving. Furthermore, the theory did not accord with two generally accepted points:

> In the first place, it has been agreed...that it is not certain that the sum saved out of a given income necessarily increases when the rate of interest is increased; whereas no one doubts that the investment demand-schedule falls with a rising rate of interest. ...In the second place, it has been usual to suppose that an increase in the quantity of money has a tendency to reduce the rate of

interest, at any rate in the first instance and in the short period. Yet no reason has been given why a change in the quantity of money should affect either the investment demand-schedule or the readiness to save out of a given income. Thus the classical school have had quite a different theory of the rate of interest in Volume I dealing with the theory of value from what they have had in Volume II dealing with the theory of money.[10]

LOANABLE FUNDS

Yet it was in their attempts to resolve the conflicts within classical theory, by introducing monetary variables directly into the analysis, that neo-classical economists were to produce the 'worst muddles of all'. In this *loanable funds* version, the classical voluntary savings (supply of funds = demand for securities) is modified in the interests of greater realism by allowing for the effects of new money creation and the dishoarding of idle balances. The supply of loanable funds onto the market can be influenced by discretionary monetary policy on the part of central government, or by switches of preference between holdings of securities and money by capital market transactors (see Figure 3.2).

Passing over the fact that in this diagram we are necessarily adding changes in stocks to flows and showing all variables as a function of

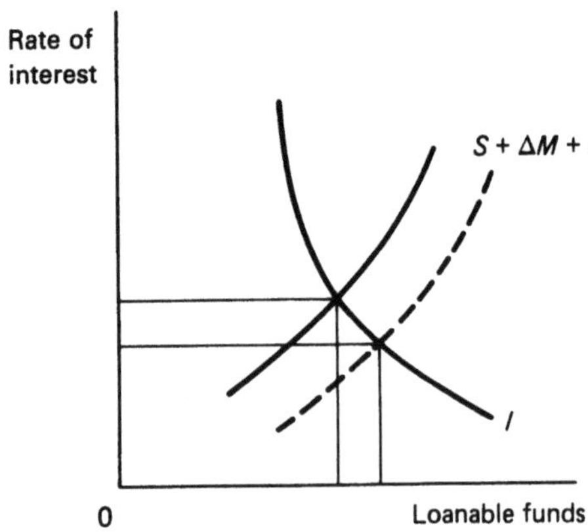

Figure 3.2

the rate of interest, the important point for present purposes is that the rate of interest determined at the intersection of the loanable-funds schedules is different from that established in the classical model. At the new market rate classical saving and investment are not equal, with the demand for investable funds exceeding the supply of voluntary savings.

This formulation clearly held important implications for the role of monetary policy. In the hands of the Austrian school of economists it was in later years to become the basis for an attack on the use of discretionary monetary policy as a stimulus to economic activity and, by extension, on the views of Keynes himself. This question is properly a matter for Chapter 20, below, but for the moment we should notice that Keynes was fully aware of the policy implications of the loanable-funds approach and that he dismissed the whole business as being based on a fundamental confusion – a confusion which, as we shall see, his own formulation precludes.

THE SIGNIFICANCE OF THE INVESTMENT–SAVING RELATION

In attempting to patch up the classical theory the loanable-funds approach had merely compounded its errors. At bottom the misconceptions arose from a failure to appreciate the essential differences between a barter-type economy, the theory of which underlay both classical and neo-classical versions of the theory, and a monetary economy, the theory of which was the substance of the Keynesian Revolution.

These differences, as we have seen, manifest themselves most clearly in the question of the relationship between investment and saving. Upon the answer to this most crucial question will depend, for example, the view we are to take of the rate of interest and its economic significance. More fundamentally, however, it will indicate our acceptance or rejection of Say's Law – in the sense of the automatic tendency of the economy to adjust to full-employment equilibrium – and hence of the need for state intervention in the organisation of economic activity.

The question of the relationship between investment and saving formed the basis of the debate between Keynes and the leading loanable-funds theorist, D. H. Robertson. Upon the outcome of this theoretical debate depended the success or failure of the Keynesian

Revolution, for it was, as we shall see, intended by Keynes to be a revolution of theory: an overthrowing of established principles.

Keynes's treatment of investment and saving contains the key to his theory of a monetary production economy and can be seen to encompass four main elements: (i) the theory of effective demand and the central role of investment within it; (ii) the nature of saving and its relationship to investment; (iii) the finance of investment; (iv) the monetary theory of interest.

We shall find, in the chapters that follow, that once we have explained the principle of effective demand, with which Keynes overturned Say's Law, and made clear the nature of saving and its relationship to investment, the Robertsonian challenge to the Keynesian Revolution can easily be met and defeated. From the conclusions thus reached will follow Keynes's approach to the finance of investment and his conception of interest as a monetary phenomenon. We shall then explain the economic significance of the rate of interest, as a regulator of employment and output, both in the general case and in the peculiar economic conditions of Keynes's special case.

Part II
The Keynesian Revolution and its Critics

1: Robertsonian Economics

4 Keynes's Revolution

A REVOLUTION IN PROGRESS

In contrast to the lucid brilliance of much of Keynes's work, the *General Theory* is often described as a badly written book. Untidy, lacking a clear design, with ideas not fully thought out and arguments flawed by obscurities, inconsistencies or actual error, etc. – the perceived defects are numerous.[1] They are considered either to be evidence of Keynes's struggles to free himself from orthodoxy or are ascribed to the hasty preparation required to bring the new ideas before a world thought to be in urgent need of them.

That the *composition* of the book had been for its author 'a long struggle of escape...from habitual modes of thought and expression' is a matter of record,[2] but the notion of ill-digested ideas and hasty preparation does not accord with the evidence we now have of the process of discussion and criticism which took place during the book's long gestation.[3]

The real problem with the *General Theory*, setting out as it did to overturn existing ideas, was that it had to face in two directions at once. It looked backwards to orthodoxy, to explain its inappropriateness for dealing with the real world and, at the same time, forwards, to construct a model of the new economics. In any revolution the process of transition from old to new will often appear to outsiders as confused, messy and inconclusive – but this, of course, is more a function of the transitional process itself than of the degree of clarity of the revolutionist's vision. Only afterwards, possibly, will observers become aware of the overall conception, the grand design.

The *General Theory* is a picture of the revolution in progress. Similarly, the extensive correspondence and journal debate which followed the book's publication look in both directions.[4] Even the article 'The General Theory of Employment',[5] credited by G. L. S. Shackle with providing 'Keynes's ultimate meaning', is largely concerned with points of departure from classical orthodoxy. From August 1936, Keynes was

> thinking of producing in the course of the next year or so what might be called footnotes to my previous book, dealing with

various criticisms and particular points which want carrying further. Of course, in fact, the whole book needs re-writing and re-casting. But I am still not in a sufficiently changed state of mind as yet to be in a position to do that.[6]

From 1937, illness and later the pressure of work brought on by the war meant that Keynes did not have the leisure to prepare a distillation of the argument, to set out the main principles and applications of his own theory, free of archaeological encumbrance. As it is, we have only the merest of indications of the future direction of his thought, in a set of draft 'footnotes to the General Theory'[7] and some lecture notes of 1937.[8]

A QUESTION OF PRINCIPLES

That Keynes was intent upon producing a revolution in economics is clear from his oft-quoted remark in a letter to G. B. Shaw in 1935:

> I believe myself to be writing a book on economic theory which will largely revolutionise – not, I suppose, at once but in the course of the next ten years – the way the world thinks about economic problems.[9]

Moreover, it is also clear that it was in the sphere of economic theory rather than policy that the principal overturning was to take place:

> my suggestions for a cure, which, avowedly, are not worked out completely, are on a different plane from the diagnosis. They are not meant to be definitive; they are subject to all sorts of special assumptions and are necessarily related to the particular conditions of the time. But my main reasons for departing from the traditional theory go much deeper than this. They are of a highly general character and are meant to be definitive.[10]

The reasons for the inappropriateness of the classical theory in dealing with the problems of a monetary economy were introduced in the previous chapter. So pressing were those problems that Keynes felt it imperative to bring the classical economists to battle on questions of pure theory without delay. Keynes thought that 'the matters at issue are of an importance which cannot be exaggerated',[11] and he saw the publication of the *General Theory* as

> an attempt by an economist to bring to an issue the deep divergencies of opinion between fellow economists which have for the time being almost destroyed the practical influence of economic theory, and will, until they are resolved, continue to do so.[12]

He spoke of 'putting all the driving force I know how behind arguments which for me are of painfully practical importance'.[13]

A STRATEGY FOR REVOLUTION

The major question that remained was that of presentation: of how best to confront his fellow economists with the new ways of thinking so that his assault upon them should be successful. For he was well aware that 'in economics you cannot convict your opponent of error – you can only convince him of it'.[14]

Here Keynes faced a dilemma. He perceived that his own theories, taken by themselves, were simple and straightforward and would only appear difficult and complicated when argued out against a background of classical theory and classical assumptions. Nevertheless, by generalising from his own experience in moving from old to new, he concluded that for his revolution to be successful he must start with the classical view and argue his case step by step towards his own position.

Keynes had clearly set himself a task of heroic proportions, and the inherent difficulties are apparent in the book as published, with Keynes's own arguments often cast in both old and new terms and with the distinction not always made clear. He wrote:

> the ideas which are here expressed so laboriously are extremely simple and should be obvious. The difficulty lies, not in the new ideas, but in escaping from the old ones, which ramify for those brought up as most of us have been, into every corner of our minds.[15]

He feared that 'those who are strongly wedded to what I shall call "the classical theory", will fluctuate, I expect, between a belief that I am quite wrong and a belief that I am saying nothing new'.[16]

It was thus vitally necessary to bring into clear focus the points of distinction between Keynes and those whom he sought to convince; to establish, that is, definite points of departure, in an attempt to prevent the new ideas simply being absorbed and incorporated as special cases into the old. Because of this, Keynes deliberately employed in his attack the tactic of an overtly controversial style of argument.

He was to explain his reasons clearly in a lecture given in Stockholm later in 1936. Notes for the lecture read as follows:

> What I have to say [is] intrinsically easy / Difficulty lies in its running against our habitual modes of thought / It is only to an audience of economists that it is difficult / I also make it more difficult than I need because I myself am so much bound to the past. I am extremely anxious to emphasise and bring to a head my difference from orthodox theory precisely because I was brought up in this faith /.../ And for me it is difficult to mark my departure except, so to speak, controversially – by comparing what I now believe with what I used to believe.[17]

However, despite the inclusion in the Preface to the *General Theory* of a plea for 'forgiveness if, in the pursuit of sharp distinctions, my controversy is itself too keen', Keynes was soon to find that he had, in an uncertain world, imperfectly foreseen the impact of his adopted approach. Although Keynesian economics would soon be widely adopted in the industrialised world, within a few months of the publication of the *General Theory* in February 1936 there are signs that Keynes already sensed that he was not succeeding in his main purpose – of convincing those who like himself had been trained in the classical economics of the need to re-examine the basic assumptions which underlay their position.

In dealing with the dilemma posed by the intrinsic simplicity of his ideas on the one hand, and the strongly felt need to fight the argument out step-by-step, Keynes began to feel that his emphasis had perhaps been wrongly placed. To R. F. Harrod he wrote:

> what some people treat as unnecessarily controversial is really due to the importance in my own mind of what I *used* to believe, and of the moments of transition which were for me personally moments of illumination. You don't feel the weight of the past as I do. One cannot shake off a pack one has never properly worn. And

> probably your ignoring all this is a better plan than mine. For experience seems to show that people are divided between the old ones whom nothing will shift and are merely amazed by my attempts to underline the points of transition so vital in my own progress, and the young ones who have not been properly brought up and believe nothing in particular.[18]

Perhaps Keynes was naive or over-sanguine in expecting his own generation to set to work with a will to clear out the intellectual lumber from their attics, for he was plainly taken aback to find the old ones 'so much occupied with my manners that my thought passes by unnoticed'.[19] It does not seem to have occurred to Keynes that, for his critics, questions of too-sharp distinctions, too-strident claims to originality, and disregard and disrespect for previous ideas and their authors, should loom more important than the ideas themselves.

A REVOLUTION AGAINST WHOM?

It is also interesting to note that to the 'badly brought up' young ones the 'controversy with old views would mean practically nothing';[20] for, in correspondence with J. R. Hicks over the draft of Hicks's famous 'Mr. Keynes and the Classics' paper, [21] Keynes claimed that:

> what you are giving is a representative belief of a period when economists had slipped away from the pure classical doctrine without knowing it and were in a much more confused state of mind than their predecessors had been. The story that you give is a very good account of the beliefs which, let us say, you and I used to hold.[22]

Before looking at the precise point of Keynes's remark, the prior questions arise of what is to be regarded as classical economics, and who are to be thought of as classical economists. It is the generally accepted view that Keynes set up a 'straw man' theory as the object of his attack; also he expressed some sympathy with D. H. Robertson's complaint that he applied the label 'classical economist' or 'classical theory' to the 'vacuous countenance of some composite Aunt Sally of uncertain age'.[23] But while it is fair to say that there is some imprecision in Keynes's apportionment of the term as between names and dates, it is clear that he had a serviceable working definition which contained the essential elements.

The issue appears confused because Keynes employed terminology which is at odds with the usual history-of-thought classification. He explained that:

> 'The classical economists' was a name invented by Marx to cover Ricardo and James Mill and their *predecessors*, that is to say for the founders of the theory which culminated in the Ricardian economics. I have become accustomed, perhaps perpetrating a solecism, to include in 'the classical school' the *followers* of Ricardo, those, that is to say, who adopted and perfected the theory of the Ricardian economics, including (for example) J. S. Mill, Marshall, Edgeworth and Prof. Pigou.[24]

That is, he included those whom we should generally think of as 'neo-classical'.[25]

Keynes justified his broader definition by the application of a single criterion, in that he considered a classical economist to be 'one who, whether he knows it or not, requires for his conclusions the assumption of something in the nature of Say's Law'.[26] That is, a belief in the doctrine that aggregate demand will always accommodate itself to aggregate supply as given by the level of employment determined in the labour market, so that the economy will, free of constraint, move naturally to full-employment equilibrium.[27]

Keynes perceived that this doctrine had been consciously held by the earlier classical economists but that, latterly, questions relating to the supply of and demand for output as a whole had ceased to be discussed:

> To me, the most extraordinary thing regarded historically, is the complete disappearance of the theory of the demand and supply for output as a whole, i.e. the theory of employment, *after* it had been for a quarter of a century the most discussed thing in economics.[28]

The importance of this is that because the equilibrium level of employment and output would be given by the point at which 'the supply of output as a whole and the demand for it would be in equilibrium', Keynes had made the centrepiece of his attack on Say's Law the proposition that the level of aggregate demand is determined, *independently of conditions of aggregate supply*, by states of expectations affecting investment, consumption and the demand for money. Therefore the economy could be in equilibrium at any of a range of levels of employment and output.

But whereas, increasingly, orthodox economists had moved away from explicit reliance on Say's Law, their conclusions regarding the self-righting properties of a free-market economy tacitly depended upon it. Consequently, if Keynes's attack on Say's Law were to prove successful the orthodox position would lose its (implicit) theoretical support.

Keynes's difficulty is now apparent, for he was seeking to convince orthodox economists that their views were wrong (or, more precisely, that they had no theoretical basis for their policy prescriptions)[29] on the basis of theories to which they might no longer claim to subscribe. The Keynesian Revolution, that is, was aimed at a target which had wholly 'slipped out of sight'.[30]

It was due to their failure to keep in mind the premises upon which their theoretical position depended, that accounted for the 'much more confused state of mind' of latter-day classical economists, to which we made reference earlier. For it allowed them to give a role to money which could not be justified on strictly classical assumptions and which led, therefore, to the creation of an 'inconsistent hotch-potch':

> The inconsistency creeps in, I suggest, as soon as it comes to be generally agreed that the increase in the quantity of money is capable of increasing employment. A strictly brought up classical economist would not, I should say, admit that (Letter to Hicks, March 1937, in Keynes, *CW*, XIV, p. 79).

That is, Keynes distinguished between pure classical economics, based upon what, in stylised form, we should now refer to as the 'dichotomised' classical model, in which real and monetary forces operated independently to determine (a full-employment level of) employment and the price level respectively; and the later classical economics which recognised the 'non-neutral' powers of money to stimulate employment and output but which failed to reconcile this with the notion of interest determined by investment demand and saving out of a given income. Only when Keynes had successfully unravelled the former confusion between saving and investment and the finance of investment, did it become clear that saving would vary as income varied with investment; and that investment would (with given expectations) vary with a rate of interest determined by the quantity of money in relation to the demand for it.

THE NEO-CLASSICAL 'MUDDLES'

But this is moving on too fast, for while the classical economists had made no attempt to bridge the gap between the two theories of interest the attempt had been made by those economists whom Keynes classified as neo-classical: that is, those who had rejected Say's Law and become 'enlightened', but who had, in their attempt to reconcile real and monetary influences in the determination of the rate of interest, produced the 'worst muddles of all'.[31] This they did, as will be explained at length in the next chapter, by allowing changes in the quantity of money to swell the quantity of loanable funds available for investment; so giving rise to an actual inequality of investment and saving and the consequent creation of *supplementary* saving, which was not voluntary as in classical theory but 'forced' out of consumers by a rise in the price level.

Keynes mentioned as examples of neo-classical economists, R. G. Hawtrey, D. H. Robertson, B. Ohlin and F. A. Hayek.[32] Of these we shall later deal at length with F. A. Hayek[33] and refer briefly to Ohlin's 'Swedish', 'loans', theory of interest. But for the moment we shall concentrate our attention on D. H. Robertson, whose version of the 'loanable funds' theory of the rate of interest illustrates the possibilities and limitations of developing a classically based theory of interest, as compared with Keynes's alternative approach of abandoning classical theory and beginning afresh.

That is, Robertson is interesting because, like Keynes, he had become dissatisfied with orthodoxy but, unlike Keynes, he attempted to propagate new strains from the existing plant rather than pull it up by the roots and plant anew. He is particularly interesting because after the publication of the *General Theory* he was to become one of Keynes's keenest critics, and in so doing helped Keynes to elucidate and refine his thinking on the key concepts of investment, saving and the rate of interest.

ROBERTSON AND KEYNES

Robertson was successively Keynes's pupil, his colleague and collaborator and, finally, his most intellectually threatening and tenacious critic. Though erstwhile friends, the two grew apart over the period of the *General Theory* and the Keynesian Revolution; and although a warm working relationship developed during the busy wartime period of preparation for the Bretton Woods conference (after 1943), the breach was never healed.

On matters of policy they shared a common view (as did many economists of different theoretical persuasions), and on purely intellectual questions Keynes several times suggested, in guarded terms, that the distance between them could not be great. But there was to be no meeting of minds, and on Keynes's death in 1946 their views were unreconciled.[34]

Robertson, as is well known, was an intellectually brilliant man but by nature shy and sensitive. In commenting on various drafts of ideas sent to him over the years by Keynes, he had found himself cast in the part of 'keeper of Keynes's conscience', an emotionally draining role which he found increasingly difficult to sustain. Nevertheless, in arguing the case, after 1936, for continuity and evolution in the development of economic doctrines, Robertson was to provide the perfect foil to Keynes's cocksure confidence and revolutionary inconoclasm.

There are various possible reasons for Robertson's rejection of the Keynesian Revolution. It has, for example, been suggested that because Robertson was himself 'enlightened' and had moved away from the classical position, he was unable to grasp the full significance of Keynes's innovations.[35] This explanation is unconvincing, for two reasons. The first is that Robertson explicitly denied that he had 'found it difficult to appreciate the revolution in thought' which followed the publication of the *General Theory*, on the grounds (significantly, as we shall see below) that the term 'Keynesian Revolution' implied greater advances in thought than were in fact contained in the *General Theory*.[36] The second is that it doesn't really square with Robertson's awareness of the development of economic doctrines and his own and Keynes's position as major participants in that development. Robertson was conscious that both he and Keynes had departed from orthodoxy – and indeed it was Robertson who had initiated the move.[37] Nevertheless, when assessing the theoretical innovations represented by individual elements of the *General Theory*, it was not to his own work that he turned for a benchmark but to the economics of Marshall and Pigou, the very targets at which Keynes's attack had been aimed.

Another possibility is that Robertson felt it necessary to view the development of economic theory as a process characterised by continuity; proceeding, that is, by way of evolution rather than revolution and with due recognition for the contributions of predecessors.

Now whether this was merely a 'desire to see justice done, an attempt to make Keynes give credit where credit was due'[38] or, less charitably, an example of Robertson's 'piety', is a matter of taste and judgement. For Keynes, however, it was unquestionably the latter, for in 1933 he wrote:

> My differences, such as they are, from Mr. Robertson chiefly arise out of my conviction that both he and I differ more fundamentally from our predecessors than his piety will allow.[39]

Keynes had earlier attempted to explain to Robertson their relative positions *vis-à-vis* classical theory, and it is clear that he perceived the source of their differences to lie in Robertson's attempts to effect a reconciliation between received theory and the insistent demands of his (Robertson's) own insights:

> I see that you are saying that it all makes no difference, that Marshall related it all to a Royal Commission in an affirmative sigh, that it has been well known to Pigou for years past and is to be found in a footnote to *Industrial Fluctuations*, that Neisser's bunk comes to the same thing, and the like; though in truth, *you* are the only writer where much of it is to be found in embryo and to whom acknowledgements are due. But I would rather you said this, than that it was wrong! You are like a man searching for a formula by which he can agree without changing his mind.[40]

It was Robertson's attempts at reconciliation between old forms and new ideas that caused him to concentrate his attention on the detail or individual parts of Keynes's argument – the better to see to what extent there was correspondence with, or departure from, the individual elements of orthodox theory. It was, in turn, this attention to detail which prevented Robertson from making a generous and open-minded attempt to catch the sense of Keynes's new conception, his overall design. Replying to Keynes's letter, from which the above was taken, Robertson wrote:

> Both over the *Treatise* and this book [the *General Theory*] I have gone through real intellectual torment trying to make up my mind

> whether, as you often seem to claim, there is some new piece on the board or rather a rearrangement, which seems to you superior, of existing pieces.[41]

The point is, of course, that it is perfectly possible to achieve a revolution by brilliant new design, using materials which are in themselves neither wholly nor even preponderantly new. In Keynes's case not only was the overall conception new, with, say, the level of demand determining employment and the real wage, rather than the real wage determining employment and the level of demand; but in his treatment of saving, investment and the rate of interest the contrast between Keynes and the classics is complete.

ROBERTSON'S DILEMMA

Robertson's approach to economics, like that of every other economist, must to some extent have been shaped by his personality. This, in Robertson's case, could perhaps account for his fastidious over-emphasis on detail at the expense of the whole, his scrupulous concern with the apportionment of credit and, as we shall see, a step-by-step 'realistic' approach to economic analysis. That he should have been in 'intellectual torment' in attempting to assess Keynes's contribution is itself significant, and it is clear from his response to Keynes's criticism during the period preceding the publication of Robertson's *Banking Policy and the Price Level*[42] (the period, it must be noted, from which Keynes dated all his emancipation)[43] that Robertson was not of the stuff that revolutionaries are made – at least when working in the shadow of Keynes:

> I am afraid of being swayed into publishing by the desire to avoid disappointment and loss: but I am also afraid of being swayed against publishing by my tendency to believe you are always right! Sometimes when I have stood out against this weakness, I have been justified![44]

But there was more to Robertson's problem than his relationship with Keynes. The due apportionment of roles in the post-1936 debate, referred to earlier, was the product of deeper influences, which manifested themselves in Robertson's need to retain links with the orthodoxy from which his own ideas desired to lead him.[45]

Keynes sensed the nature of Robertson's dilemma, and in commenting on a paper sent to him by Robertson in 1937 he gently chided its author in words vivid with imagery and symbolism. He described the paper as 'a brilliant effort ... But it is an extreme example of your chivalry towards the underdog argument and your sentimental attachment to words which have once meant something to you.' With what is plainly an adaptation of lines by Swinburne, Keynes suggested:

> 'Even the muddiest river winds somewhere safe to sea' would be a good title. I feel, after reading it, that the strictly intellectual differences between us are probably very small indeed at bottom. But I am trying all the time to disentangle myself, whilst you are trying to keep entangled. You are, so to speak, bent on creeping back into your mother's womb; whilst I am shaking myself like a dog on dry land.[46]

Keynes's choice of metaphor and simile cannot be fortuitous. A sense of the urge to return to beginnings is strongly marked, as the direct reference to 'mother's womb' and the oblique reference via the river winding to sea make clear; for the personification of the sea as mother-figure is a recurrent strain in Swinburne's poetry. In addition, the choice of allusion itself suggests that Keynes regarded Robertson's undue attachment to his intellectual origins as potentially dangerous, for in Swinburne's representation the sea can be both mother and lover,[47] 'whose embraces are at once more fatal and sexually keen than others'.[48]

If this allusion to Swinburne *identifies* Robertson's problem, then there is a related reference which: (i) draws attention to its consequences; (ii) indicates Keynes's desire to help Robertson to solve it – both in Robertson's interest and in his own; (iii) exposes the dilemma of the counsellor who is seeking the correct approach to his subject. In the *General Theory* Keynes had dismissed neo-classical attempts to graft on monetary influences to the classical (saving-and-investment) theory of the rate of interest, with a paraphrase quotation from Ibsen's play *The Wild Duck*:

> But at this point we are in deep water. 'The wild duck has dived down to the bottom – as deep as she can get – and bitten fast hold of the weed and tangle and all the rubbish that is down there, and

it would need an extraordinarily clever dog to dive after and fish her up again.'[49]

Though the literary reference is different, it contains the same symbolic elements. The sea again enters, as a means of escape but also of destruction: Keynes's 'we are in deep water' clearly means 'in difficulties'; while Ibsen's play refers to 'the sea-deeps'. Also we have 'tangle' as against 'keep entangled' and 'disentangle'. Finally, the dog, which previously had been rather cryptically juxtaposed with the mother's womb, is now seen to play an important role *vis-à-vis* the wild duck – and to have a reason for shaking itself on dry land.

At the centre of Ibsen's play is the legend that a wounded wild duck, rather than face the humiliation of capture by the hunter, will dive down and drown herself by clinging to the bottom-weed. In the play, however, a wounded wild duck is rescued from its chosen fate by a dog of extraordinary powers, and lives on in an attic as the symbol of a creature out of its element but outwardly (and perhaps inwardly) content with its new life.

In the *General Theory* the *dramatis personae* are referred to only in general terms, as members of the neo-classical school who had fatally entrapped themselves in the weedy depths of the loanable-funds approach. The identity of the clever dog is not given.

In the later (December 1937) reference, however, it becomes clear that the central characters are Robertson and Keynes; and in their respective roles we see the predicaments of both. While Robertson is perceived to need the comfort and security of his intellectual origins, in creeping back into his mother's womb, for Keynes the waters had broken, there could be no going back. But how was Keynes to take Robertson with him, both to release him from the self-imposed captivity which stultified his intellectual development *and*, by the same token, to establish the superiority of his own (revolutionary) approach over that of Robertson?

Two interpretations of the wild-duck symbolism when applied to the condition of the central character, Hjalmar Ekdal, are given in the play: (i) that of Gregers Werle, which sees the creature in the attic as still the wild duck in the sea-deeps: capable of being rescued by a clever dog and therefore requiring only a 'sight of heaven and sea' to make it abandon its life of illusion and unreality; (ii) that of Dr Relling, which sees the wild duck not as she *was* but as she *is*: in the attic, damaged and in captivity but domesticated and content, and from which state she does not wish to be, nor cannot be, rescued.[50]

The first interpretation implies that Hjalmar Ekdal can be shocked back into acceptance of the reality he requires for his fulfilment, by being confronted with the truth about his present position. The second interpretation, on the other hand, sees Hjalmar as a willing and necessary prisoner of an illusory but comfortable existence.

When applied to the position of Robertson, a clue to Keynes's interpretation is suggested by the general strategy he adopted to get his *General Theory* accepted by the orthodox school. That is, he believed that by confronting them with the 'truth' (by challenging them directly on points at issue) he would make them face 'reality' and so accept the new approach. He failed and was surprised.

In the *General Theory*, therefore, he possibly takes the first interpretation and sees himself as the extraordinarily clever dog able to effect a rescue. Later, suitably chastened, he shows more insight into Robertson's problem (as indicated by his mother–womb symbolism) but still makes reference to his former view (the dog shaking itself on dry land) *because* Robertson is the key critic whom he feels he must convince. Therefore, while he increasingly takes the second interpretation of Robertson's position, he nevertheless feels it necessary to indicate to Robertson the true reason for his inability to follow Keynes: that is, that Robertson senses his view is flawed but is unable to abandon it and start again because of his need to retain the link with the past.

Consequently, in Keynes's letters, arguments over points of theory at issue go hand-in-hand with hints at the true source of Robertson's difficulties. But, for Robertson, too much was at stake, so that his response to Keynes is a stone-walling insistence on the need to argue out theoretical punctilios; there can be no effort of will on Robertson's part to reach out for and grasp Keynes's main thesis. He is emotionally incapable of, and unwilling to make, the leap of faith.

As in the play, with the death of Hedvig, there is 'tragedy' in the outcome of the Robertson–Keynes controversy, ending as it does with the estrangement of the two former friends and colleagues.

There is a widespread unease among commentators that perhaps Robertson's achievements as an economist have, despite the many academic honours accorded him, been generally underestimated.[51] An assessment of Robertson's contribution to economics is far beyond the scope of this book, but in relation to the Keynesian Revolution the issue is fairly clear-cut. To the extent that it was necessary to see that the provision of a proper basis for commonly accepted policies required a fundamental overturning of the core of classical theory, Robertson's achievement was of a lower order than that of Keynes. Robertson was too deferential to past thought and past personalities. It is perhaps the least-remarked aspect of Keynes's individual achievement that he was prepared to reject openly the inherited views of much respected teachers and colleagues for what he believed to be the correct approach. Keynes's revolution displays on the part of its author a degree of intellectual honesty and moral resolution which is wholly admirable.

IRRECONCILABLE DIFFERENCES

There is a third possible reason for Robertson's rejection of the Keynesian Revolution, which follows on directly from the above and which has generally been underemphasised. That is, that there were differences on intellectual grounds which could not be resolved except by either Robertson or Keynes admitting definite and fundamental error. Neither was to do so. Keynes, because his argument followed on from principles which derived from the working of a monetary economy, was successfully able to withstand Robertson's relentless probing. On the other hand, Robertson's attack was conditioned by his chosen approach, of modifying and adding to the existing body of theory. This approach, however, had three important but inhibiting consequences.

The first is that Robertson was led into error in his own theory. That is, he inherited along with the classical forms some classical assumptions, and these, when incorporated into his own analysis, were to flaw his argument to such an extent that his attack on Keynes was nullified.

The second is that he was presented with some knotty problems of reconciliation between old and new. In particular he was compelled through his confusion over the nature of saving and the finance of investment to invoke, as a keystone of his loanable-funds theory, the doctrine of forced saving upon which Keynes had deliberately turned his back. This in turn entirely depended for its validity on his adopted methodology of period analysis or the step-by-step approach, which again was completely at odds with Keynes's states-of-expectations approach. These matters will be examined in Chapters 5 and 8.

Finally, his own conception of the saving–investment relationship, based as it was on classical assumptions, led him seriously to misinterpret Keynes's argument; and it was upon this misinterpretation that much of his criticism of Keynes was founded.

That Robertson himself believed that his differences from Keynes were substantive and not merely cosmetic is suggested by Dr Presley in his major study of Robertsonian economics. Presley points out that while Robertson rejected Say's Law and a belief in any automatic mechanism for generating full employment in the economy, he saw his own theoretical contribution as growing out of the Cambridge orthodoxy – which he felt it necessary to defend against Keynes and the Keynesian Revolution. In this regard, Presley argues:

> His defence did not arise from any personal loyalty to Marshall and Pigou, he was much closer to Keynes than to either of them ... Rather he believed Keynes to be mistaken on a purely intellectual level.[52]

It is to intellectual differences that we shall turn below for a resolution of the conflict between Keynes and Robertson. Notice in this regard that it was Keynes rather than Robertson who on several occasions reached out by suggesting that there was in reality little ground to traverse for agreement to be reached. In addition, it was Keynes who at a late stage was to introduce a concept, 'finance', which he intended should not only make his own analysis more complete but also build a bridge to those who were approaching the same set of phenomena from a different direction.[53]

Both these examples of attempts at reconciliation lend support to the idea that, though Keynes correctly identified the seat of Robertson's misunderstanding (a confusion between 'the revolving fund of money in circulation and the flow of new saving'),[54] he may not have realised fully the implications for Robertson of making the step towards Keynes that could have brought agreement.

For, in one sense, Robertson had been right to concentrate attention on the detail of Keynes's argument: that is, on certain points the validity of which was fundamental to the success of Keynes's new approach. These were, of course, those topics (relating to saving, investment and the rate of interest) which we earlier identified in Chapter 3 as key indicators. If Robertson had succeeded in defeating Keynes on these theoretical points he would effectively have drawn the teeth of the Keynesian Revolution.

The catch, however, was that the argument worked entirely symmetrically. That is, if Robertson were forced to admit the validity of Keynes's approach on these points, his own loanable-funds theory would immediately fall to the ground. For, despite the formal equivalence which can be shown to exist between them, Keynes's and Robertson's theories are incompatible and to accept one is to reject the other. And in this respect Robertson was at a fatal disadvantage, for his theory contained a basic weakness. Robertson failed to understand the nature of saving and the 'paradox of thrift', and the implications of this failure ran through the strata of his argument like a geological fault. Once the error was recognised, the loanable-funds theory, the whole intricate apparatus of reconciliation between old orthodoxy and new insights, would be revealed as invalid.

The ramifications of this weakness for Robertson's argument will become apparent in the following chapters. However, we may notice at the outset that Presley's thorough and well-documented study, which is strongly sympathetic to Robertson and seeks to demonstrate the superiority of his arguments, explicitly recognises this weakness, though the recognition is tucked away in a footnote with scarcely an inkling of its significance.[55]

5 The Robertsonian Critique

INTRODUCTION

In keeping with his philosophy of evolution in economic doctrines, Robertson's own theories were developed continuously throughout his professional lifetime, with none of the fundamental overturning of previously held views such as marked Keynes's progress.

It is, therefore, possible to discuss Robertson's principal ideas without specific reference to the fact that they were developed over a period of time and encompassed a number of his major publications. For Keynes, on the other hand, we refer only to the economics of the *General Theory* and the post-1936 debate.

Our starting-point is with the 'forced saving' theory, the theory which underlay Robertson's position on questions of theory and policy during the inter-war period and beyond. The elements relevant to an understanding of forced saving and of its importance for Robertson can be set out as follows.[1]

INVESTMENT AND SAVING

Though Robertson remained in some fundamentals decidedly classical, he did pioneer the view in Britain that the acts of saving and investment are not synonymous and that there must be a clear distinction between decisions to save and decisions to invest.

Taking the investment side first, Robertson distinguished between two types of capital. Fixed capital or 'man made material wealth' consists of those physical instruments of production which can be used to produce goods and services in the future. Of greater interest here, however, is circulating or working capital, which can be thought of as the stock of goods and services used up during the production process and without which it could not take place.[2] This concept derives from the real-saving theory, which in turn has its origins in the economics of Robinson Crusoe's island.

Here the opportunity costs of producing capital goods, as against producing consumer goods or taking leisure, have an immediately practical, as against a purely academic, interest. This is because in order to be able to devote the necessary time to the production of capital goods Crusoe must first accumulate a sufficient stock of consumption goods. These goods will provide subsistence during the period of investment and so constitute the *real capital* required for the project.

It is important to notice that for this approach the notion of the necessity of real prior accumulation carries over into the monetary economy, where real provision must be made for consumption during the investment period whatever the stock of fiat money available.

Whereas for Crusoe's economy circulating capital consists almost entirely of the accumulated stock of consumption goods, in a modern capitalist economy the preponderance will consist of work in progress and the stock of raw materials used up in the production process. With a stable level of output, the amount of circulating capital required will vary directly with the average length of the production period, with, conversely, the implication that the larger is the stock of circulating capital the longer can be the production period and/or the volume of production.

This, then, explains the derivation of the classical proposition that saving is equal to investment, because saving, which is represented by the accumulated stock of consumption goods, determines the quantity of investment which can be undertaken.

On the saving side, therefore, Robertson in his early work equated the quantity of saving which is available for investment with the community's stock of consumption goods accumulated for subsistence purposes, and at first he applied the analysis to a monetary economy without taking account of the influence of banking policy on saving. Later, however, the scope of the 'loanable funds' concept was broadened to include the forced saving provided as a result of banking activity, so that there was not only the notion of saving *determining* investment but also the possibility of confusion between saving and the means available to finance investment.

Robertson referred to saving in the Keynesian sense as 'lacking'; total lacking, consisting of spontaneous lacking (or voluntary saving), and forced lacking (or forced saving). The function of lacking is to provide the capital required in the production process. Long lacking is the lacking used up in the provision of fixed capital; while short lacking provides for working capital. The concept of forced lacking – or forced saving – applies to working capital, rather than fixed capital, and hence to the provision of short lacking, rather than long lacking, because of bank lending patterns prevalent at the time Robertson was writing.[3] The process of forced saving itself can be explained as follows.

FORCED SAVING

Short lacking is necessary because the average length of the production period is greater than zero; that is, because the production of consumer goods cannot be instantaneously expanded. As a preliminary to increased production, entrepreneurs need to expand their working capital. The creation of additional working capital requires increased employment of labour. In turn the higher level of incomes generated leads to increased expenditure in the consumption-goods market *in advance of* the requisite increase in output. As consumption-goods prices are pushed upward some consumers are forced to reduce their consumption; the reduction being, of course, the saving required to match the investment in working capital.

The role of the banks in the process is to expand their lending in response to the demands of entrepreneurs and so provide the finance required to increase the quantity of working capital. From this there follows a standard quantity theory result of the Cambridge Equation type, of a rise in the money supply followed by direct expenditure in the goods market and a rise in the price level. Therefore, by utilising the credit-creating capacities of the banks, entrepreneur-investors force would-be consumers to increase their saving.

There are three further points to notice about the forced-saving process. The first is that it is heavily dependent for its validity on Robertson's adopted methodology of period analysis or the step-by-step approach. We will pass over questions relating to the *sequence* of events postulated by Robertson and accept it as it is. The important point to bear in mind is that because period analysis played a crucial role in Robertson's theory, its absence from Keynes's approach was a central feature of Robertson's criticism. The irrelevance of this criticism will become apparent in due course.

The second point is that Robertson's account of forced saving in no way depends upon inelasticity in the supply of output such as would occur at full employment, but only on the existence of lags inherent in the production process. Here again we see the key role of period analysis, since, for forced saving to occur in the presence of unemployed resources the rise in the price level must precede the expansion of output.

The third point is that the forced-saving process is accompanied by a shift in relative prices. Entrepreneurs' increased expenditure financed by bank loans will cause the prices of capital goods to rise faster than those of consumer goods and there will be an incentive for resources to move from consumer to capital goods industries. Though this point is not relevant for present purposes it will become so in our discussion of the Austrian theory of money.[4]

THE FLAW IN ROBERTSON'S ARGUMENT

In order to understand the weakness in Robertson's argument[5] we must bring together two related aspects of his analysis: (i) his adopted methodology of adding to and amending existing theory; from which followed (ii) his acceptance of the real-saving theory, based on the economics of the Robinson Crusoe economy.

Because Robertson failed to understand the paradox of thrift, he saw voluntary (prior) saving as a source of finance for investment. However, in attempting to make classical theory more realistic Robertson added two new sources of finance, namely, new money creation by banks and dishoarding of idle balances. Therefore, while in classical theory voluntary saving and investment were equal, both being functions of the rate of interest and, therefore, flowing in a kind of natural harmony, for Robertson a desire for increased production could give rise to a demand for increased investment financed not by voluntary saving but by new money and dishoarding. Consequently saving and investment might not be equal – in the sense that investment could be greater than *voluntary* saving. Hence the crucial importance of *forced* saving, to supply the deficiency of saving.

In other words: (i) it was *necessary* in the loanable-funds theory to provide the extra saving to match the extra investment financed by credit creation and dishoarding; and (ii) it was *possible* to do so because of Robertson's period analysis and postulated sequence of events.

It is clear that Robertson understood both that there must be funds (actual money) to finance investment *and* that the increased investment must be matched by an equal amount of abstinence or saving.

The problem lies in confusing the two processes: to believe that the one embodies the other.

The source of inspiration for Robertson's forced-saving thesis is not obvious but it may lie in a paper written by Keynes in 1913.[6] This, of course, would be the work of the unreformed Keynes, who saw the source of finance for investment to be saving of some kind. The interesting point for present purposes is that Keynes envisaged the possibility that saving might exceed the amount of present resources set aside for investment ('deliberate saving') due to the activities of banks in mobilising balances deposited with them as the basis for loans to finance investment projects (undeliberate saving).

Keynes's paper did not enquire as to the effect of banking activity on the structure of prices and the consequent shift between consumption and investment, but here, none the less, we have clearly the classical version of the finance of investment, modified to take account of the operations of the banking system.

The root of all Robertson's trouble can be traced back to his attempt to develop this classically based approach. It caused him to neglect the question of the nature of saving itself and the phenomenon of the paradox of thrift, based upon the expenditure–income identity, which rendered the classical approach untenable.

It is this neglect which accounts for his continued acceptance of the notion that saving determines investment, for his confusion in attributing to saving the dual role of abstinence or waiting and of providing funds for investment, and for his belief that investment and saving can be unequal in the sense that there is excessive investment relative to voluntary saving.

This conclusion can be confirmed by examining the sequence of the causal relationship between (i) the provision of funds for investment and (ii) the element of abstinence or waiting, in each of Robertson's sources of lacking:

(1) Spontaneous lacking (voluntary or prior saving out of income):

[income] → saving → money for finance of investment.

(2) Forced lacking (due to banking operations):

money for finance of investment → [expenditure → prices] → saving.

(3) Forced lacking (due to net dishoarding):

[dishoarding] → money for finance of investment [expenditure → prices] → saving.

(4) (Induced) forced lacking (due to attempts to restore real balances after rise in price level):

money for finance of investment → [expenditure → prices → real balances] → saving.

Notice that only in the case of (1), spontaneous lacking, does saving initiate the sequence, does abstinence precede finance; in all other cases it follows as a *consequence* of prior expenditure. In other words, voluntary saving is the 'odd man out', in that it provides the funds to finance investment; whereas forced saving is *determined by* the extent of the prior provision of funds to finance investment and consequent expenditure. Voluntary or prior saving is the strictly classical element in Robertson's theory and is included because of his policy of building on existing analysis.

The fault in this element lies in applying the real-saving theory of a Robinson Crusoe economy to a monetary economy. In a developed 'social' economy (an economy with a number of interacting participants), in which *exchange* takes place mediated by money, the necessary equality of purchases and sales, of expenditure and income, will ensure the operation of the paradox of thrift. That is, in a simple Income = (Consumption) Expenditure model an attempt to save more will result in a *fall* in the rate of saving. In a simple Income = (Consumption + Autonomous Investment) Expenditure model an attempt to save more will reduce the level of income but leave the rate of saving unchanged.

This is obviously not just a semantic point. It means that saving does not determine investment, and therefore that a policy of attempting to encourage investment by the stimulation of saving will be self-defeating. It is the point which distinguishes Keynes's theory from classically based theories. It implies that the loanable-funds approach can be at best misleading and that it cannot be validated by incorporation into some composite approach such as the *IS–LM* model.[7]

This is the basic weakness in Robertson's argument, the recognition of which would have meant conceding victory to Keynes. What is left? The cases in which lacking arises as a consequence of prior expenditure are more promising. The question remains, however, does lacking arise as a consequence of rising prices – even at under-employment levels of output – or as a consequence of changes in real income?

It is in this regard that the importance of Keynes's multiplier analysis is revealed – an importance that Robertson clearly sensed, for he centred much of his attack on Keynes around its function and mode of operation. Indeed, any doubts which remain concerning the above interpretation of Robertson's position are dispelled as soon as we turn to Robertson's criticism of Keynes.

ROBERTSON'S CRUCIAL QUESTION FOR KEYNES

Robertson formulated his criticism of Keynes by reference to three main considerations. The first is Robertson's acceptance of the principle that prior saving determines investment and provides not only the necessary element of abstinence from consumption but also the funds required to finance investment in a non-barter economy. The second is that Keynes had turned this causal sequence on its head by claiming that investment determines saving, with saving made equal to investment through changes in the level of real income rather than the rate of interest.[8] The third is that in the *General Theory* Keynes was critical of the Robertsonian resort to forced saving as an under-employment phenomenon and did not utilise the forced-saving device in his own analysis.

Consequently, the question to which Robertson directed his attention was: if for Keynes investment is to be financed wholly from voluntary saving and saving is determined by investment, how is the necessary finance to be provided for investment to take place? Robertson sought for an answer as follows.

ROBERTSON'S VIEW OF THE MULTIPLIER

In Keynes's view the quantity of saving equal to a given amount of investment was generated through the successive rounds of the multiplier. By taking this in conjunction with the commonly held belief that Keynes employed only static analysis and proceeded by comparing 'snapshot' views of positions of equilibrium, a conclusion seemed clear enough. That is, that the multiplier was being assumed to work *instantaneously* and so provide the saving and the funds for investment at the very moment they were required.

This conclusion, based as it was on the view that Keynes considered only positions of equilibrium and neglected intervening states of change, seemed to be confirmed by Keynes's 'other' theory of saving and investment which contended that they are always equal by definition. Both approaches precluded the possibility of disturbance, which might lead to the inequality of investment and saving such as existed in Robertson's theory, from banking operations in creating new money or from changes in hoarding behaviour. Keynes was able to hold these views, it was alleged, because of his failure to distinguish between *ex ante* and *ex post* concepts, between planned saving and realised saving.

Consequently, not only was Keynes of the *General Theory* critical of the Robertsonian conception of forced saving itself but his methodology obviated any *need* to resort to it. Below full employment the multiplier automatically and instantaneously provided the amount of saving required to finance the investment without resort to the banks or the need for a rise in the price level.

On this view Keynes's multiplier analysis provided a completely alternative account of the saving-and-investment process and a most powerful challenge to Robertson's forced-saving doctrine. Nevertheless, from a loanable-funds standpoint the multiplier approach depended for its validity on assumptions which in the real world were demonstrably untenable. Keynes's attack could therefore be defeated by reference to these crucially important assumptions. The argument would go as follows.

Because to a loanable-funds theorist voluntary saving was a principal source of funds for investment, it was clear that the funds must be provided in step with the increments of saving through the multiplier. However, not until the last increment of income was generated would saving be equal to investment. But if these funds were to finance the initial investment they would have to be provided instantaneously.

This could only be done if the multiplier were assumed to operate without a lag and in the real world this would clearly be a nonsense. Thus the necessity of having to recognise the existence of lags in the working-out of the multiplier was seen as a body-blow to Keynes's attack. Furthermore, because sufficient voluntary saving was only generated *after* the multiplier had worked itself out there was a need to identify an interim source of finance, and this, from a Robertsonian standpoint, led the argument back to forced saving.

Indeed, confirmation for Robertson that Keynes had been forced to recognise this weakness in his argument, was provided by Keynes's introduction, subsequently to the *General Theory*, of a new source of funds which operated in advance of capital formation, at the time the investment decision was taken. This source of funds, provided by the banks, Keynes called 'finance', and with its introduction Keynes was seen to signify his recognition of the dynamic nature of the saving–investment process.

Even now, however, Keynes sought to avoid any suggestion that he had been compelled to accept the forced-saving thesis. He did this by denying the usual quantity theory result of a rise in the money supply – a rise in the price level – by continuing to assume that below full employment the supply of output was highly (perfectly) elastic so that prices need not rise.

THE MULTIPLIER, CONSUMPTION BEHAVIOUR AND THE ACCELERATOR

The main plank of Robertson's attack on the multiplier was, therefore, that it must be recognised as a dynamic rather than a static process.

In addition, however, Robertson believed that the existence of influences on consumption behaviour apart from income would produce instability in the propensity to consume and so destroy the predictability of the multiplier and the essential symmetry of Keynes's argument.

Furthermore, Robertson claimed that Keynes had neglected to take account of the accelerator hypothesis. Working in conjunction with the multiplier the accelerator would ensure that a rise in income consequent upon an increase in investment expenditure would in turn induce a further increase in investment. This would give rise to a further demand for funds to finance the induced investment and so pose the question of where the *additional* funds were to come from.

DID KEYNES RECANT?

It followed that the approach Keynes adopted in the *General Theory* made it impossible for him to accept the loanable-funds theory of the determination of the rate of interest. He therefore had to cast about for an alternative explanation and adopted the familiar liquidity-preference theory.

This was a purely monetary theory which denied any major role for the real forces of 'productivity and thrift'. And, as much else in Keynes's approach, it was cast in purely static terms, with the rate of interest being determined by the demand for money in relation to the available stock. It thus stood directly opposed to the dynamic approach of Robertson in which the rate of interest was determined by *flows* of loanable funds.

Nevertheless, under pressure from Robertson in the post-*General Theory* debate, Keynes was seen to recant his interest theory and accept the neo-classical elements of productivity and thrift as major determinants of the rate of interest. He was thus no longer able to claim that a change in investment due to the increased productivity of capital would leave the rate of interest unchanged.

This recantation was confirmed for Robertson by Keynes's apparent acceptance of the *IS–LM* reconciliation between the loanable-funds and liquidity-preference theories, which, because it was a reconciliation which owed more to Robertson's theory than to Keynes, involved a move backwards towards neo-classical theory. This acceptance also involved Keynes's acknowledgement of the influence of the rate of interest on saving, though indirectly via changes in investment and income.

Finally, it is not possible to help Keynes out of the need to recant his interest theory by arguing that his liquidity-preference approach was essentially concerned with the short term where monetary forces are dominant. This is because Keynes's market rate of interest is determined by reference to some safe, future rate – the 'normal' rate – in relation to which individuals make the choice between holding money or bonds. Keynes failed to explain how the normal rate is determined, though enquiry would have forced him to recognise the influence of the long-term forces of productivity and thrift.

THE CENTRAL ISSUE: THE RELATIONSHIP BETWEEN SAVING AND THE FINANCE OF INVESTMENT

It should now be clear that in distinguishing between the two approaches everything hinges on the view taken of the relationship between abstinence, saving or lacking on the one hand and the provision of funds to finance investment on the other. Keynes regarded them as essentially different processes and kept them separate. Robertson, by contrast, confused them, and as a consequence fatally flawed his own argument and made nugatory his attack on Keynes.

This is a very important conclusion, and in case there is any lingering doubt about the argument upon which it is based it can be recapitulated as follows.

Robertson believed in the efficacy of saving as a determinant of investment. Prior saving not only performed the necessary act of abstinence but also supplied the funds by which the investment should be financed. Because, in a real-world economy, purchasing power could be supplied through the operations of the banking system and also through dishoarding, a demand for funds to finance an increase in investment could be supplied without a change in prior saving.

It was thus possible at this stage for saving and investment to be unequal; where then was the extra abstinence to come from? In Robertson's view it was forced out of consumers with laggard incomes. That is, expenditure on investment put purchasing power onto the market in advance of any increase in consumption goods output, so that prices would rise and some would-be consumers would have to make do with less. The rise in prices thus transferred resources to capital goods industries.

We have, therefore, a sequence of events in which saving precedes investment and supplies the necessary funds, and then investment precedes saving and the funds are introduced from the banks in advance of saving. It is, consequently, not surprising that Robertson should regard Keynes's multiplier as a major threat, for the multiplier denied this sequence in its entirety. Now investment determined saving throughout and there was, moreover, no need for *forced* saving.

However, because of his confusion between the essentially separate processes of saving and of financing investment, Robertson thought that the multiplier, in generating new income and the requisite saving, had also to produce the funds for investment *out of that saving*. It followed that the only way that Keynes could supply the funds to finance the original investment was to assume that the multiplier operated instantaneously. That is, Keynes allowed only static analysis for the key element in his theory, in contrast with the dynamics which characterised Robertson's whole approach.

Here, it seemed, was the weak link in the Keynesian chain. Once Keynes was compelled to accept that the multiplier operated with a lag he had to introduce a new source of finance for investment *in advance of saving*. From Robertson's viewpoint this was a fundamental shift in the *sequence* of events admitted by Keynes and to Robertson indicated a move towards forced saving.

THE STRATEGY FOR A REPLY TO ROBERTSON

The reply to Robertson's attack must begin in general terms, with an examination of Keynes's fundamentally original contribution to the theory of the monetary production economy, the principle of effective demand, with which he overturned Say's Law as the tacit basis of the classical macroeconomics.

This will also explain the importance of investment as the key element of expenditure in the determination of employment and output in a 'capitalistic' free-market economy. In addition, we shall gain an understanding of Keynes's preferred 'states-of-expectations' methodology for 'taming the real world' as a necessary aid for his demonstration of the role of effective demand.

The next step will be to explain the nature of saving and its relationship to investment, before replying in detail to the Robertsonian charges relating to saving and investment. Then after dealing at some length with the question of the finance of investment we shall be ready to introduce the controversy over Keynes's theory of the rate of interest.

6 The Principle of Effective Demand

INTRODUCTION

The neutral-money, real-exchange economy of economic orthodoxy is typically encapsulated in a theoretical model which assumes away the uncertainties and foibles of the real world by allowing full information and perfect foresight. With given resources and known wants, it would be possible to formulate plans which would produce optimal results for each individual; while for the economy as a whole a path consistent with equilibrium would be determined from the outset.

It would, of course, be possible to relax the assumptions of the model to allow for the imperfections of the real world and to approximate its actual events. For example, the trade cycle was a well-observed phenomenon, and orthodoxy recognised its existence by thinking in terms of a general *tendency* (subject to constraints and shocks) towards full-employment equilibrium rather than of its permanent maintenance. Though Say's Law still underlay the theory, it would be in terms of what has been dubbed 'Say's Equality' rather than the very restrictive 'Says Identity' so far considered.

KEYNES AND EXPECTATIONS

Similarly, though Keynes's explanation of persistent unemployment is often depicted as depending on the necessity for entrepreneurs to make plans under conditions of uncertainty, with the consequent possibility that expectations will be disappointed, it should be borne in mind that 'the traditional explanation of unemployment linked the mistaken expectation of entrepreneurs (too optimistic in the boom and too pessimistic in the slump) to fluctuations in output and employment'. It has been pointed out[1] that, for example, F. Lavington, writing in 1922, had argued that probably the most important single cause of unemployment was cyclical changes in business activity; that the state of business activity at any time depended on entrepreneurs' estimates of future market conditions; and that these estimates were in turn shaped by the general state of business confidence which had a tendency to rise or fall cumulatively. Moreover, Lavington had indicated that his summary represented the views of leading contemporary (neo-classical) economists such as Marshall, Pigou and Robertson, so that 'Keynes could thus hardly claim anything novel in his emphasis on expectations'.[2]

EFFECTIVE DEMAND: KEYNES'S PRINCIPAL INNOVATION

It is true that expectations play a leading part in Keynes's approach and indeed we have to think in terms of expected rather than actual magnitudes as the determinants of employment and output. Nevertheless, Keynes went to considerable lengths to make clear that the principal innovation in his theory of a monetary production economy was not expectations as such but the *principle of effective demand*, which he referred to as 'the substance of the General Theory of Employment'.[3]

The main idea can be concisely stated as follows:

> *effective demand* is simply the aggregate income (or proceeds) which the entrepreneurs expect to receive, inclusive of the incomes which they will hand on to the other factors of production, from the amount of current employment which they decide to give. The aggregate demand function relates various hypothetical quantities of employment to the proceeds which their outputs are expected to yield; and the effective demand is the point on the aggregate demand function which becomes effective because, taken in conjunction with the conditions of supply,[4] it corresponds to the level of employment which maximises the entrepreneur's expectations of profit.[5]

Therefore, corresponding to the point of effective demand there will be a determinate and equilibrium level of employment. If, on the other hand, for any given level of employment the expected proceeds exceed the aggregate supply price, entrepreneurs will be motivated to expand employment and output up to the point at which rising costs make supply price equal to expected proceeds. It follows that in making their employment decisions entrepreneurs will be guided by their expectations of aggregate demand. By definition their choice will be that of the expected equilibrium employment.

> The amount of labour N which the entrepreneurs decide to employ depends on the sum (D) of two quantities, namely D_1, the amount which the community is expected to spend on consumption, and D_2, the amount which it is expected to devote to new investment. D is what we have called above the *effective demand*.[6]

THE ROLE OF CONSUMPTION

With regard to the consumption component, it was one of Keynes's innovations to make the distinction between the propensity to consume as against the amount consumed; where the propensity to consume refers to the functional relationship between a given level of income and the expenditure on consumption out of that level of income. The importance of this for present purposes is that, as employment increases, aggregate real income is increased. Now, the propensity to consume is assumed to be such that as aggregate real income is increased aggregate consumption increases but not by as much as income (that is, the marginal propensity to consume is greater than zero but less than unity). The implication is that:

> employers would make a loss if the whole of the increased employment were to be devoted to satisfying the increased demand for immediate consumption. Thus, to justify any given amount of employment there must be an amount of current investment sufficient to absorb the excess of total output over what the community chooses to consume when employment is at the given level ... It follows, therefore, that, given what we shall call the community's propensity to consume, the equilibrium level of employment, i.e. the level at which there is no inducement to employers as a whole either to expand or to contract employment, will depend on the amount of current investment. The amount of current investment will depend in turn, on what we shall call the inducement to invest; and the inducement to invest will be found to depend on the relation between the schedule of the marginal efficiency of capital and the complex of rates of interest on loans of various maturities and risks.[7]

THE ROLE OF INVESTMENT

It was of the essence of Keynes's approach to the determination of investment in a monetary economy that the 'marginal efficiency of capital' is not the same thing as the ruling rate of interest. While the schedule of the marginal efficiency of capital will govern the terms upon which entrepreneurs *demand* funds to finance new investment, the rate of interest will govern the terms upon which funds are *supplied*.[8] Keynes defined the marginal efficiency of capital as 'being equal to that rate of discount which would make the present value of the series of annuities given by the returns expected from the capital-asset during its life just equal to its supply price', where supply price is 'the price which would just induce a manufacturer newly to produce an additional unit of such assets, i.e. what is sometimes called its replacement cost'.[9] Keynes further explained that continued investment in any given type of capital would cause its marginal efficiency to decline, partly because the prospective yield would fall and partly because pressure on resources would cause the supply price to rise.[10] It followed that 'There will be an inducement to push the rate of new investment to the point which forces the supply price of each type of capital-asset to a figure which, taken in conjunction with its prospective yield, brings the marginal efficiency of capital in general to approximate equality with the rate of interest'.[11] It also followed that investment would not be increased *beyond* this point, so the nature of the rate of interest and its crucially important role in a monetary economy will be the subject of investigation below.

EQUILIBRIUM

With the causal sequence clearly in mind we can now see that with a given propensity to consume and rate of new investment there can be only one level of employment consistent with equilibrium. However, there is no reason to believe that the equilibrium employment that results will be equal to the full-employment level; for this level can be seen as only the limiting case of a range of possible outcomes set by the condition that the real wage cannot be less than the marginal disutility of labour (as we shall see in Chapter 22). Keynes points out that the effective demand associated with full employment is a special case, 'only realised when the propensity to consume and the inducement to invest stand in a particular relationship to one another', that is, 'when, by accident or design, current investment provides an amount of demand just equal to the excess of the aggregate supply price of the output resulting from full employment over what the community will choose to spend on consumption when it is fully employed'.[12] Here, the operation of Say's Law will, put in terms of Keynes's analysis, ensure that,

> the aggregate demand price (or proceeds) always accommodates itself to the aggregate supply, so that, whatever the value of N may be, the proceeds D assume a value equal to the aggregate supply price Z which corresponds to N. That is to say, effective demand, instead of having a unique equilibrium value, is an infinite range of values all equally admissible; and the amount of employment is indeterminate except in so far as the marginal disutility of labour sets an upper limit.[13]

But with, of course, the clear implication that competition between entrepreneurs would cause employment and the level of effective demand to increase up to the point at which output ceases to expand – that is, to full employment.

However, the important conclusion which follows from Keynes's own approach and which provides the main feature distinguishing it from orthodoxy is, therefore, that:

> except on the special assumptions of the classical theory according to which there is some force in operation which, when employment increases, always causes D_2 to increase sufficiently to fill the widening gap between Z and D_1 – the economic system may find itself in stable equilibrium with N at a level below full employment, namely at the level given by the intersection of the aggregate demand function with the aggregate supply function.[14]

Clearly, the 'force in operation' which absorbs savings and increases investment sufficiently to maintain Say's Law is the working of the classical capital market, by which an act of saving is given the power to create a corresponding increment of investment, as we saw above, in Chapter 3.

Having worked through the mechanics of Keynes's principle of effective demand, we must now give the theory operational validity for the real world of uncertainty by introducing the role of expectations.

THE ROLE OF EXPECTATIONS

Entrepreneurs will be motivated by the desire to maximise profits to offer that quantity of employment which will coincide with the point of effective demand: that is, the point of intersection of the aggregate demand and supply schedules. Because in an uncertainty economy the point of effective demand cannot be known directly, entrepreneurs must attempt to reach it by acting on their *expectations* of the relevant magnitudes.

It may be, of course, that even if plans are realised, *expectations* will prove to have been wrong, so that firms will not be in profit-maximising equilibrium and entrepreneurs will have to revise their plans as soon as practicable and offer employment on the basis of revised expectations. It should therefore be possible by successive revisions of individual, short-period expectations to reach a given point of effective demand by simple trial and error over a time period.

However, even if we leave on one side the possibility that entrepreneurs' *plans* will not be realised, so that the quantity of employment offered does or does not coincide with equilibrium independently of the expectations of entrepreneurs, there is, as noted earlier, no reason to believe that effective demand is represented by a fixed point. Because aggregate demand is composed of the expenditures of investors and consumers, the point of effective demand will shift with every change in the marginal efficiency of capital, the propensity to consume and the state of liquidity preference. In this way, effective demand will be influenced by changes in the state of long-period expectations operating on these three 'psychological' variables.

Entrepreneurs will thus be attempting to hit a target they cannot see and which is, moreover, continually shifting. The final complication is that the actions of entrepreneurs themselves, in reacting to disappointed expectations, will bring about changes in the 'psychological' variables independently of any *autonomous* change in long-period expectations.

This was Keynes's vision of the real world – the world in which entrepreneurs had to operate and to make the decisions which would determine the level of employment. It presents a picture of great complexity but, as J. A. Kregel has argued:

> such a picture with unpredictable shifting functions and unforeseen change was ill-suited to the exposition of what Keynes felt to

be his most fundamental contribution, the principle of effective demand. The problem that had to be faced was 'how [the real world] can usefully be tamed to serve the analyst and the practitioner' ... to serve the simple exposition of effective demand in determining the level of employment.[15]

THE PROBLEM OF EXPOSITION

In demonstrating how Keynes chose to 'tame the real world', Dr Kregel has provided valuable insights into the methodology of the *General Theory*. Most significantly Keynes did not choose the orthodox course, of eschewing the real world and of conducting his experiments within the wholly abstract framework of a world with perfect foresight and full information. The adoption of such a course, even with the introduction of constraints and the relaxation of assumptions sufficient to approximate the conditions of the real world, would have been unconvincing and inconsistent; for it would have trivialised Keynes's insight and placed him firmly with the neutral-money men whose theories he was attacking because of their inappropriateness as a basis for their policy recommendations. Indeed, as we shall see in Chapter 21, with one notable exception neo-classical economists were forced to prescribe policies which were actually inconsistent with their theories. In any case, 'such a method would have implied rejecting those very features which he considered crucial in a monetary production economy, and without which there would be no need for a theory of effective demand, since under neutral money conditions all money income would be fully spent on current output'.[16]

The essence of the difference between Keynes's approach and that of the orthodox economists clearly lay (and still lies) in the assumptions from which theorising should begin. Keynes's approach was to take the real world as it was – with uncertainty and the need to take decisions based upon expectations – and then to make assumptions about both long- and short-period expectations so as to provide a choice of more or less complex versions of the model which could be used as a vehicle for the exposition of his main thesis.

STATES OF LONG- AND SHORT-PERIOD EXPECTATIONS

Keynes's full version or complete dynamic model is that of *shifting equilibrium*; it is the version outlined above. Not only are entrepreneurs attempting to find equilibrium but equilibrium itself is moving, under the influence both of autonomous shifts in long-period expectations and of entrepreneurs' reactions to disappointed short-period expectations. This model will 'describe an actual path of an economy over time chasing an ever changing equilibrium – it need never catch it'.[17] It is to be contrasted with the model Keynes employed to 'tame the real world' for expository purposes in the *General Theory*. In this version, of *stationary equilibrium*, long-period expectations are assumed constant, and although short-period expectations may be disappointed, the reaction to disappointment is assumed to have no effect on long-period expectations. Because equilibrium does not now shift, it becomes possible for entrepreneurs to reach the point of effective demand by trial and error, successively revising their expectations and their employment decisions and so moving along a stationary aggregate supply curve. By means of this model Keynes was able to demonstrate the importance of uncertainty and expectations, in conjunction with a given equilibrium level of output and employment which could be clearly shown to be below full employment.

It was this model, of *stationary equilibrium*, that Keynes chose in preference to the alternative Swedish approach based on the *ex ante* and *ex post* concepts. This was because of the impossibility of establishing a definite relationship between any given *ex ante* aggregate expectation and a corresponding *ex post* aggregate outcome.[18] Nevertheless, in conceptual terms, to every given state of long-period expectations – no matter how briefly held – there would be a corresponding equilibrium or long-period level of employment. Keynes's method of making the relationship precise was to assume that a given state of long-period expectations would continue long enough for employment to assume its equilibrium level. Hence the emphasis in the *General Theory* on the problems of short-period adjustment to equilibrium.

Unfortunately, this approach led to confusion, and interpreters of the *General Theory* continued to accord to 'expectations' an excessive degree of importance as compared with the theory of effective demand. As a consequence, Keynes, in lectures given after the publication of the *General Theory*, suggested a *static equilibrium* version of the model, in which not only were long-period expectations held constant and kept independent of short-period effects, but short-period expectations were now assumed always to be realised – in the sense that entrepreneurs correctly predicted the point of effective demand so that the system moved immediately into equilibrium. This, Keynes felt, would be the most suitable way to show that the point of effective demand could occur at less than full employment for a given state of expectations, and that this would be *irrespective* of the process by which the system reacted to disappointed expectations.[19]

Note that this analysis makes it clear that we are dealing with various levels of unemployment as *equilibrium* rather than disequilibrium states, so that interpretations and extensions of Keynes's thesis are properly centred on the model of shifting equilibrium in a monetary production economy and not on the analysis of 'unemployment and disequilibria' referred to earlier, in Chapter 2. In addition, Keynes's approach can be seen to provide an 'economics for all seasons' and not just for the deep-slump conditions of half-a-century ago.

IN SUMMARY

The preceding argument can be summarised as follows. Effective demand is the fundamental principle upon which Keynes's system was founded, and it occupies a position parallel to that of Say's Law in the classical economics. For Keynes:

(1) The level of employment is determined by the level of effective demand.
(2) The point of effective demand is that point at which the aggregate demand curve intersects the aggregate supply curve; it need not, obviously, be at the full-employment level.
(3) Entrepreneurs, to maximise profits, seek to determine output and employment at the level which corresponds to the point of effective demand.
(4) Even when output and employment are in equilibrium at this level, they need not be at the full-employment level. That is, there can be equilibrium with unemployment, so that under-employment equilibrium is determined by effective demand which

depends upon the state of liquidity preference, the marginal efficiency of capital, and the marginal propensity to consume. Once the assumption of an automatic tendency to full-employment equilibrium is dropped, long-period expectations governing liquidity preference, the m.e.c., and the m.p.c. will not be set with full employment in mind for there is no reason why they should be.

(5) Effective demand is the principle with which Keynes overturned Say's Law. It implies a reversal of the classical causal relationship between saving and investment, and so has consequences for the way in which investment is financed and for the determination of the rate of interest.

7 Keynes's Theory of Investment and Saving

INTRODUCTION

We now turn to the second of the four elements encompassed by Keynes's treatment of saving and investment, namely, the nature of saving and its relationship to investment.

We have so far thought only in terms of modifications to the classical approach by which the flow of funds arising from voluntary saving might be augmented by changes in the stock of money(net new money) or diminished by hoarding – the 'idle savings' being thus withheld from the purchase of financial claims. This loanable-funds approach still saw investment as being financed by saving and a change in investment as being determined by a change in prior saving. The equilibrium rate of interest is a function of the supply and demand for loanable funds, combining the forces of 'productivity' and 'thrift', hoarding and money creation.

All in all, it was still possible to argue that income not spent in one way would (though imperfectly) be spent in another. In Keynes's approach, on the other hand, aggregate income *is determined by* the level of aggregate expenditure, so that it was crucially important for Keynes to get the saving–investment causal sequence reversed in order to knock away this prop to the maintenance of Say's Law in a monetary economy. Without the establishment of a sequence in which causation flowed from investment to saving there could be no meaning to the principle of effective demand and no possibility of under-employment as an equilibrium state.

INVESTMENT, SAVING AND THE FINANCE OF INVESTMENT

Keynes's view of saving and its relationship to investment has been widely misunderstood, and we shall avoid many pitfalls if at the outset we make the distinction between 'saving', which is the consequence of devoting resources to the production of capital goods rather than consumption goods and which in effect takes place at the same time as investment, and 'savings', which is the part of received income not spent to satisfy immediate consumption and which accumulates initially in the form of money balances. Because these money balances are part of the economy's total money stock used to finance transactions in general, we shall in the following discussion deal separately with the *investment–saving relation* (in the present chapter) on the one hand, and the *finance of investment* (in Chapter 9) on the other. We shall see that these must be regarded as essentially separate processes, for the investment–saving relation manifests itself entirely through changes in real income, or at full employment through a change in the composition of real income; whereas the finance of investment is accommodated *as part of* the finance of aggregate economic activity by the available stock of money and its velocity of circulation.

In this way we shall (a) obviate the contortions of thought necessary to sustain the (erroneous) belief that investment is somehow financed by saving; (b) direct our attention instead to the process of *finance*, which is the means by which in a monetary economy money balances are transferred, in exchange for financial claims, from those whose money holdings exceed their requirements for planned expenditure to those who wish to finance expenditure on a greater scale than their ready access to money will allow;[1] (c) see clearly how, with a given money stock, changes in the demand for money to finance transactions or to hold as an asset will influence the rate of interest which is, in a monetary economy, wholly a monetary phenomenon.

INVESTMENT DETERMINES SAVING

Taking the investment–saving relation first, we have already established from our discussion of effective demand that investment and saving are the *determinates* of the system; while the *determinants* are 'the propensity to consume, the schedule of the marginal efficiency of capital and the rate of interest'. Keynes notes that 'these determinants are, indeed, themselves complex and each is capable of being affected by prospective changes in the others', but he also points out that the determinants 'remain independent in the sense that their values cannot be inferred from one another'.[2]

The next step is to recognise that saving, in the sense of output not devoted to consumption, is merely a residual, and that we shall get the relationship straight if we think in terms of:

> decisions to consume (or to refrain from consuming) rather than decisions to save. A decision to consume or not to consume truly lies within the power of the individual; so does a decision to invest or not to invest. The amounts of aggregate income and aggregate saving are the *results* of the free choices of individuals whether or not to consume and whether or not to invest; but they are neither of them capable of assuming an independent value resulting from a separate set of decisions taken irrespective of the decisions concerning consumption and investment.[3]

Furthermore, Keynes saw that, because of the (entirely normal and logical) way in which they were defined, saving and investment would always be equal, a conclusion which mystified some commentators and led, as we shall see, to the widespread adoption of the (misleading in some contexts) concepts of *ex ante* and *ex post* saving and investment.

> Whilst, therefore, the amount of saving is an outcome of the collective behaviour of individual consumers and the amount of investment of the collective behaviour of individual entrepreneurs, these two amounts are necessarily equal, since each of them is equal to the excess of income over consumption...
>
> Income = value of output = consumption + investment
>
> Saving = income − consumption
> Therefore saving = investment.[4]

It will help to clarify matters if we keep in mind the idea that as investment is taking place, so, in effect, is saving of an exactly equivalent amount, since in the creation of real assets for investment purposes, investment is constituting that part of total realised real income which will not be devoted to consumption. This crucial idea must be emphasised. When investment has taken place, so, in effect, has saving, because investment has already appropriated a part of whatever amount real income turns out to be.

INVESTMENT, CONSUMPTION BEHAVIOUR AND THE CHANGE IN REAL INCOME

The share of realised real income to be made available for consumption will depend upon the community's propensity to consume out of a given increment of real income. At less than full employment real income must increase just sufficiently to accommodate the demands of both investors and consumers. The marginal propensity to consume will determine *by how much extra to the change in investment* real income must change in order to meet both demands. Hence the marginal propensity to consume will give the value of the (investment) multiplier, which is the coefficient of expansion of the initial expenditure which will produce the requisite change in real income.

Because the marginal propensity to consume has a value which is greater than zero but less than unity, each successive round of expenditure out of received incomes will be diminished by the proportion of income not to be devoted to consumption, so that a proportion of potential purchasing power in each round is deleted by individuals' saving. As the multiplier works itself out, savings (money balances) will accumulate until they equal that part of realised income not to be devoted to consumption, which in turn will be equal to the quantity of real income (physical assets) already devoted to investment. Therefore, realised investment will bear a relation to total realised real income equal to the proportion of income not devoted to consumption to income – and equal to the reciprocal of the multiplier value.

THE MULTIPLIER

The concept of the multiplier itself is well known and receives a standard treatment in the textbooks. The principle involved is extremely simple but follows from two of Keynes's fundamentally important insights: (i) the national income identity and causal nexus, by which *expenditure* on the part of one individual or group will be received as *income* by another individual or group; (ii) the 'psychological law' that as income increases so will consumption but not by as much as the increase in income. It follows that an injection of extra expenditure consequent upon an increase in (autonomous) investment will accrue as increased income to the recipients of the expenditure. They will spend part on consumption according to their marginal propensities and save the remainder. The increased spending will again accrue as incomes so that the recipients will in their turn increase their expenditure. The process continues with recipients in each round spending the same proportion[5] of a declining absolute amount of received income.

When the process comes to an end the increase in aggregate income is greater than the increase in the initial expenditure by the value of the multiplier. For example, with a marginal propensity to consume of $b = 0.75$ the multiplier will have a value of $k = 1/(1 - b) = 4$. Therefore, for an initial investment expenditure of £100m, the change in aggregate income will be £400m. That is, the change in real income is made up of: investment goods £100m (one-quarter and equal to the reciprocal of the multiplier value); and consumption goods £300m (three-quarters and equal in proportion to the given marginal propensity to consume).

Note also that with a marginal propensity to save $1-b$ of 0.25, aggregate accumulated *saving*, £100m, will be equal to the proportion of realised income not devoted to consumption and equal to the amount of realised income already devoted to *investment*.

Consequently the system is again in equilibrium, either when real income has changed sufficiently to satisfy the demands both of investors and consumers, or when the change in aggregate saving is equal to the change in investment. These are, of course, but two ways of looking at the same set of circumstances, and when one is defined so is the other.

Nevertheless, it is preferable, as noted earlier, to think in terms of the satisfaction of consumption and investment demands, as this has the effect of defining equilibrium without any recourse to the unsound ideas inherent in the terms '*ex ante*' or 'intended' or 'desired' *saving*. It is also more in sympathy with the spirit of Keynes's approach, and although he recognises that any increase in investment must always give rise, via the effect of the multiplier on incomes, to increased savings in the hands of the public of exactly equivalent amount,[6] he formulates his theory of the multiplier in terms of investment and consumption expenditure:[7]

> Let us define, then, $\frac{\partial Cw}{\partial Yw}$ as the *marginal propensity to consume.*
>
> This quantity is of considerable importance, because it tells us how the next increment of output will have to be divided between consumption and investment. For $\Delta Yw = \Delta Cw + \Delta Iw$, where ΔCw and ΔIw are the increments of consumption and investment; so that

we can write $\Delta Yw = k\Delta Iw$, where $1-\frac{1}{k}$ is equal to the marginal propensity to consume.[8]

We shall turn in the next chapter to a consideration of the notions of *ex ante* and *ex post* saving and investment, but for the moment there are two comments to be made about the investment multiplier which will be of central importance for later discussion.

The first is that the *logic* of the multiplier always holds and that in a discussion of *principles* its operation may safely be regarded as instantaneous:

> In general ... we have to take account of the case where the initiative comes from an increase in the output of the capital goods industries which was not fully foreseen. It is obvious that an initiative of this description only produces its full effect on employment over a period of time. I have found, however, in discussion that this obvious fact often gives rise to some confusion between the logical theory of the multiplier, which holds continuously without time lag, at all moments of time, and the consequences of an expansion in the capital goods industries which take gradual effect, subject to time lag and only after an interval ... But in every interval of time the theory of the multiplier holds good in the sense that the increment of aggregate demand is equal to the product of the increment of aggregate investment and the multiplier as determined by the marginal propensity to consume.[9]

The second point, which must be borne very clearly in mind, is that we have so far dealt only with changes in real income consequent upon an increase in investment, and have said nothing about the *finance* of investment, as part of the finance of an increased level of economic activity in general. This point is to make clear that the finance of investment does not depend in any sense on 'special effects' produced by taking liberties with the multiplier analysis. Because we are dealing with a monetary economy we have, of course, tacitly assumed that the expenditure–income transactions of the multiplier, involving both investment and consumption, would necessitate the use of money, but we have not yet made this explicit in terms of the demand for and supply of money.

We have also seen money balances (savings) accumulating to the extent of aggregate saving – and so allowed ourselves to assume that the increase in aggregate wealth deriving from the increase in investment has been accompanied by a corresponding increase in the demand for money. But this is by no means necessary or likely and we shall shortly need to look more closely at the portfolio choices open to wealth-holders.

THE PROPENSITY TO SAVE AND THE RATE OF SAVING

For the moment, however, we must deal further with changes in real income and notice that a change in investment will always give rise to a change in saving of equal amount, whatever decisions are made by individual consumers and savers and whether the economy is in deep recession or nearing full employment. Table 7.1, which is constructed on the basis of alternative states of long-period expectations, clearly shows that the *absolute* amount of saving (the *rate* per time-interval) will be determined by the *absolute* amount of investment (the *rate* per time-interval), whereas the marginal propensity to consume (the marginal propensity to save as m.p.c. + m.p.s. = 1) will determine the change in the level of income necessary to accommodate the demands of consumers as well as investors.

Therefore, if the rate of investment remains constant so will the rate of saving; and changes in the marginal propensity to consume will give rise to income changes only. Note that the higher the m.p.c. the larger the value of the multiplier and the greater will be the change in income so as to accommodate the increased consumption demand.

Misunderstanding will therefore be avoided if we do not confuse the *rate* of investment and saving per time-interval, which will always be equal, and the propensity or *desire* to consume and save out of a

Table 7.1

I	*m.p.c.*	k	ΔY	ΔC	*m.p.s.*	S
100	0.50	2	200	100	0.50	100
100	0.75	4	400	300	0.25	100
100	0.80	5	500	400	0.20	100

where I = investment, Y = income, C = comsumption and S = saving.

given (increment of) income. It is only in this latter sense that it is possible to talk about 'desired' or 'intended' saving.

We can see from the table that because saving depends upon income, a change in the *desire* to save (consume) will give rise to a change in spending and therefore in income, such that there will be no change in the resulting rate of saving which will remain equal to investment. This is, of course, because a decreased desire to save will cause the rate of income flow to rise, so that savers will be saving a smaller proportion of a larger income. Keynes stated the point shortly as follows:

> It is ... impossible for the community as a whole to save *less* than the amount of current investment, since the attempt to do so will necessarily raise incomes to a level at which the sums which individuals choose to save add up to a figure exactly equal to the amount of investment.[10]

The point was elucidated by Mrs (Professor) Joan Robinson in her 'simplified account of the main principles of the Theory of Employment':[11]

> change in the desire to save means that people are inclined to save more out of the same income. But with the same desire to save, the actual amount of saving will depend upon the income they have to dispose of ... Investment causes incomes to be whatever is required to induce people to save at a rate equal to the rate of investment. The more willing people are to save, the lower is the level of income corresponding to a given rate of investment, and the smaller the increase in income brought about by a given increase in the rate of investment.

It is now possible to understand clearly what Keynes means in the following passage, in terms both of the desire to save and the rate of saving – and not to misunderstand the direction of causation implied:

> An increment of investment in terms of wage-units cannot occur unless the public are prepared to increase their savings in terms of wage-units. Ordinarily speaking, the public will not do this unless their aggregate income in terms of wage-units is increasing. Thus their effort to consume a part of their increased incomes will stimulate output until the new level (and distribution) of incomes

> provides a margin of saving sufficient to correspond to the increased investment. The multiplier tells us by how much their employment has to be increased to yield an increase in real income sufficient to induce them to do the necessary extra saving.[12]

It is, of course, of crucial importance for Keynes's thesis that the argument does not hold in the opposite direction; that is, that the desire to save does not promote investment:

> whatever the attitude of individuals to saving may be, the amount that they will actually save, taken together, is determined for them by the decisions of the entrepreneurs as to the amount of investment goods that it suits them to produce. Any one individual it is true can increase his rate of saving, but the very fact that he is saving more, which means that he is spending less, leads to a decline in other people's incomes to such an extent that they save less, and his saving makes no change in the total rate of saving. The individual saver has no direct influence upon the rate of investment. If entrepreneurs see a profit to be made by investment, investment will take place, and if they do not it will not. The initiative lies with the entrepreneurs not with the savers.[13]

If, therefore, it is not possible for savers to influence the aggregate rate of saving there can be no route to full employment via the classical capital market. In fact, to explain the existence of unemployment at all, in the classical system, it is necessary to account for the lack of demand for securities by the existence of (irrational) hoarding, but this, as we can now see, is a myth:

> The error connected with the idea of 'hoarding' arises, no doubt, from the desire to find where the vanished savings have got to. It is clear enough that if the desire of individuals to save has increased, but the desire of entrepreneurs to invest has not increased, then actually savings do not increase, and the explanation is put forward that the missing savings have somehow got lost on the way by going into money instead of into securities. But this is not a tenable explanation. The savings are nowhere. They have failed to come into existence, because as fast as one man increases his saving, by reducing his spending, other men's incomes fall off and they save less as much as he saves more.[14]

THE PROPENSITY TO SAVE AND THE RATE OF INVESTMENT

This, however, is not the end of the story, for not only will the attempt to stimulate investment by an increased desire to save prove useless, but it may, by its depressing effect on current income, actually act as a *discouragement* to investment:

> the expectation of future consumption is so largely based on current experience of present consumption that a reduction in the latter is likely to depress the former, with the result that the act of saving will not merely depress the price of consumption-goods and leave the marginal efficiency of existing capital unaffected, but may actually tend to depress the latter also. In this event it may reduce present investment-demand as well as present consumption demand.[15]

The conclusion that a fall in the propensity to consume is likely to have a depressing effect on employment prospects becomes entirely understandable once we see that the only possible free-market justification for employment is the expectation of consumption.[16]

We must notice here, however, that it is *possible* for an increased desire to save to stimulate investment, because the fall in current incomes will reduce the (transactions) demand for money relative to the supply and so bring about a fall in the rate of interest; but this effect of the fall in income is unlikely to be strong enough to outweigh the dampening effect on expectations, as we shall see.[17]

SAVING AT FULL EMPLOYMENT

We must, finally, deal with the case in which investment is undertaken as the economy nears full employment. As in the under-employment case, investment will give rise to an equal amount of saving for, as Keynes points out, 'assuming that the decisions to invest become effective, they must in doing so either curtail consumption or expand income'.[18] 'Moreover, except in conditions of full employment, there will be an increase in real income as well as of money income.'[19]

That is, as the economy approaches full employment, at which point output becomes completely inelastic, a portion of aggregate expenditure will raise prices rather than output, so that the increase in consumption will be constrained by the inability of real income to rise and the excess demand will be absorbed by rising nominal income; the rise in investment thereby curtailing consumption.

Notice here that the difference between full-employment and under-employment positions is *not* that prices rise at full employment. The difference is that below full employment the multiplier will produce the requisite change in real income whether or not prices rise as well. It is, however, only at full employment that we might observe the phenomenon of 'forced saving' or 'forced frugality': that is, the reduction in real consumption expenditures caused by rising prices as investment is increased at full employment.

8 Robertson and Keynes on Investment and Saving

INTRODUCTION

From Robertson's point of view there are two versions of Keynes's analysis of investment, saving and the rate of interest.

There is first what we might call the Perceived Initial Version, which is cast entirely in static terms and which is dominated by the multiplier analysis. The multiplier plays a key role in this version because: (i) it supplies saving *and* finance automatically and so allows Keynes to avoid a rise in interest rates in the finance of investment; (ii) there is consequently no need for prices to rise as there is no requirement for an increase in bank credit; (iii) therefore there is no *need* for forced saving – as saving is automatically supplied to match investment – and there is no *possibility* of forced saving because prices do not rise; (iv) productivity and thrift are brought together in a neat relationship which does not allow them to interfere with the determination of the rate of interest; (v) this leaves the rate of interest to be determined entirely by changes in the supply and demand for money.

This version is obviously completely at odds with Robertson's own theory, but in the second, or what we might think of as the Perceived Revised Version, there is a welcome return to the Robertsonian fold, for this version reflects Keynes's alleged reaction to the revelation that lags operate in the real world.

With the introduction of 'finance' in advance of saving, Keynes is seen to accept a sequence of events compatible with the forced-saving process and to defend himself against this interpretation only by assuming output to be perfectly elastic. By the same token he admits that the productivity of investment can influence the demand for money and so the rate of interest. The admission is confirmed by Keynes's approval of the *IS–LM* model, which also allows for a functional relationship between the rate of interest and saving, so that Keynes finally accepts the loanable-funds view that the rate of interest is determined jointly by real and monetary forces.

In either version, this view of Keynes is almost wholly wrong and stems entirely from Robertson's confusion over saving and the finance of investment. By dealing separately with the real-income adjustments of the investment–saving process on the one hand and the financing of investment on the other, we are exploiting one of Keynes's most important insights, and also developing a framework which will enable us to think clearly about the real world and come to correct conclusions on questions of policy.

Before moving on to deal with the finance of investment in the next chapter, there are important questions central to the Robertson–Keynes debate which relate to the equality of saving and investment and to the static nature of Keynes's theory.

KEYNES'S 'TWO THEORIES' OF $S = I$

It is an established tenet of the Keynesian critical heritage that Keynes was confused over the question of the equality of saving and investment. Keynes's confusion is perceived to arise from his attempt to reconcile what were taken to be his two alternative explanations of why saving must always be equal to investment: namely, that they are equal by definition, and that they are made equal through the working of the multiplier. J. C. Gilbert, for example, has noticed that 'Samuelson in 1946 pointed out that Keynes's thinking remained fuzzy on this important analytical distinction throughout his life. In 1963, Samuelson referred to Robertson having rightly pointed out this mistake.'[1]

An attempt at a reconciliation between the two approaches to equality was made many years ago by Alvin Hansen, who argued that the 'source of confusion arose from the failure of his [Keynes's] critics to realise that while investment and saving are always *equal* they are not always in *equilibrium*'.

That is, for the cases with which Keynes was mainly concerned – comparative statics or moving equilibrium – variables are always in a normal or desired functional relationship to each other, so that saving and investment will not only be *equal* but also in equilibrium. However, on the numerous occasions on which Keynes was dealing with processes of change which involved the lagged adjustment of certain variables, such as the adjustment of expenditure to changes in income, this will not be the case, because until the lag has worked itself out, '*actual* consumption will not be equal to *desired* consumption (and *actual* saving will not be equal to *desired* saving)', so that saving and investment though *equal* will not be in equilibrium.[2]

It is clear that Hansen gained an inkling of what Keynes was driving at, though he did not identify stationary equilibrium as Keynes's typical case, and helped only further to confuse matters by not explaining how investment and saving could be equal while a system with lags is still adjusting to equilibrium. He does not tell us how investment and saving can be equal by definition and at the same time equal as a condition of equilibrium for the system.

There is a similar resort to the idea of desired as against actual magnitudes as an explanation of Keynes's position, by Presley, who argues from the loanable-funds standpoint – to which the doctrine of the necessary equality of saving and investment was a direct challenge – that Keynes's adherence to the two alternative explanations stemmed from his failure to distinguish between *ex ante* and *ex post* concepts.[3]

This point is, of course, but part and parcel of the Robertsonian argument that Keynes's analysis is entirely static, that he was concerned only with comparing alternative positions of equilibrium. In other words, he only examined states of the economy *after* the various adjustments had taken place, so that the multiplier, which was a dynamic process, had to be assumed to work instantaneously.[4]

It was very necessary for the loanable-funds school to cultivate this interpretation of Keynes because it rendered his analysis vulnerable to attack from the application of 'real-world' conditions; for without the imposition of this transparently clear weakness Keynes's challenge would have been far more menacing.

But how, according to his critics, was Keynes able to persist with his static multiplier analysis, which made saving depend entirely on investment with no independent power for saving directly to influence investment? The answer which lay conveniently to hand was the Swedish distinction between *ex ante* and *ex post*, 'between actual saving and attempted saving' – a distinction which Keynes had clearly failed to make.

$S = I$ AND THE QUESTION OF CAUSALITY

The *ex ante–ex post* distinction was a necessary part of classically based theories, for it allowed, for example, loanable-funds theorists to handle the apparent inequalities between saving and investment which resulted from attempts to make classical analysis more realistic by the introduction of sources of finance for investment other than voluntary saving. Keynes noted:

> The theory of the rate of interest which prevailed before (let us say) 1914 regarded it as the factor which ensured equality between saving and investment. It was never suggested that saving and investment could be unequal. This idea arose (for the first time so far as I am aware) with certain post-war theories. In maintaining the equality of saving and investment, I am, therefore, returning to old-fashioned orthodoxy. The novelty in my treatment of saving and investment consists, not in my maintaining their necessary aggregate equality, but in the proposition that it is, not the rate of interest, but the level of incomes which (in conjunction with certain other factors) ensures this equality.[5]

Keynes was concerned to demonstrate the necessary equality of saving and investment because of the potential misunderstandings which could arise; that is, that the correlative saving and investment must always be exactly equal – as he pointed out when commenting on a League of Nations Report on capital formation:

> the amount of saving which is taking place *at the same time* as the investment must be exactly equal to it ... This corollary is not merely a neat truism. For unless it is kept in mind the reader is very likely to be led to false conclusions. For example, he might naturally suppose ... that the right way to prepare for an increase of investment is to save more at an appropriately prior date. But the corollary shows that this is impossible. Saving at the prior date cannot be greater than the investment at that date. Increased investment will always be accompanied by increased saving, but it can never be preceded by it. Dishoarding and credit expansion provides not an *alternative* to increased saving, but a necessary preparation for it. It is the parent, not the twin, of increased saving.[6]

Nevertheless, for loanable-funds theorists the inequality of saving and investment due to credit-creation and dishoarding was as much an article of faith as the efficacy of prior saving:

> This proposition was central to the forced saving thesis and, in turn, to Robertson's loanable funds theory. The inequality of saving and investment was practically guaranteed by the interference of changes in the money supply and hoarding habits upon the supply of, and demand for, loanable funds. If they were equal it was purely coincidental.[7]

In as much as the difference between this and Keynes's equality doctrine is to be accounted for by way of the methodologies employed – by the use, that is, of dynamic analysis as against static analysis – that difference is trivial. Much the more important point of departure is, of course, in the direction of causation postulated, and here the two approaches are irreconcilable. Here again we can see that failure to recognise the nature of saving and its relationship to investment can lead to serious misunderstanding:

> this possible inequality is determined largely by the dynamic nature of Robertsonian analysis compared with the static analysis of Keynesian economics. The time lags in the adjustment of output to monetary expenditure flows, and the lag of some money incomes behind price changes, are responsible for saving being not only spontaneous and voluntary but also forced.[8]

But this, of course, is very confusing. Whether the analysis we employ is static or dynamic, saving will always end up being equal to investment. The important thing is to get the direction of causation right and to start with investment expenditure. It will then be clear that if we begin with a given quantity of investment, it will produce an equal quantity of saving.

If, for example, we allow Robertsonian analysis its Saving–Investment : Investment–Saving sequence, we shall in equilibrium find that: Investment = Saving (Keynesian) = Lacking (spontaneous and forced). If we now impose a Keynesian sequence, by removing prior saving as a source of finance for investment so that the funds to pay for new investment must come entirely from the banks, the quantity of lacking generated is the same but the composition is different. We now have: Investment = Saving (Keynesian) = Lacking (forced).

The misunderstanding, of course, arises from the attempt to equate Keynes's voluntary saving with Robertson's voluntary (spontaneous) saving or lacking. Keynes's voluntary saving, which is always *ex post*, is equal to Robertson's total saving or lacking, part of which is *ex ante* (voluntary saving – a decision variable) and part of which is *ex post* (forced saving).

Hansen approached the question from a slightly different angle, and pointed out that expenditure from whatever source will create income, part of which will be saved:

> in Robertson's way of looking at the problem, the new money plus the reactivated idle balances are thought to be *in addition* to income. In the Keynesian definition the new funds, having in fact been expended in the current period, swell the current income ... And that part of current income which is not spent on consumers' goods is in fact saved. The Keynesian saving (from current income) would thus exceed Robertsonian saving (from yesterday's income). The difference between the two is the expenditure made from new money and from reactivated idle balances.[9]

Hansen treated the Keynes and Robertson approaches as purely formal equivalents which differed only in the alternative methodologies they employed. But Keynes was not only concerned with the formal equivalence of alternative statements. He was seeking to show that saving and investment could be unequal only in the sense that they related to different periods or, more properly, to different states of expectations.

To any given state of long-period expectations there will *ceteris paribus* be a corresponding level of investment and therefore of effective demand. A change in long-period expectations could, therefore, raise the level of investment and effective demand relative to current effective demand and income; and therefore the level of investment relative to current saving.

Consequently, adjustment of employment and output to equilibrium will begin with entrepreneurs making estimates of effective demand, so that, in the terminology of Keynes's *A Treatise on Money*, in which the *inequality* of saving and investment was regarded as the chief cause of fluctuations,[10] the argument would run:

> the expectation of an increased excess of Investment over Saving, given the former volume of employment and output, will induce entrepreneurs to increase the volume of employment and output. The significance of both my present and my former arguments lies

> in their attempt to show that the volume of employment is determined by the estimates of effective demand made by the entrepreneurs, an expected increase of investment relatively to saving as defined in my *Treatise on Money* being a criterion of an increase in effective demand.[11]

We can now see that to every given state of long-period expectations there will be a corresponding level of investment. To every level of effective demand there will in equilibrium be an equivalent level of income. Consequently, in equilibrium there will be a level of saving out of income equal to the level of investment corresponding to a given state of long-period expectations.

To bridge the gap between a given state of expectations and level of investment and saving on the one hand and an equilibrium level of employment and output on the other, we must reintroduce the multiplier.

The multiplier determines the position of effective demand for any given state of expectations, and gives the proportionate relationship between investment goods and consumption goods which must exist in final output if equilibrium is to be achieved. Keynes explained the principle in simple terms as follows:

> If, for example, the public are in the habit of spending nine-tenths of their income on consumption goods, it follows that if entrepreneurs were to produce consumption goods at a cost more than nine times the cost of the investment goods they are producing, some part of their output could not be sold at a price which would cover its cost of production ... Thus entrepreneurs will make a loss until they contract their output of consumption goods down to an amount at which it no longer exceeds nine times their current output of investment goods.[12]

Notice that there is no reference to saving in Keynes's exposition, despite the fact that we know that when the multiplier has worked itself out saving will be equal to investment. This is so whether the propensity to consume is assumed to be constant or variable, or whether the multiplier is assumed to work instantaneously or with a lag. Increasingly Keynes preferred to conduct his analysis without reference to saving at all and chose instead to direct attention towards decisions to invest and decisions to consume.[13]

KEYNES'S 'TWO THEORIES' RECONCILED

A reconciliation of the ideas of saving and investment being equal by definition and as an equilibrium condition should now be possible.

We recall that in the simple Income = (Consumption + Autonomous Investment) Expenditure model of the textbooks, equilibrium is established with saving equal to investment. A favourable change in long-period expectations will produce extra investment which will increase aggregate expenditure and income by the product of the change in investment and the multiplier.

Each successive increase in investment will shift the aggregate demand curve upward and establish a new equilibrium level of income (see Figure 8.1).

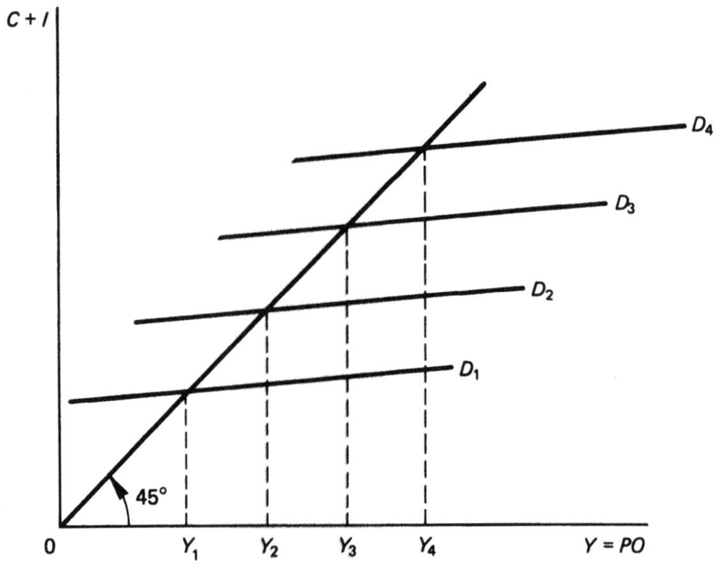

Figure 8.1

Because $Y = PO$, where O is real output and P is the average price level of output, each level of income can be represented by a rectangular hyperbola giving a range of possible combinations of output and the price level to which it might correspond.

If we now impose supply conditions in the form of the aggregate supply function,[14] we shall find that the points of intersection of the nominal income curves and the aggregate supply curve will indicate points of effective demand, at which each level of aggregate demand is equal to aggregate supply.

It is also possible to see that as the economy approaches full employment, successive increases in aggregate expenditure will produce larger increases in the price level for any given increase in real output (see Figure 8.2).

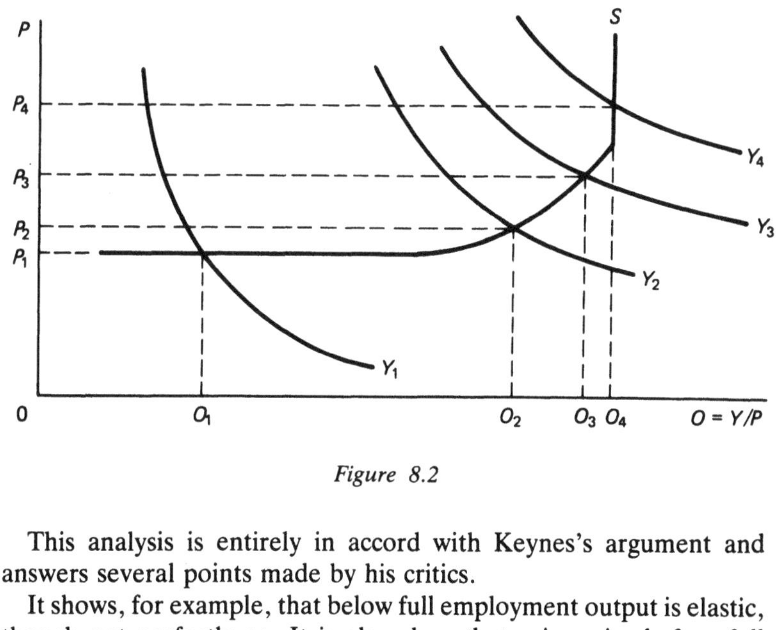

Figure 8.2

This analysis is entirely in accord with Keynes's argument and answers several points made by his critics.

It shows, for example, that below full employment output is elastic, though not perfectly so. It is also clear that prices rise before full employment is reached because short-run costs increase as output rises. Where money wages are variable this tendency is reinforced.[15]

Note also that the emphasis of critics on the 'static' nature of Keynes's theory really refers to his method of 'taming the real world' by assuming long-period expectations as given at any time and then analysing the effects of entrepreneurs' attempts to reach profit-maximising equilibrium.

In other words, with a *given* capital equipment corresponding to a *given* state of long-period expectations we are concerned with adjustment to equilibrium in the short period. Keynes's analysis is not, therefore, as several writers claim, set in static terms in the sense that it views the economy in a series of 'snapshots' of equilibrium positions. In replying to E. S. Shaw, Keynes specifically states that:

> I am not concerned with instantaneous snapshots, but with short-period equilibrium, assuming a sufficient interval for momentary decisions to take effect.[16]

With a given quantity of investment, the extent and composition of aggregate demand facing entrepreneurs will be determined by the multiplier. Because the marginal propensity to consume reflects preferences for consumption now as against deferred consumption out of an increase of income, the purpose of the multiplier is to indicate by how much aggregate expenditure and real income must change so as to accommodate the demands of consumers as well as investors.

To find profit-maximising equilibrium, entrepreneurs must plan output and therefore employment to coincide with the point of effective demand. Equilibrium will not be attained unless the quantity of consumption goods and investment goods produced stand in the same relation to each other in aggregate output as do consumption expenditure and investment expenditure in aggregate demand.

It should now be clear that with given long-period expectations saving must be equal to investment as a condition of equilibrium, otherwise the multiplier would still be in operation and income would still be changing. In equilibrium, saving must by definition be identically equal to investment, as they both bear the same relation to the level of *realised* income; as $Y \equiv I + C$ and $S \equiv Y - C$ so that $S \equiv I$.

In long-period equilibrium, with expectations realised, the level of employment and its distribution between consumption-goods and investment-goods industries will be such that expenditure, income and (the value of) output will all stand in the same relation to each other.

EX ANTE AND *EX POST* INVESTMENT AND SAVING

Evidently Keynes did *not* have two theories of the equality of investment and saving and there is no necessary conflict between the notions of their being equal by definition and as a condition for equilibrium. Nor is it the case that Keynes neglected a superior mode of analysis by his failure to make the distinction between *ex ante* and *ex post* concepts. The fact is that he experimented with this approach but abandoned it as inexact and unsuitable for his purposes.[17] He recognised the usefulness of the method for expositional purposes but remained convinced that:

> when one comes to prove something truly logical and properly watertight, then I believe there are advantages in my method and that the *ex post* and *ex ante* device cannot be precisely stated without very cumbrous devices. I used to speak of the period between expectation and result as 'funnels of process', but the fact that the funnels are all of different lengths and overlap one another meant that at any given time there was no aggregate realised result capable of being compared with some aggregate expectation at some earlier date.[18]

But did Keynes perhaps abandon this approach because he failed to understand it? A. Leijonhufvud has argued that:

> There is no doubt whatsoever that Keynes misunderstood completely the Swedish '*ex ante-ex post*' terminology ... Thus, in his 1937 *Economic Journal* debate with Bertil Ohlin, he assumed '*ex ante*' to have a purely temporal connotation, i.e. meaning 'in advance of', or 'in anticipation of' ... Keynes' revealing statement that: 'As for the concept of "*ex ante*" saving, I can attach no sound sense to it', is certainly understandable, since he interpreted the term to refer to current income withheld from consumption *in anticipation* of a future increase in income.[19]

It is certainly the case that Keynes would have thought of *ex ante* saving in terms of *prior saving*, income withheld from consumption as a way of increasing investment and hence future income. He would, of course, have regarded any such idea as nonsensical *because of* his expenditure-determines-income : investment-determines-saving causal sequence.

For the same reason he would have rejected the notion of *desired* saving because it gives the impression that saving is an independently determined decision-variable. Yet this is precisely the way in which Leijonhufvud himself understands and gives credence to *ex ante* and *ex post* (a usage which corresponds with the Swedish). For in suggesting that an 'instantaneous' multiplier would imply that *desired* saving and investment must be equal through time and that observed rates of income must therefore be interpreted as short-run equilibrium rates, Leijonhufvud points out that:

> This would raise problems with respect to the explanation of movements in income, since such movements must be conceived of as essentially continuous and as adjustments in response to disequilibrium forces, saving and investment being the income-determining factors.[20]

Leijonhufvud's reference to saving and investment as the income-determining factors would seem to confirm that in his use of the *ex ante–ex post* terminology he misunderstands Keynes's approach and lends support to the view of saving and investment as two independently determined flows, which though more often than not are unequal *ex ante* will always be reconciled and made equal *ex post.*

This is because the use of *ex ante–ex post* can lead to a failure to make clear the crucial distinction between the rate of saving and the propensity to save. To talk in terms of a desired (*ex ante*) aggregate *rate* of saving is plainly absurd, whereas an actual or *ex post* aggregate *rate* of saving, as determined by the rate of interest, is understandable enough.

More reasonable might seem to be the idea of desired or *ex ante* saving when applied to the *propensity* to save, for here there lies the possibility of individual decision-making. But there are two problems with this.

The first is that because aggregate desired saving is the sum of individual desired saving, the consumption-saving decision will be made as the multiplier is working and income is changing. Therefore, as an increment of income is presented to each recipient, consumption and saving *ex ante* will immediately become consumption and saving *ex post*: for each individual desired and actual consumption and saving will always be equal.[21]

The second is that because the two propensities, to save and to consume, sum to unity, they are determined together. Consequently, when the consumption function is specified so is the saving function, and any influence of, for example, the rate of interest on consumption behaviour is by the same token applicable also to saving behaviour.

Keynes, despite what his critics might aver, recognised the influence of the rate of interest on saving but was careful to distinguish between its influence on the propensity to save on the one hand and the rate of saving on the other. His conclusion was that the principal determinant of consumption behaviour is the level of income and that this includes current income, past income and expectations of future income, so that the propensity to consume should be considered fairly stable.[22]

In addition to this decidedly modern-sounding (permanent income) determinant, the influence of the rate of interest on the decision to consume or save out of a given level of income is only one among several others, and is likely to be relatively unimportant in the short period.[23] On the other hand, the influence of the rate of interest on the *rate* of saving is substantial, but in the opposite direction to that claimed by the classically based theories. For example:

> we can be certain that a rise in the rate of interest will have the effect of reducing the amount actually saved. For aggregate saving is governed by aggregate investment; a rise in the rate of interest (unless it is offset by a corresponding change in the demand-schedule for investment) will diminish investment; hence a rise in the rate of interest must have the effect of reducing incomes to a level at which saving is decreased in the same measure as investment.[24]

Though Leijonhufvud accuses Keynes of conceiving *ex ante* in purely temporal terms, it is interesting to note that he does allow that 'Keynes' manifest misunderstanding of this terminology does not prove that he was incapable of distinguishing between "desired" and actual magnitudes'.[25]

And this distinction Keynes did make, though only in the case of investment. It was not that Keynes misunderstood the idea of *ex ante* and *ex post*; it was rather that he understood it only too well. But he had to make sense of it – to apply it – in terms of his own theory of the economy, and to do this he could conceive of *ex ante* and *ex post* investment, but only of saving *ex post*; there could be no place for *ex ante* saving. In addition to his being able to attach 'no sound sense' to the notion (see above), he variously referred to *ex ante* saving as 'a very dubious concept';[26] as 'much the worst' of the very many bad ideas advanced in this connection;[27] and as 'surely a chimera, which it is much better not to mention'.[28]

Keynes thought of *ex ante* and *ex post* as the difference between 'planned' or 'designed', and 'actual'.[29] But because of the causal sequence he envisaged there was also, given the existence of lags, a temporal element to allow for. Keynes's investment–saving sequence would be: *Ex Ante* Investment→*Ex Post* Investment→*Ex Post* Saving (equal to *Ex Post* Investment).

He was quite taken with Ohlin's distinction between investment *ex ante* and investment *ex post* because it directed attention to the factors, including expectations, that influenced investment plans and that led to the *decision* to invest a certain amount *ex ante*. It also led Keynes to extend his theory of the demand for money, liquidity preference, to allow for the fact that money to finance investment might be required from the time the investment decision is taken as well as during the actual currency of the investment project. There is, in other words, a lag of finite length between the time at which a decision is taken and the time at which investment takes place. It may, during this interval, be necessary to acquire money in connection with the financing of the project.[30]

THE CO-ORDINATION OF INVESTMENT AND SAVING PLANS

One reason why the *ex ante–ex post* approach became popular in the wake of the Keynesian Revolution, was that it allowed classically based theories to come to terms with reality. In an essentially timeless world of perfect knowledge, problems of inter-temporal choice are largely accounting problems. But if economic decision-making is constrained by insufficient information, then the inability of the theory to predict full-employment equilibrium is put down to the failure of the information system to allow the proper co-ordination of saving and investment plans. The plans of savers and investors, it is said, cannot be made 'consistent'.

Such a view, as we now see, is untenable, because investment will always produce an equal quantity of saving regardless of the individual decisions of savers and consumers; and the only sense in which the *inequality* of saving and investment can legitimately be seen to produce under-employment states is that in which *ex ante* investment will no longer produce a full-employment rate of saving. More generally, we should merely argue that if current *ex ante* investment is less than (greater than) current *ex post* investment, then income and saving will be falling (rising).[31]

Keynes's insistence on the necessary equality of saving and investment was to emphasise that investment can never be excessive in relation to the flow of (voluntary) saving, and that at less than full employment there can be no resort to the notion of forced saving.

However, even though Keynes's approach does not require saving to be forced out of those whose incomes fail to adjust quickly enough, it does depend upon there being a rise in prices as employment and output increase. In other words, contrary to the claims of the Robertsonian school, Keynes not only allows for a rise in prices as output increases but (in the *General Theory*) positively requires there to be one. It is the method by which real wages are reduced as demand raises employment and output. We shall return to this point in Chapter 22.

INVESTMENT, SAVING AND THE PRICE LEVEL

In Keynes's theory, investment goods and consumption goods are complementary in supply on the assumption that unemployed resources exist. The nature and course of the disturbance to the system following an increase in investment will depend on the extent to which the increase is foreseen.

With a nod towards our later discussion of the 'rational expectations' hypothesis, we may note that a rise in prices will occur whether or not the increase in aggregate investment is completely foreseen.

In the first case, a rise in aggregate investment which is sufficiently foreseen for the consumption goods industries to advance in step with the investment goods industries, will ensure that there is no more 'disturbance to the price of consumption-goods than is consequential, in conditions of decreasing returns, on an increase in the quantity which is produced'.[32]

In the second polar case we assume that the expansion of output and employment in the capital goods industries is so entirely unforeseen that in the first instance there is no increase in consumption goods output. The increased demand for consumption goods from those workers drawn into employment in the capital goods industries will force up the prices of consumption goods,

> until a temporary equilibrium between demand and supply has been brought about partly by the high prices causing a postponement of consumption, partly by a redistribution of income in favour of the saving classes as an effect of the increased profits resulting from the higher prices, and partly by the higher prices causing a depletion of stocks.[33]

Eventually, consumption-goods output adjusts to meet demand, and the marginal propensity to consume will rise temporarily, to compensate for the previous fall, before resuming its normal level.[34] Despite, therefore, the temporary departure of consumption behaviour from its normal pattern, the principle of the multiplier will always hold good.

THE ELASTICITY OF SUPPLY

If investment goods and consumption goods are to be complementary in supply, rather than competitive, the expansion of consumption goods to absorb the expansion of demand resulting from the increase in investment requires that there be unemployment of resources. This does not mean, however, that consumption goods must be in perfectly elastic supply. In fact Keynes explicitly conducts his analysis on the assumption that they are not.[35]

Yet the argument of the Robertsonian school is that because the introduction of lags into the multiplier leaves Keynes tacitly dependent on forced saving, he attempted to avoid this conclusion by assuming that output was perfectly elastic below full employment. If, therefore, it could be shown that output was less than perfectly elastic, so that prices would rise as output expanded, the reliance of Keynes's analysis on forced saving could no longer be in doubt.

But this argument fails completely. Not only does Keynes allow that output will be less than perfectly elastic in supply below full employment, but also that prices must be expected to rise in the normal course of events.

In correspondence with Sir William Beveridge in 1936, Keynes argues only that at less than full employment the elasticity of supply of consumption goods will be greater than zero.[36] Similarly, in writing to J. R. Hicks soon afterwards, he said:

> I should say that my theory provides for the supply of consumption goods and of goods in general having, or being capable of having, some elasticity, whereas the classical theory assumes that the supply of output as a whole is wholly inelastic; increase in one direction being necessarily offset by a decrease in another.[37]

In other words, supply is not required even to be highly elastic ('I do not see why you require me to assume that the elasticity should be *high*'[38]), let alone perfectly elastic. Keynes would claim only that at less than full employment, and taking into account the degree of foresight on the part of consumption goods manufacturers and the lags in the working of the multiplier, output will be in some degree elastic.

To argue that the validity of Keynes's theory depends on the supply of output being (perfectly) elastic is to believe in a need for forced saving which Keynes explicitly denies. It is simply not the case that for Keynes there must be no increase in the price of consumption goods. It is an integral part of his theory that prices will rise but that this is a consequence of increasing output as such and not of increasing investment.

That is, an expansion of output and employment in the short run will normally be associated with rising prices 'on account either of the physical fact of diminishing return or of the tendency of the cost-unit to rise in terms of money when output increases'.[39] Elasticity in supply simply means that production must be 'balanced' so as to limit the rise in the price of consumption goods.[40]

In any case, the necessary rise in prices as employment is expanded in the short run, has nothing to do with forced saving, for the rising costs which underly it

> are characteristic of a state of increasing output as such, and will occur just as much if the increase in output has been initiated otherwise than by an increase in bank credit. They can only be avoided by avoiding any course of action capable of improving employment.[41]

We might note, finally, that the distinction between situations characterised by elastic supply and inelastic supply defines the spheres of competence of Keynesian economics and classical economics respectively. If full employment is defined as that point at which output becomes wholly inelastic, then, when full employment is achieved, Keynes's theory is no longer *required*.[42] But this is only to say that in full-employment equilibrium, with which Keynes's theory deals as a special case, the classical economics comes into its own.

9 The Finance of Investment

THE 'SAVING FINANCES INVESTMENT' MYTH

Keynes attacked the widespread belief that investment is somehow financed by saving. The persistence of this myth must no doubt be attributed partly to its inherent plausibility: that because saving is a withdrawal from the income stream and investment is an injection, and because in equilibrium saving is equal to investment, it seems only commonsense to suppose that that which is saved must supply that which is invested.

In addition, there is apparent support for this view in the manner in which the saving–investment equilibrium is to be achieved. Within mainstream economics teaching, the Keynesian innovation is generally identified as the reversal of the classical saving–investment causal sequence; so that sufficient saving to finance any given level of investment is automatically generated through the working of the investment multiplier. Because saving is *always* made equal to investment there need be no concern about the provision of sufficient voluntary saving to finance a desired level of investment. Professor Gilbert, who in his recent book has surveyed and digested a wide range of opinion on Robertson and Keynes and the relationship between investment and saving, must reflect a view which is commonplace when he twice argues in identical terms that:

> The equality of saving and investment by definition in the *General Theory* obscured somewhat the fundamental point that an increase in investment could be matched by an increased amount of saving out of a higher level of income. This is a very important point for government economic policy during a period of mass unemployment. Investment can be increased, for example, by public works and the levels of employment and real national income raised. There is no need to worry about the source of the savings to finance the increased rate of investment.[1]

The fact that savings accrue *after* investment has taken place would on this view seem to raise the question of how precisely funds which have not yet become available can be used to finance prior investment. For the Robertsonian school, as we have seen, the only possible answer could be that the multiplier must be assumed to work instantaneously; while, more ingeniously, Horwich has suggested the operation of a 'transfer effect', whereby an increased demand for funds to finance investment projects will bring about a rise in the rate of interest which will bid out the requisite funds from idle balances and transfer them to investors.[2]

This at least is half-way towards an understanding of Keynes's position, for we must be clear that investment is a form of expenditure which in a monetary economy must be financed, like any other, by means of a money balance. It is money which finances expenditure, not saving.

Nevertheless, may it not be argued that because income is received in the form of money, and consumption is effected by spending money, then that portion of income not devoted to consumption – saving – will accumulate as savings in the form of money balances and hence can be made available, via the financial system, to investors who will use the same money balances to finance projects in hand? In other words, does not saving finance investment?

We have already seen that this cannot be the case. The problem is that we tend to think of the investment–saving relationship in terms of the circular flow of income with, in equilibrium, a flow of saving equal to investment being somehow mediated through the financial system and brought back into the flow of expenditure. We are thus encouraged to think of saving and the money flow which represents it as being in some sense a separate flow in a distinct channel or circuit, so that saving and investment, though integrally bound up with each other, have little to do with the income–consumption expenditure flow and the money flow which represents it in real life. In other words, it is the flow of money in the saving channel which seems especially suitable for financing investment.

But, of course, the danger with this view is that it might lead us to imagine that an inadequate rate of investment could somehow be remedied by encouraging saving – as a way of promoting the flow of funds available for investment – and that the rate of interest must be determined as the equilibrating price of loans in the capital market.

Once, however, we get behind the separately labelled flows we can see that economic activities of all kinds, including consumption and investment expenditure, or the receipt of income and the accumulation of savings, must all, in a monetary economy, find expression in a monetary transaction. Consequently, in order to consume, invest or accumulate a stock of wealth it will be necessary first of all to gain control of a money balance either momentarily or for a more or less extended period of time.

Therefore, regardless of their labels, all forms of activity will be financed via the circulation of a common fund or stock of money and, reduced to this universal form, changes in the level or pattern of economic activity will give rise to changes in the aggregate demand for money relative to the available stock. Seen in this light the type of activity considered is interesting only in so far as it will determine the period of time for which balances will be required and, therefore, the terms on which money balances may be obtained for loans of different maturities.

In other words, to gain an understanding of the process whereby economic activity in general is financed and to prepare the ground for a discussion of the rate of interest, we must, to turn the old maxim on its head, *pierce the veil of income to reveal the monetary reality within*.

FINANCE IN A MONETARY ECONOMY

Keynes originally (in the *General Theory*) dealt with the finance of investment and of economic activity in general in the course of his analysis of the factors determining the rate of interest, a topic to which we shall turn below. Having established to his own satisfaction that the rate of interest could not be (proximately) determined by investment and saving ('productivity' and 'thrift'), Keynes was able to cast aside the shards of old theories, beliefs and assumptions which littered the loanable-funds approach and to begin afresh, taking as his starting-point the elementary principles on which a monetary economy operates.

Keynes's principal insight was into the implications of the fact that in a monetary economy it is necessary to follow what we should now call a 'trading rule'. That is, that the exchange of non-money assets must be mediated by money; which means that to undertake any form of expenditure will require the prior or contemporaneous acquisition of a money balance on terms appropriate to the transaction in question. This in turn leads to a consideration of the factors determining the demand for and supply of money.

We have come to regard Keynes's main innovation in the theory of the demand for money as being his emphasis on the asset demand based upon money's store of value function; as against the medium of exhange function which was supposedly adequately recognised by classical orthodoxy. However, it is more illuminating to think, in Keynes's own terms, of money as liquidity; the unique distinguishing characteristic of money, as against close substitutes, being its 'spendability' (implying acceptability together with the cognate attributes outlined above, in Chapter 1), the quality of being able immediately to finance transactions and to settle debts by transfer.[3]

On this view, the asset demand is properly interpreted as the outcome of the choice between liquidity (holding resources in instantly spendable form) and illiquidity (holding future command over goods and services in a form which yields a return but is not suitable for spending). Consequently, whether for purposes of wealth-holding or for financing transactions, we can in general speak of a person's or firm's demand for liquidity (liquidity preference) and of their desire to become more or less liquid.

Keynes's emphasis on money as liquidity and on the need in a monetary economy to acquire sufficient resources in spendable form as a prerequisite of economic activity, is perhaps best illustrated by the modern theory of finance, which deals with the mechanism developed to allow deficit spending units – those who wish to spend in excess of their immediate access to money balances – to acquire the funds they need from surplus spending units, those whose holdings of liquidity are surplus to current spending requirements. The process may be direct, as when the deficit spending unit issues a financial claim direct to a surplus spending unit in exchange for a money balance; or, more likely in an economy with a developed financial system, indirect via financial intermediaries.

Financial institutions, which perform the intermediary function, are of particular interest here because their activities can encompass both a financial and a monetary role. All financial institutions will, through specialisation, absorb risk, and so are able to reconcile the needs of deficit spending units for longer-term, high-risk borrowing, with the needs of myriad surplus spending units for short-term, low-risk lending.

In addition, those financial institutions which operate as banks and so provide a payment-transfer system will, because their issued claims are in spendable form and so count as money, be able not only to provide access to liquidity but to add to the total stock through the process of credit creation. The significance of this point will become apparent below.

LIQUIDITY SUPPLY AND DEMAND

In the *General Theory* Keynes did not deal specifically and explicitly with the means by which investment is financed. Rather, his approach subsumed the point within his analysis of the finance of economic activity in general, as part, in turn, of his theory of the determination of the rate of interest. The lack of a specific statement was to have unfortunate consequences, for it led his critics to interpolate explanations of their own derived for the most part from orthodox views of saving and investment.

This development not only produced such absurdities as the 'instantaneous multiplier' thesis, dealt with earlier, but also paved the way for the claim that despite appearances to the contrary Keynes never broke away from neo-classical interest theory and that ultimately he was forced to acknowledge the fact.

More generally, it disguised the revolutionary simplicity of Keynes's approach, which unites a variety of economic activities around a common mode based on the first principles of monetary exchange. Concern with outward forms falls into the background as Keynes leads us behind the scenes to examine the monetary framework of economic life. In place of detailed descriptions of transactors, markets and institutions there is a single-minded concentration on the central concept of *liquidity* and on the factors determining its demand and supply.

If we turn first to the demand for liquidity we find that Keynes relates demand not to particular kinds of economic activity, such as consumption or investment expenditure, but rather to broad categories of requirements which stem from the two principal functions which are normally ascribed to money.

These functions are that money acts as a medium of exchange in the finance of transactions and that money can be held as a store of wealth. In turn these functions derive from the two distinctive characteristics of a monetary economy which are, respectively, that transactors must follow the trading rule that money mediates exchange, and that financial as well as other forms of economic activity are subject to uncertainty.

It is this 'ancient distinction' between money as a medium of exchange and as a store of wealth which provides the starting-point for Keynes's familiar analysis of the 'motives' for holding money.

THE DEMAND FOR MONEY: TRANSACTIONS MOTIVE

From money as a medium of exchange in the finance of transactions, Keynes derived his *transactions motive*, which is 'the need of cash for the current transaction of personal and business exchanges'.

Within this category the idea of a *personal* need for money-holding is further developed as the income motive, which is based upon the need to 'bridge the interval between the receipt of income and its disbursement'. The extent of the demand under this heading will, therefore, depend upon the level of income and the relationship between the length of the pay period and the pattern of disbursement.

These ideas, of course, would have seemed unexceptional to a classical economist, being of a purely technical nature, but their significance lies in the underlying rationale which sees the demand for money to finance transactions as part of the overall demand for liquidity in a monetary economy.

Similarly, Keynes developed the idea of money held for transactions purposes on the part of the business community as the business motive, which encompasses the demand for money to 'bridge the interval between the time of incurring business costs and that of the receipt of the sale proceeds; cash held by dealers to bridge the interval between purchase and realisation being included under this heading'.[4] The amount to be demanded for this motive will depend mainly on 'the value of current output (and hence on current income) and on the number of hands through which output passes'.[5]

This motive, therefore, is entirely the parallel of the previous one. In both cases the existence of a positive balance at any time will be due to the lack of synchronisation of payments and receipts, but also to the inadequacy of available facilities to provide suitable funds *at the moment when they are required*. The amount of money to be held for this purpose would also be influenced by the 'relative cost of holding cash', that is, by the net rate of return produced by the purchase of a non-money asset. And here, we should note, the position is complicated by the fact that interest may be earned on holdings of money – for example, by holding bank deposit-account deposits.[6]

For present purposes the most striking feature of the business motive is that it is defined so sparingly. It is clear that Keynes intends it to cover balances held to finance business expenditure – to meet costs which, due to the roundaboutness of the production process, will necessarily be incurred prior to the receipt of revenue.

Consequently, it must be intended to apply equally to money held in connection with the finance of investment, the production of consumer goods and day-to-day outgoings. Bearing in mind the 'lumpiness' of investment expenditure in a firm's budget, Keynes's treatment seems barely adequate even when we have made allowance for the fact that the 'motives' only apply to money balances which for the reasons stated must be *held* in anticipation of expenditures; and specifically excludes cases in which the requisite money balances can be acquired as and when they are needed through the financial system. The obvious example would be a bank overdraft facility which would allow a firm to bring a money balance into existence at the time payment was to be made.

In any case, Keynes was preoccupied with the establishment of his liquidity-preference theory of interest and was thus concerned to emphasise reasons for which there might be a demand for money to hold *in relation to* an available stock. Consequently, he neglected the mechanics of finance in the *General Theory* and only later sought to remedy the defect, not only because of the confusion caused by his omission but also because he came to realise that he had left his liquidity-preference theory incomplete. We shall return to this point below.

THE ROLE OF UNCERTAINTY

In what has been said so far there is no apparent departure from previously accepted theory; but Keynes saw that the desire to hold money in preference to profitable assets was also to be explained by that other characteristic feature of a monetary (real world) economy, the state of uncertainty. He argued:

> it is obvious that up to a point it is worthwhile to sacrifice a certain amount of interest for the convenience of liquidity. But, given that the rate of interest is never negative, why should anyone prefer to hold his wealth in a form which yields little or no interest to holding it in a form which yields interest (assuming, of course, at this stage, that the risk of default is the same in respect of a bank balance as of a bond)? ...There is ... a necessary condition failing

> which the existence of a liquidity preference for money as a means of holding wealth could not exist.[7]

That necessary condition, Keynes explained,

> is the existence of uncertainty as to the future of the rate of interest, i.e. as to the complex of rates of interest for varying maturities which will rule at future dates. For if the rates of interest ruling at all future times could be foreseen with certainty, all future rates of interest could be inferred from the *present* rates of interest for debts of different maturities, which would be adjusted to the knowledge of the future rates.[8]

Uncertainty as to the future of the rate of interest gives rise to two motives for holding money: the precautionary motive and the speculative motive.

THE DEMAND FOR MONEY: PRECAUTIONARY MOTIVE

Keynes defined the purpose of the precautionary motive as being:

> To provide for contingencies requiring *sudden* expenditure and for *unforeseen* opportunities of advantageous purchases and also to hold an asset of which the value is fixed in terms of money to meet a subsequent liability fixed in terms of money.[9]

This motive is based upon a more subtle idea than the previous one, and has two components. First, because the future is unknowable there will be a desire to have on hand balances to meet future unplanned expenditures. In addition, there will be a need to provide for future expenditure the date of which is known.

In neither case would it be appropriate to make provision by holding financial claims, because uncertainty as to the future of the rate of interest means that capital values at any future date (prior to maturity where the security has a maturity date) cannot be known. Consequently, the holding of a money balance satisfies 'the desire for security as to the future cash equivalent of a certain proportion of total resources'.[10] The precautionary motive gives rise, then, to the holding of a genuinely 'idle' balance.

As in the case of the transactions motives, Keynes makes the precautionary motive to depend upon 'the general activity of the economic system and of the level of money income'.[11] In the same way, the strength of demand under this heading will be influenced by, for example, the availability of overdraft facilities, the payment of interest on financial claims which count as money (bank deposits), and the opportunity or relative cost of holding money.

More significantly, in the case of the precautionary motive the demand for money will be influenced by the existence of opportunities for resale of assets from portfolio in a secondary market, for 'in the absence of an organised market, liquidity-preference due to the precautionary motive would be greatly increased'.[12]

Here, be it noted, Keynes implicitly recognised the economic importance of a secondary, resale, market in conferring 'liquidity' on financial claims and other assets, which in the absence of such facilities would represent a more certain 'lock-up' of money balances and so provide a disincentive to the provision of funds for investment.

At the same time, however, he drew attention to the opposite influence of an organised capital market, which taken in conjunction with the separation of ownership and management of firms, could have a deleterious effect on investment by directing attention towards short-term movements in secondary market prices and away from the estimation of prospective returns from new investment projects.

Keynes's assessment of the relative usefulness of primary and secondary markets and of 'enterprise' as against 'speculation' is dealt with below, in Chaper 14. For present purposes the problem raised for the demand-for-money function is that whereas the absence of a secondary market would greatly strengthen the precautionary motive for money-holding, the 'existence of an organised market gives an opportunity for wide fluctuations in liquidity preference due to the speculative motive'.[13]

THE DEMAND FOR MONEY: SPECULATIVE MOTIVE

In comparison with the precautionary motive, Keynes's speculative motive is a much more 'positive' idea and the balances to which it gives rise are much more 'active'; not indeed in the same way as balances held for transactions purposes in financing income, but in the sense that they are held *as against* holding profitable assets as part of a continuous strategy to maximise dealing profits.

The speculative motive is the most novel element in Keynes's analysis of the demand for money and for that reason is the most familiar. It is money-holding with 'the object of securing profit from knowing better than the market what the future will bring forth'. Because the prices of fixed-interest securities vary inversely with the market rate of interest,[14] individual investors can benefit by estimating more accurately than predominant market opinion how interest rates will move over the immediate future.

For example, an individual who believes that future rates will be above the rates assumed by the market (security prices will be lower) will be motivated to sell securities and hold cash, delaying his repurchase of securities until after their prices have fallen. Conversely, an individual who believes that future interest rates will be below the level assumed by the market will be motivated to borrow money at short term in order to purchase debts of longer term at the current lower price. Taken together the sales produced by 'bear' opinion and the purchases produced by 'bull' opinion will determine the market price of securities and the market rate of interest.

Keynes saw the rate of interest as a 'highly conventional' phenomenon, 'for its actual value is largely governed by the prevailing view as to what its value is expected to be'.[15] While the stability of the interest rate is dependent on there being 'a *variety* of opinion about what is uncertain',[16] for each individual contributing to the variety of opinion, the prediction as to the future movement of the rate will be based upon observation of the current market rate and 'the degree of its divergence from what is considered a fairly *safe* level of *r*, having regard to those calculations of probability which are being relied on'.[17]

Consequently, the quantity of money demanded to satisfy the speculative motive will depend on the dealer's opinion as to the future course of the rate of interest, and this in turn will be determined by his estimate of the relationship between the current rate and the 'safe' rate. For any given state of expectations the speculative demand will increase as the rate of interest falls, because each fall both reduces the market rate relative to the 'safe' rate and so increases the risk of a fall in capital values, and at the same time reduces the returns from holding non-money assets and therefore the offset to the risk of illiquidity.

MONEY MARKET EQUILIBRIUM

Keynes's aggregate demand for money function taken in conjunction with the quantity of money available to satisfy the demand can be written as a condition for money market equilibrium:

$$M = M_1 + M_2 = L_1(Y) + L_2(r)$$

where L_1 represents demand for transactions and precautionary purposes shown as a function mainly of income; and L_2 represents demand for speculative purposes, shown as dependent mainly on the relation between the current rate of interest and the state of expectation. M_1 and M_2 are, respectively, money balances held to satisfy these demands.

This is a useful representation of the essential distinction in Keynes's analysis which lies between the demand for money on the one hand and the quantity of money available to satisfy demand on the other. Changes in the relationship between demand and supply will produce changes in the state of liquidity, which changes will be indicated by movements in the rate of interest.

Different kinds of economic and financial activities will, therefore, have their effect on the general state of liquidity – and therefore on the rate of interest – by way of their contribution to the aggregate demand for money. Consequently, an increase (for example) in the level of activity of whatever kind will *ceteris paribus* increase the demand for money and cause the rate of interest to rise.

In addition, a change in long-period expectations could, as we shall see, cause the rate of interest to rise or fall independently of any change in liquidity preference which emanates from a rise or fall in the level of economic activity. It is important to make this observation at this juncture, as developments in Keynes's analysis subsequent to the *General Theory* gave rise, despite Keynes's best efforts, to misunderstandings among his critics.

STOCK VERSUS FLOW: MONEY DEMAND AND VELOCITY

The Robertsonian school claim to find yet another 'static' element in Keynes's theory in as much as the role of money is stated in stock terms, whereas a 'dynamic' theory would be expressed in terms of money's velocity of circulation.[18] In fact, Keynes was careful to explain why he took his chosen line. We shall look first at Keynes's treatment of velocity and the demand for money, and then (in the next section) at his solution to the all-important problem of the relationship between saving and hoarding.

Keynes recognised that his analysis of the motives for holding money:

> is substantially the same as that which has been sometimes discussed under the heading of the Demand for Money. It is also closely connected with what is called the income-velocity of money; for the income-velocity of money merely measures what proportion of their incomes the public chooses to hold in cash, so that an increased income-velocity of money may be a symptom of a decreased liquidity preference.[19]

However, the problem with the use of the income-velocity approach is that it:

> carries with it the misleading suggestion of a presumption in favour of the demand for money as a whole being proportional, or having some determinate relation, to income, whereas this presumption should apply, as we shall see, only to a *portion* of the public's cash holdings; with the result that it overlooks the part played by the rate of interest.[20]

In Keynes's view, income velocity should be defined not as the ratio of Y to M (equal to $M_1 + M_2$); but rather as the ratio of Y to M_1, money demanded to satisfy the transactions and precautionary motives.

$$L_1\,(Y) = \frac{V}{Y} = M_1$$

The value of V would depend upon the state of economic and financial organisation, the distribution of incomes and the opportunity cost of holding idle cash. Over a short time-period these factors will not change significantly so that V can be regarded as pretty well constant. Therefore, under this heading, money is held more as a necessity than as a preference as against other assets.

In other words, the problem with the income-velocity idea is that it is too limited: it includes only part of the total money stock and leaves out of account M_2, money holding as determined by the rate of interest, 'since it is in respect of his stock of accumulated savings, rather than of his income, that the individual can exercise his choice between liquidity and illiquidity'.[21]

Only in the world of pure theory, or under some form of economic organisation which precludes uncertainty as to the future course of the rate of interest, will the speculative demand for money be zero in equilibrium. In this case M_2 will be equal to zero and M will be equal to M_1. Therefore, because $M_1V=Y$ and Y(income)$=OP$ (the quantity and price of current output), we quickly arrive at $MV=OP$: 'which is much the same as the Quantity Theory of Money in its traditional form'.[22]

The amount of money held under M_1 is money in 'active' circulation and is determined by those longer-run institutional arrangements which are subsumed under the expression 'income velocity of circulation'. In this context 'demand' and 'velocity' are but alternative formulations of the same economic phenomenon.

The traditional quantity theory result cannot be obtained, however, because part of the total money stock will be held under M_2, money held on inactive account. Here the essential distinction in Keynes's analysis between the demand for money and the quantity available to satisfy demand, provides the clearest point of departure from the loanable-funds approach with its unhappy agglomeration of saving, dishoarding and credit creation.

SAVING AND HOARDING

Having made clear the nature of saving and its relationship to investment, Keynes turned the corner into monetary analysis by way of a novel dual-decision theory of time preferences, which introduced the concept of liquidity preference and explained its central importance in Keynes's scheme. With this analysis Keynes was to eclipse and supersede the loanable-funds theory, by clarifying on established microeconomic principles the previously confused and uncertain relationship between 'saving' and 'hoarding'.

Individuals' time preferences will take effect as the result of two sets of decisions.[23] The first is to determine 'how much of his income he will consume and how much he will reserve in *some* form of command over future consumption'. Here the outcome will be governed by the individual's propensity to consume.

However, the individual must further decide 'in *what form* he will hold the command over future consumption which he has reserved, whether out of his current income or from previous savings'. Here the individual's liquidity preference, the choice between holding liquid money or profitable assets, will be in respect of his *stock* of wealth. As expectations change so will the demand for money for speculative purposes, but only in equilibrium will the demand for money under L_2 be equal to the quantity available under M_2, where $M_2 = M - M_1$.

Keynes's essential distinction between the demand for money on the one hand as against the quantity available to satisfy demand on the other, gives us the correct approach to the concept of hoarding. For hoarding reflects the *desire* to hold money, and the 'propensity to hoard' is the equivalent of liquidity preference. It is to be distinguished from the quantity available for hoarding, which is given by the money stock, minus what is required to satisfy the transactions motive. Therefore the desires of the public cannot *proximately* determine the quantity of hoards; they will, rather, determine the rate of interest at which the propensity to hoard is made equal to the amount available for hoarding.[24]

A later refinement was the point that, over time, the size of the individual's wealth stock will increase as new savings flow in from income, and that this also could give rise to an increased demand for money to hold without at the same time doing anything to satisfy it. In the course of examining various concepts of hoarding, Joan Robinson was to explain that:

> Investment is going on at a certain rate, individuals, taken one with another, are adding to their wealth at a rate equal to the rate of net investment, and they wish to hold a part of the increment of their wealth in the form of money. Thus the demand for money is rising gradually through time, and, if the quantity of money is constant, there is a gradually increasing upward pressure on the rate of interest.[25]

It follows that the adjustment to equilibrium must involve a change in the composite demand for money until it is equal to the available supply. With a given quantity of money an increase in the amount hoarded is achieved by way of a fall in the level of incomes and economic activity, 'which releases money from the active circulation, and is another name for a fall in the average velocity of circulation of money'.

In any case, the demand for money to hold as part of a stock of wealth is only a component of the aggregate demand for money; and at the same time the income velocity of money in the active circulation is merely an arithmetical ratio of a stock of money to the flow of income with given payments habits etc. The stock-flow point is not at all helpful, and the use of the velocity concept leads only to confusion, being, as Keynes points out, 'merely a name which explains nothing'.[26]

ECONOMIC CAUSATION AND CHANNELS OF FLOW

To accuse Keynes of thinking only in static terms when his theory depends so much on the effect of expectations can only be the result of misunderstanding: misunderstanding not only of his overall methodology (see Chapter 6, above); but misunderstanding also engendered by a confusion between economic causation and channels of flow.

For Robertson the loanable-funds theory provided a 'commonsense account of events' and was intended to portray the way in which the money market actually worked and reflecting the modes of thought of those who operated in it.[27] In support of this view, Dr Presley has quoted Professor Tew's remark that when assessing the state of the stock market 'all my arguments seem to present themselves in terms of flows'.[28] In addition a leading textbook of financial economics informs us that 'the loanable funds theory of interest rate determination is the theory most often used by financial market analysts'.[29]

However, we should not perhaps be overly surprised at differences of opinion between economists and market operators as to the nature of reality. Do we not castigate bankers for thinking of their institutions as 'cloakrooms' rather than as engines generating bank deposits from a reserve base? In the same way, we can argue that the Robertsonian 'dynamic' view of the market in loanable funds is in reality to take an accountant's, a flow-of-funds analyst's, or even an ornithologist's view of the finance of economic activity.

It might, for example, be of interest for certain purposes to know where money balances have actually come from, and how they circulate to finance different kinds of economic activity, and how one balance can finance several financial claims. The provision of such information is the purpose of the financial accounts, of the flow-of-funds table.

We could, like the ornithologist tagging a wild goose (or a wild duck!) somehow identify a particular money balance and trace its progress from one account to another and from one ownership to another. By this means we might find that the money employed to finance a particular piece of investment actually came in part from current savings, in part from dishoarding and in part from new money creation.

The relevance of this approach clearly depends on the nature of our underlying economic model; on our view of the causal relationship between economic variables. Given Keynes's view of the working of a monetary production economy and in particular his analysis of the relationship between investment and saving, such an approach would be less useful than one which immediately directed attention to the state of liquidity and hence to the determination of the rate of interest.

THE DEMAND FOR MONEY: FINANCE MOTIVE

After publication of the *General Theory* Keynes was to modify his specification of liquidity preference, both to allow for the effects of Bertil Ohlin's distinction between *ex ante* and *ex post* investment[30] and in addition to provide:

> a bridge between my way of talking and the way of those [the loanable funds school] who discuss the supply of loans and credits etc. ... to show that they were simply discussing one of the sources of demand for liquid funds arising out of an increase in activity.[31]

Keynes was to admit that he had been 'seriously at fault' in the *General Theory* in omitting any discussion of the process whereby capital formation is financed. He had, it is true, allowed for the effect of an increase in *actual* activity on the demand for money but now he saw the need in addition to allow for the effect of an increase in *planned* activity.

This was to take account of the entrepreneur's requirement for finance at the time the investment *decision* was taken (investment *ex ante*), and was to cover the period – the interregnum – up until the time the investment was actually made (became *ex post*). Not only would this command of liquid resources mean that the entrepreneur could 'go ahead with assurance', but it would also encompass the possibility that *ex post* investment would turn out to be different from *ex ante* investment – but that it is at the *ex ante* stage that decisions concerning finance will have to be made.[32]

To get the finance motive in perspective we should be clear that the principal distinction between Keynes's various motives for holding money is the length of time for which money is likely to be held and hence how quickly each will contribute to the restoration of liquidity.

In receiving income an individual is given command of a money balance from the common stock which then is literally at his disposal. Part will be returned immediately or within a very short time as expenditures are made in accordance with consumption behaviour taken in conjunction with the pay period etc. Part, however, will be left over as savings and will be added to the individual's wealth stock. Because a decision may be taken to hoard rather than engage in financial investment, the aggregate money stock may be depleted to the extent of hoards and the restoration of liquidity delayed for an indeterminate time, depending on the rate of interest and state of expectation etc.[33]

The finance motive, however, being a demand for money initiated at the planning stage of investment, is governed as to the time that will elapse before its release into circulation by the length of the lag between the investment decision and its execution. Consequently, the firm's demand for money to finance *planned* activity may be seen as of greater significance for the state of liquidity than demand for the finance of actual activity, in as much as 'the cash which it requires may be turned over so much more slowly'.[34]

Therefore, money held for the finance motive 'may be regarded as lying half-way, so to speak, between the active and inactive balances'.[35] In other words, though it is an active balance in the sense that it is held in connection with planned expenditure, it cannot be relied upon for the restoration of liquidity to the same extent as money held for transactions purposes.

Nevertheless, in common with transactions demand, balances held for purposes of finance are 'self-liquidating', in the sense that they in turn reduce and then restore overall liquidity as they are respectively taken up and then used to finance investment expenditure. Therefore:

> 'finance' is essentially a revolving fund. It employs no savings. It is, for the community as a whole, only a book-keeping transaction. As soon as it is 'used' in the sense of being expended, the lack of liquidity is automatically made good and the readiness to become temporarily unliquid is available to be used over again.[36]

For, with a given state of liquidity the desire of someone to become more liquid can only be accomplished if someone else is prepared to become temporarily less liquid for the appropriate period. This, of course, applies not only to individuals but also to the financial institutions, and it was to the banks that Keynes looked to become temporarily less liquid in turn to a series of firms wishing to invest; that is 'to organise and manage a revolving fund of liquid finance'.[37]

Therefore, with a given rate of investment the demand for finance can be satisfied from a given quantity of money, revolving endlessly to finance a succession of investment projects. In *ex ante–ex post* terms it means that because funds required to finance current *ex ante* investment are provided by finance released by current *ex post* investment, it is only when the current rate of investment *ex ante* is different from the current rate of *ex post* investment that there will be a change in the liquidity position.

In this case, with a given money stock and given liquidity preferences on the part of the public and the banks, an increase in planned investment will, in increasing the aggregate demand for money, lead to a rise in the rate of interest. It was this point which Keynes saw as providing 'the coping stone of the liquidity theory of the rate of interest' which he had overlooked when writing the *General Theory*.[38]

It is, therefore, a lack of finance – a shortage of money relative to the increased demand causing the rate of interest to rise – which can put a brake on an increase in the rate of investment. By the same token, it is an increase in the amount of money available to meet the demand which can restore the situation and allow the investment to go ahead.[39]

It follows that 'in general the banks hold the key position in the transition from a lower to a higher scale of activity'. And here, Keynes noted, the British practice of allowing overdraft facilities to suitable customers would greatly facilitate the provision of finance for an increased rate of investment. Because of the existence of unused overdraft facilities, entrepreneurs would have finance to hand at the time the investment *decision* was taken, so enabling them to go ahead with assurance. But no pressure would be exerted on the banks' liquidity position until the overdraft facilities were used to finance actual activity. Investment is thus encouraged due to the absence of disincentives at the planning stage.[40]

The entrepreneur's demand for 'finance' is added to his existing financial requirements, about which Keynes was now more forthcoming:

> The entrepreneur when he decides to invest has to be satisfied on two points: firstly, that he can obtain sufficient short-term finance during the period of producing the investment; and secondly, that he can eventually fund his short-term obligations by a long-term issue on satisfactory conditions. Occasionally he may be in a position to use his own resources or to make his long-term issue at once; but this makes no difference to the amount of 'finance' which has to be found by the market as a whole, but only to the channel through which it reaches the entrepreneur.[41]

It is perfectly clear that though Keynes elaborated on and added to his liquidity-preference approach after publication of the *General Theory*, there was no wavering from the main principle that the finance of economic activity is a matter of the demand for and supply of money and that changes in the state of liquidity will bring about changes in the rate of interest.

THE SIGNIFICANCE OF THE FINANCE MOTIVE: TWO VIEWS

Although Keynes could confidently claim that the introduction of the 'finance' motive made no 'really significant change' in his previous theory and that his theory 'substantially' was 'exactly what it was' when he first published his book,[42] this is not how things appeared to his critics.

For the loanable-funds school this innovation signified a major reverse for Keynesian theorising. In the first place it was taken as a sign that Keynes accepted Robertson's interpretation of the multiplier as a dynamic rather than a static process, so that finance had to be provided for investment in anticipation of the voluntary saving that would eventually be provided out of newly created income.

Second, the reopened question of how investment was to be financed in the absence of instantaneously provided voluntary saving, seemed to provide good grounds for the reinstatement of the forced-saving thesis.

Third, it was an apparent indication that Keynes had moved closer to the Robertsonian transmission mechanism, thus accepting a direct rather than an indirect link between 'the productivity of investment' and the rate of interest.

Whereas previously an increase in investment was seen to affect the rate of interest only indirectly via an increase in the level of income and hence the demand for money, now because an increase in *ex ante* investment would cause the demand for money to increase directly through the finance motive, a link was established between the 'productivity of investment' and the rate of interest. In this way Keynes's introduction of the finance motive was taken as confirmation of his acceptance of neo-classical interest theory.

SAVING, THE FINANCE OF INVESTMENT AND THE RATE OF INTEREST: A REPLY TO ROBERTSON

Discussion of productivity, thrift and the rate of interest is best delayed until after our examination of the nature of interest, but there are three points involving liquidity preference which can be dealt with here.

The first is that although the finance motive allows increased *ex ante* investment to increase the demand for money directly, this does not establish a link of any peculiar significance between investment and the rate of interest.

Because it is the aggregate demand for money taken in conjunction with the available supply that determines the rate of interest,[43] no special distinction can be claimed by investment, because precisely the same result could be achieved by an increased demand for money to finance an increased propensity to consume or to hoard. The distinction between the finance demand and demands previously specified is not that it is based upon the finance of investment *per se*, but that it is based upon an activity which is *planned* and could apply equally well to planned consumption.[44]

The second point is that the finance motive, and the revolving fund of money which supplies it, carries no implication that the rate of interest will be invariant over the cycle. While *ceteris paribus* the revolving fund will be of constant amount, the demand for money will expand and contract over the cycle and so affect the rate of interest:

> the increased demand for money resulting from an increase in activity has a backwash which tends to raise the rate of interest; and this is indeed a significant element in my theory of why booms carry within them the seeds of their own destruction.[45]

The third point concerns the influence of 'thrift'. It is perfectly possible for saving to change the rate of interest, but it is important to bear in mind that this result can only be achieved through the effect of a change in the *propensity* to save (consume) on the level of income and hence the demand for money. The *rate* of saving cannot change unless the rate of investment is changing.[46] The possibly adverse effects on the incentive to invest were touched on earlier.

Also it should now be clear from the point of view of our discussion of the investment–saving relation and the nature of saving and of the role of money in the finance of economic activity, that the 'finance of investment by saving instantaneously generated by the multiplier' myth is completely scotched. Indeed any idea of saving as a source of finance for investment must be firmly resisted; as when investment is *ex ante* no saving has taken place and when investment is *ex post* savings only accumulate with a lag.

It is, however, quite possible to consider saving in relation to other activities as a means of *restoring liquidity* and here it will be seen to be inferior to both consumption and investment. An attempt to increase the amount of money available in the market by saving *ex ante* can only refer: (i) to an increase in the propensity to save so that transactions demand falls with the fall in income which must result, as noted above; or (ii) to the attempt by individuals to become less liquid themselves – to reduce their own holdings of *money* – in order to make others more liquid. With a given level of income and interest rates and without a change in expectations it is difficult to see how this could occur.[47]

In the more relevant case of an increase in activity, if there is no change in the money stock,

> the public can save *ex ante* and *ex post* and *ex* anything else until they are blue in the face, without alleviating the problem in the least – unless, indeed, the result of their efforts is to lower the scale of activity to what it was before.[48]

Similarly, though savings initially accumulate in liquid form they are a less reliable means of restoring liquidity than consumption and investment, due to the effects of hoarding on the part of wealth-holders.[49]

Note, in this regard, that when money is taken up to satisfy the finance motive it is subsequently released not from saving but from investment, as *ex ante* becomes *ex post*, for 'there will always be *exactly* enough *ex post* saving to take up the *ex post* investment and so release the finance which the *latter* had been previously employing'.[50]

These particular points lead us to the more general point that one of Keynes's most important insights was to make clear the relative roles of money and saving. He pointed out that:

> We have been all of us brought up ... in deep confusion of mind between the demand and supply of money and the demand and supply of savings; and until we rid ourselves of it, we cannot think correctly.[51]

In regard to his keenest adversary in particular, Keynes saw this confusion as the chief obstacle to a reconciliation of ideas:

> It is Mr Robertson's incorrigible confusion between the revolving fund of money in circulation and the flow of new saving which causes all his difficulties.[52]

It remains only to point out that the Robertsonian criticism that the induced investment arising from the operation of the accelerator would exacerbate the shortage of voluntary saving to finance investment, is merely an extension of the original error. And in this connection we should note that the alleged static nature of Keynes's thought is partly based on the belief that Keynes had failed to take account of the acceleration principle. But there is abundant evidence that Keynes was centrally concerned with the relationship between current investment and expected future income. Meltzer, for example, has interpreted Keynes's investment theory explicitly in terms of the accelerator. In addition, Keynes linked expected income to his m.e.c. theory in his correspondence with Hicks over the 'Mr. Keynes and the Classics' article. Finally, there are apposite references both in the *General Theory* and in his interpretative 'The General Theory of Employment' article which followed.[53]

Keynes's thesis has so far emerged intact. An increase in *ex ante* investment relative to current *ex post* investment will, if the banking system agrees to increase the money stock, increase incomes to the point at which aggregate saving is equal to realised investment. There is no call for the rate of interest to rise. If, on the other hand, the money stock fails to expand in line with the increased demand, the rate of interest will rise and investment will be checked. For Keynes,

> The investment market can become congested through shortage of cash. It can never become congested through shortage of saving. This is the most fundamental of my conclusions within this field.[54]

10 The Rate of Interest

KEYNES'S APPROACH: A STYLISED VIEW

We have now reached the last of the four topics encompassed by Keynes's treatment of investment and saving.

Robertsonian criticism of Keynes's approach to the nature of interest and the determination of the rate of interest is criticism based on a version of Keynes's theory which is familiar from the stylised accounts of the textbooks. This stylised version is in two parts or stages.

In the first stage, Keynes seeks to correct the classical theory but in so doing falls into error of his own. In the second stage, Keynes's innovations are successfully reconciled with mainstream neo-classical thinking to produce the composite 'modern' version which forms the basis of the standard macroeconomic teaching model.

In the first stage, the 'crude' Keynesian theory has the following features. The rate of interest is determined solely by the supply and demand for money, where the supply is fixed exogenously and demand is analysed according to the three familiar motives for holding money. Here the novelty of Keynes's theory lies in his introduction of the speculative motive which is interest-elastic and reflects the preferences of wealth-holders for liquidity as against holdings of interest-bearing bonds. The amount demanded for speculative purposes is seen to be a function of expectations of future movements of the interest rate, being high when rates are expected to rise and low when rates are expected to fall. In turn, expectations themselves are determined in the psychology of individual transactors by reference to some largely unexplained 'normal' or 'safe' rate of interest.

So far, the theory though interesting is simply an alternative hypothesis to existing theories, but three qualifications are relevant which provide the basis for criticism of Keynes's approach. First, it is a purely 'stock, theory, dealing with a given stock of money and the level of demand for that stock. Second, it is a purely monetary theory, and as such excludes 'real' influences. Third, it is intended to be a determinate theory, in contrast to the classical theory which is indeterminate, being appropriate only to an economy with a given (full-employment) level of income. Once Keynes had pointed out the dependence of saving on the level of income the uniqueness of the classical solution disappeared, since there would now be a different level of income and saving for each level of the rate of interest.

This left the way open for Keynes to introduce his revolutionary liquidity approach, but, unfortunately, in his eagerness to show that the rate of interest was determined by the activities of wealth-holders in choosing between holdings of bonds or money, Keynes forgot the influence of the level of income on the (transactions) demand for money. Because each increase in the level of income would increase the demand for money, the total demand for money and, therefore, the rate of interest could not be known until the level of income was known.

Therefore, Keynes had left his own theory indeterminate and it was only with the advent of the Hicks–Hansen *IS–LM* system that a determinate solution for the rate of interest could be obtained. This modern composite theory, which incorporates both real and monetary elements, not only reconciles alternative classical (loanable-funds) and Keynesian approaches but by the same token maintains an unbroken line of development from previous theory.

All this, of course, is familiar from numerous textbook accounts but it is misleading as a guide to Keynes's interest theory. By allowing Keynes's insights to be neatly and conveniently slotted back into mainstream (neo-classical) theory the composite version gives currency to classical modes of thought. In particular, by maintaining the classical view of the relationship between saving and investment it can provide a dangerously misleading guide to economic policy.

Before turning (in Chapters 11–13 below) to Keynes's own view of the nature of interest, the determination of the rate of interest and the peculiar role of the interest rate in determining the level of economic activity, we must first rebut some specifically Robertsonian criticisms based on the 'qualifications' introduced above. Because these criticisms stem from problems inherent in the loanable-funds approach, much of the spadework of rebuttal has been done in previous chapters, as we have dealt successively with the relationship between investment and saving, the nature of saving and the finance of investment.

A PURELY STOCK APPROACH?

The standard textbook comment that Keynes's interest theory employs only stock concepts,[1] looms large in Robertsonian criticism of

Keynes, where it is taken as a manifestation of the typically 'static' approach of the *General Theory* as a whole. It is contrasted unfavourably with Robertson's 'dynamic' approach, in which the rate of interest is determined by flows of loanable funds.

There is little more to say in reply to this point. We have already dealt at length with the implications of Keynes's adopted methodology for 'taming the real world'. We have also explained why it is more appropriate to talk in terms of the supply and demand for money rather than the supply and demand for 'loanable funds'. In addition, the attempt by Robertson to provide a 'true account' of the operation of the loanable-funds market, giving emphasis to the sources of the supply and demand for loanable funds, lays his theory open to the charge of being a flow-of-funds accountant's approach or, as we have dubbed it, an ornithologist's approach. This in itself would be unexceptionable – apart, of course, from the inclusion of the fundamental flaw which derives from Robertson's misconception of saving as a source of finance.

However, there is the further point that criticism which lays emphasis on the purely stock aspect of Keynes's theory may be part and parcel of the indeterminacy charge. That is, it may stem from the belief that Keynes saw the rate of interest as being determined solely by the decisions of wealth-holders, and therefore by the speculative demand for money (L_2) and the quantity of money available to satisfy that demand (M_2) rather than by the aggregate demand for and supply of money (L and M). We shall look at this point further when we deal with interpretations of the *IS–LM* system.

Finally, it must be said that the purely methodological question of the appropriateness of stock versus flow analysis is not one of crucial importance in the present context and does not constitute the main point of departure between loanable-funds and liquidity-preference theories. Keynes was clear that it was largely a matter of appropriateness and convenience, arguing that:

> I should myself claim that I deal sometimes with flows and sometimes with stocks, but not with both at the same time. At any rate that is what I try to do.[2]

A TWO- OR THREE-FOLD MARGIN?

Another criticism of Robertson's, which clearly betrays the classical ambience of his thinking and which it will be as well to dispose of here in preparation for what is to follow, concerns the relationship between the rate of interest, saving and the demand for money.

Robertson argued that having established a relationship between saving and income, Keynes made the rate of interest the reward for not hoarding rather than for not spending and so abandoned the connection between the rate of interest and saving. Robertson, however, maintained the classical link, with voluntary saving out of disposable income being determined by the 'desire to save', which he saw as principally and positively related to the rate of interest.

Furthermore, Robertson could see no necessary inconsistency between the view of interest as the reward for not spending and as the reward for not hoarding. If saved income is not to be invested in financial securities and is still to earn interest, it could simply be held in an interest-bearing account with a bank. The interest rate so earned is, therefore, a reward for hoarding, rather than for dishoarding as claimed by Keynes. This makes the true reward for dishoarding the difference between interest on money dishoarded and on that hoarded in interest-bearing accounts.

Therefore, instead of a relationship between the rate of interest and *either* the marginal convenience of holding money *or* the marginal inconvenience of going without consumption, the rate of interest could be related to *both*, so that there is a *three-fold margin* rather than a *two-fold margin*:

> such phrases as that interest is not the reward of not spending but the reward of not hoarding seem to indicate a curious inhibition against visualising more than two margins at once. A small boy at school is told that if he wins a race he may have either an apple or an orange: he wins the race and chooses the orange. When his mother asks him how he got it, must he reply 'I got it for not eating an apple'? May he not say proudly 'I got it for not losing a race'?[3]

But this, of course, is to give a very classical answer to a very classical question. Bearing in mind Robertson's difficulties over the nature of saving and the paradox of thrift, we must ask whether, if interest is to be the reward for not spending, it is therefore held to follow that the aggregate quantity of saving is a positive function of the interest rate. If so, there is clearly a conflict with Keynes's view. For while Keynes specifically acknowledges the influence of the rate of interest on both the propensity to save out of a given income and on the aggregate rate of saving, the relationship is different in each case.

We have seen that, at least in the short run, Keynes thought the rate of interest to be a weak and uncertain influence on the propensity to consume, which he regarded as largely determined by a consumer's accustomed standard of life based on some longer-run or permanent notion of income.[4] On the other hand, Keynes saw changes in the rate of interest as having a most important influence on the amount actually saved – that is, on the rate of saving – but the relationship is, of course, *negative* rather than positive as in the classical case.[5]

The second point concerns the holding of accumulated wealth in the form of interest-bearing bank deposits rather than 'barren cash' as an alternative to the purchase of bonds. This is a perfectly feasible solution and Keynes specifically allows for it.[6]

The earning of deposit interest or the avoidance of bank charges (for example, on bank advances by overdraft) enter as the 'relative cost of holding cash'. For what we are concerned with is liquidity preference: that is, with the holding of assets other than bonds and consequently with the implications of a possible change in the demand for bonds on bond prices and therefore on the long-term rate of interest. The precise degree of liquidity of the assets to be held instead of bonds is therefore a question of secondary importance.

Though Keynes is prepared to 'draw the line between "money" and "debts" at whatever point is most convenient for handling a particular problem', he quite justifiably assumes that 'money is co-extensive with bank deposits'. Bank deposits are directly spendable but, even so, some forms of bank deposits are more liquid than others, and in order to be ready to take advantage of a change in their view of market movements, speculators may have to incur an interest-loss penalty for a sudden withdrawal of funds from a deposit account (time deposit), as compared with a current account (demand deposit).

Similarly, if funds are held on deposit with other financial institutions to take advantage of higher interest payments, liquidity will be correspondingly lower. Professional dealers in the market may of course make use of firms of money brokers, who will supply lines of money or bonds to meet 'bull' or 'bear' positions on appropriate terms. In general, however:

> If the cash can only be retained by forgoing the purchase of a profitable asset, this increases the cost and thus weakens the motive towards holding a given amount of cash. If deposit interest is earned or if bank charges are avoided by holding cash, this

> decreases the cost and strengthens the motive. It may be, however, that this is likely to be a minor factor except where large changes in the cost of holding cash are in question.[7]

On Keynes's insistence on the rate of interest *actually being* the reward for parting with liquidity as a matter of definition, we shall have more to say later.

The above puts Robertson's example concerning the schoolboy and his choice into proper perspective. Although not an exact parallel it would be much more in keeping with Keynes's view to think of the school year as income, term-time as consumption and the school holidays as saving. Over the school year, holidays will ineluctably accumulate as spare time and the choice of the schoolboy is how to occupy himself. If he takes a holiday job, he can show his wages to his mother as the reward for not staying idle. If the mother perceives the job to be deleterious to health and offers a small amount of pocket money in lieu of the job, the parallel is more nearly complete.

KEYNES'S ATTEMPTED EXCLUSION OF PRODUCTIVITY AND THRIFT

Potentially the most damaging Robertsonian criticism of Keynes's interest-rate theory is that Keynes failed in his attempt to fashion a 'purely monetary' theory of interest; that is, that Keynes had attempted to break with classical and neo-classical tradition by excluding the real forces of productivity and thrift from having any significant part in the determination of the rate of interest. Subsequently, and under the influence of Robertson's argument, he had been forced to recant his revolutionary creed and to move back to a position close to the loanable-funds theory.

For Robertson, the question of the importance of productivity and thrift in the determination of the rate of interest was not purely 'academic' but sprang from a strong conviction that Keynes should give due recognition to the work of Cambridge economists past and present which had successfully integrated real and monetary elements in the theory of interest. Therefore, by defeating Keynes's 'revolutionary' approach, Robertson would be able both to maintain the continuity of development in classical and neo-classical theory and to ensure due recognition for the contributions of previous theorists; for this, we have noted, was always a central concern in his dealings with Keynes.

However, we shall see that both the Robertsonian critique of Keynes's original position and the recantation which supposedly followed were based upon an egregious misunderstanding of Keynes's argument. Robertson's observations on Keynes's work were, of course, made from the somewhat shaky vantage point of his own, loanable-funds, position, the principal features of which were as follows.

In the loanable-funds theory the rate of interest is determined by flows of loanable funds, under the influence of both real and monetary factors. On the demand side real factors predominate, as changes in the marginal productivity of capital influence investment behaviour and so the demand for loanable funds. On the supply side monetary factors are dominant as the flow of finance from voluntary saving is modified by changes in net hoards and net new money. Both of these latter elements are stock concepts, as we noted earlier, changes in which are added algebraically to the flow of savings.

The real forces of productivity and thrift exert a long-run effect on the rate of interest and between them determine a quasi-natural rate around which oscillates a short-run market rate of interest under the influence of monetary disturbances.[8] Both rates are continually changing and a fragile equilibrium is temporarily established only when supply and demand are equated in the market for loanable funds.

The problems with this theory have been examined at length, but for our present purposes they derive from the unsatisfactory manner in which real and monetary influences are combined and from the central confusion over saving as a source of finance.

From Robertson's viewpoint, therefore, Keynes's 'purely monetary' theory of interest by definition excluded the influence of productivity and thrift. In Robertson's eyes this meant that the rate of interest must be *invariant* with respect to autonomous changes in investment and saving, as we have seen.

But how was it possible for Keynes to justify his neglect of productivity and thrift? The answer appeared to lie with the multiplier, whereby an increase in investment due to a rise in the marginal efficiency of capital will be financed by the equal amount of voluntary saving generated. This would certainly seem to solve the problem in loanable-funds terms, because the increase in the demand for loanable funds would be entirely offset by an equivalent increase in supply, leaving the rate of interest unaffected.

But to Robertson, of course, this result would only obtain using Keynes's original version of the multiplier. Interpreted in dynamic, Robertsonian, terms the lag in the provision of finance from voluntary saving would require a compensating increase in the quantity of money, with the result that forced saving would give rise to interest-rate effects.

Robertson saw the further problem of Keynes's case – that it cannot be guaranteed that the additional saving stemming from the multiplier process will be parted with willingly by wealth-holders, in exchange for securities resulting from the increased investment, without a rise in the interest rate. Therefore, to maintain the neutrality of interest with respect to changes in the productivity of investment it is necessary to assume that the speculative demand for money is perfectly interest-elastic, so that the system operates permanently in a 'liquidity trap'.

A similar point is that, interpreted in *liquidity preference* terms, the insensitivity of the rate of interest to changes in productivity and thrift could be taken as a sign that Keynes's original formulation was indeed indeterminate, with the elements that determined the rate of interest being insulated from the effects of changes in the level of economic activity.

APPARENT CONFIRMATION OF ROBERTSON'S VIEW

Altogether, when interpreted from a neo-classical viewpoint, Keynes's claim to have revolutionised interest-rate theory by the exclusion of real factors from his analysis, seemed to rest on very insecure foundations. When subsequent developments seemed to indicate that Keynes had accepted the arguments of his critics, and with them the influence of productivity and thrift on the rate of interest, the ascendancy of loanable-funds theory seemed complete.

The first development was Keynes's largely unqualified acceptance of Hicks's *IS–LL* equilibrium model of 1937, which was developed into the familiar Hicks–Hansen *IS–LM* system. By combining real and monetary elements from the loanable-funds and liquidity-preference approaches, a determinate solution for the rate of interest and level of income was obtained, with equilibrium in the markets for goods and money.

By signifying his acceptance of this interpretation of his theory, Keynes by the same token acknowledged a causal relationship between the productivity of investment (and thrift) and the rate of interest.

For example, an increase in the quantity of investment consequent upon a rise in the marginal productivity of investment would shift the *IS* curve to the right and so cause the rate of interest to rise to an extent determined by the slope of the *LM* curve. Similarly, an increase in the (average) propensity to save would cause the *IS* curve to shift to the left and so lower the rate of interest.

The reason in both cases is the same: that the change in investment or saving would act upon the level of income and, therefore, the transactions demand for money and so the total demand for money in relation to the available money stock (see Figure 10.1).

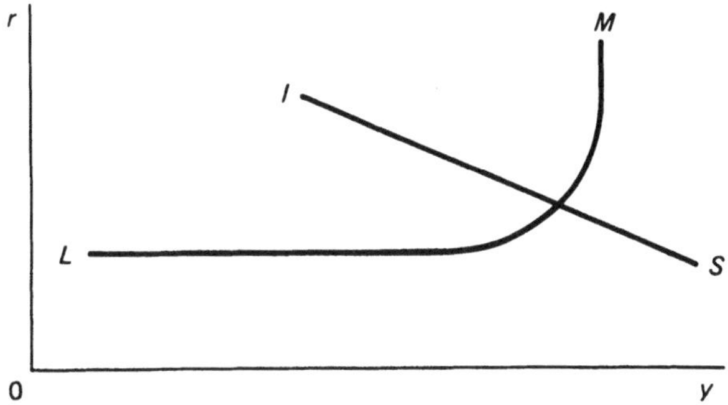

Figure 10.1

This development left the distinction between the loanable-funds and liquidity-preference theories largely a question of the route by which changes in productivity and thrift would affect the rate of interest. For Robertson the influence was *direct*, whereas for Keynes it was *indirect*, as we have seen.

With the second development, however – the introduction by Keynes of the finance motive in response to Robertson's criticism of the multiplier – the relationship between a change in the productivity of investment and the rate of interest became *direct*, since there would now be an immediate effect on the demand for money.

With this development, the only fig-leaf left to Keynes with which to protect his revolutionary gambit was the postulated existence of a 'liquidity trap'. If the *LM* curve were shown to be horizontal, so that the speculative demand for money was perfectly interest-elastic, an increase in the demand for money could be satisfied from speculative balances at an unchanged rate of interest. Consequently, whether Keynes's thesis was interpreted in loanable-funds or liquidity-preference terms, its maintenance was seen to depend on the *empirical validity* of the liquidity-trap idea.

But here again there could be no succour. It would be unrealistic to argue that the economy operated permanently within a liquidity-trap region of the *LM* curve, and in any case the existence of the liquidity trap itself could be disputed on Keynes's own admission that he knew of 'no example of it hitherto'.[9]

Finally, is it possible to help Keynes out by arguing that his theory is not a general theory but relates only to the short run where monetary factors predominate? This indeed is the usual textbook solution to the dilemma[10] and, moreover, accords well with the disposition of influences in Robertson's own theory. However, even this solution is ultimately unacceptable because of Keynes's use of the psychological 'normal' or 'safe' rate of interest, by reference to which wealth-holders make their choice between money and bonds and so determine the actual market rate.

Because for Robertson the determination of the 'normal' rate is insufficiently explained by Keynes, we are simply left with the idea that 'the rate of interest is what it is because it is expected to become other than it is'.[11] Thus Robertson dismissed Keynes's claim to have produced a purely monetary theory of the rate of interest and referred to 'an analysis which passes off as a theory of interest what is really only a theory of the divergencies of the rate of interest from some normal level left unexplained'.[12]

A ROBERTSONIAN CONCLUSION ON LIQUIDITY PREFERENCE

On Robertson's assessment there seems very little that can be salved from the wreck of Keynes's liquidity-preference theory of interest. True, Keynes had made a lasting contribution in his development of the theory of money-holding, but all-in-all it was a distinctly limited achievement when set beside his ambitious intentions.

Furthermore, it is an assessment which has endured, so that even in more recent times, when the 'reappraisal' of the Keynesian Revolution was under way and 'Keynesian economics' was being distinguished from the 'economics of Keynes', A. Leijonhufvud was in no doubt that:

> the Liquidity Preference theory is *not*, and cannot be, a complete theory of the determination of the level of interest rates. It deals merely with the determination of the *movement* of 'the' interest rate from some historically given level which will occur when the system as a whole is exposed to some specified disturbance ... It does not explain the average level around which these short-term fluctuations take place.[13]

And it is here, in Leijonhufvud's last sentence, that we have the essence of the problem. Not only is Keynes's approach misunderstood because critics interpret it by reference to their own classically based theories, but in particular there remains the impression that economists in the neo-classical tradition believe that a key variable like the rate of interest should not be at the whim of something as insubstantial as the vagaries of speculative expectations.

Indeed, they would argue that Keynes himself sensed as much, for did he not feel the need to introduce the mysterious 'normal rate' to give an element of stability and continuity to the proceedings? And though in Robertson's eyes it was an unsatisfactory expedient in as much as its determination was left unexplained, the implication was clear enough. Keynes's 'normal' rate was the rate determined by the long-run, *real* influences of productivity and thrift.

INVESTMENT, SAVING AND THE RATE OF INTEREST: A REPLY TO ROBERTSON

The major error in Robertson's criticism is to suppose that because Keynes denied that the rate of interest is determined by productivity and thrift, the rate of interest must be invariant with respect to changes in investment and saving; whereas it is an important part of Keynes's theory that this is *not* the case. Once this is understood the whole apparatus supposedly used to make it so – the instantaneous multiplier, the finance motive and the liquidity trap – all become irrelevant and redundant *in this context*.

We must be clear that Keynes did not so much *deny the influence* of productivity and thrift on the rate of interest but, rather, he *rejected the relevance* of the classical concepts of productivity and thrift to the determination of the interest rate.

In place of 'productivity' he substituted the concept of the *marginal efficiency* of capital, which varied with the scarcity of capital, such that the marginal efficiency of capital would fall as the size of the capital stock increased. Also, it was not the case that the marginal efficiency of capital determined the rate of interest; rather that the rate of interest determined the marginal efficiency of capital.

Moreover, the rate of interest could act as a brake on investment, so that it was possible for the system to be in equilibrium, with the marginal efficiency of capital equal to a rate of interest that was too high for full employment and a stock of capital insufficient to satisfy the desires of wealth-holders.

In place of 'thrift' Keynes made the distinction between the propensity to save (consume) and the rate of saving, each of which had a different relationship to the rate of interest. As in our discussion of the 'three-fold margin', it must be the propensity to consume which is relevant here.

In rejecting productivity and thrift Keynes did not, however, deny the influence of changes in investment expenditure and in the propensity to save on the rate of interest. Rather, he denied the *specificity* of investment and saving as determinants and instead viewed them simply as influences on the level of activity and income and therefore on the aggregate demand for money.

The rate of interest is not, therefore, invariant with respect to changes in investment and saving; quite the reverse, in fact, for it is a rising rate of interest which will check expansion unless steps are taken to offset the effect of a rising demand for money, by increasing the quantity of money.[14] This did not in any way constitute a concession to the classical theory. It was a conclusion which followed essentially from Keynes's own approach.[15]

With regard to the effect of saving on the rate of interest, it should be clear from previous discussion that, for example, an increase in the propensity to save, by reducing the level of activity, will bring about a fall in the demand for money and hence in the rate of interest.[16]

It should also be clear that Robertson's confusion over the nature of saving and its relationship to liquidity preference would prevent him from seeing that in circumstances in which an increase in 'thriftiness' had reduced the rate of interest but was also associated with an increase in idle balances, it was because it had *reduced* liquidity preference (propensity to hoard unchanged but level of activity lower) rather than raised it.[17]

Finally, we can reiterate the point that because it is perfectly possible for an increase in the propensity to save to reduce the rate of interest, this does not imply that it will at the same time promote investment, for reasons already stated.

With regard, next, to the role of the 'normal', or more correctly the 'safe', rate concept in Keynes's interest theory, we must reject any attempt to depict it as a sort of splint to support a sickly invertebrate. It was, rather, an attempt to describe how dealers in the market actually behave.

Moreover, it raised a terrifying possibility in the minds of orthodox economists concerning the power of expectations to determine the rate of interest, as against more tangible, quantifiable and therefore more easily controlled determinants like money supply or, more likely, saving. It suggested, for example, that if the market does not *believe* that a certain rate of interest is sustainable then policy will not be able to make it so; and conversely that the market might set a rate which would not be optimal from the point of view of macroeconomic policy. These points will be considered further in succeeding chapters.

KEYNES DID NOT RECANT

In reply to the assertion that Keynes recanted his interest theory and returned more or less to the loanable-funds position, there are three points to be considered.

The first is that for the charge to be sustained one would expect to find evidence of growing doubt, uncertainty or compromise on Keynes's part in the post-1936 literature. In fact the opposite is the case, for in articles and correspondence subsequent to the *General Theory* Keynes's tone becomes more assured as he refines and elaborates his argument. For example, the finance motive is openly introduced to remedy an omission in the original treatment which came to light as a result of Ohlin's distinction between *ex ante* and *ex post* investment. It cannot be seen in any sense as a concession to the loanable-funds school, being completely consistent with Keynes's overall approach.

Second, Keynes accepted Hicks's 1937 equilibrium model not as a more complete version of his own system but as a useful means of representing certain central features of it. We shall deal with the model in its *IS–LM* form below.

Third, instead of giving theoretical ground to Robertson in the debate, there are signs of a growing impatience with Robertson's foot-dragging criticism. For example, when in March 1938 Robertson sent to Keynes as editor of the *Economic Journal* his note 'Mr Keynes on "Finance"', Keynes wrote to Austin Robinson, his assistant editor, to say that he found Robertson's comment 'completely worthless and, what is more, intolerably boring'.[18] The reply, from Joan Robinson, was in similar vein: 'D.H.R. seems to grow more and more perverse. I can't make any sense of this at all. He seems to be wandering vaguely about in a featureless wilderness.'[19]

While this is obviously the least substantial form of evidence it is yet strongly indicative and also consistent with other forms. It is palpably not the language of recantation.

IS–LM

Keynes's acceptance of the Hicks formulation cannot be taken as evidence of his return to the neo-classical fold, because Keynes continued to think in liquidity-preference terms.

He was fully aware that it was the *aggregate* demand for money, covering the effects of investment, consumption, saving, planned consumption, etc., taken in conjunction with the available money stock, that determined the rate of interest. This much was *implied* in his discussion of the motives for money-holding in the *General Theory* and was explicitly stated on several subsequent occasions:[20] pointing out to Robertson, for example, that the difference between them stemmed, perhaps, from Robertson's taking liquidity preference 'to relate solely to the demand for inactive balances'.[21]

Not only does Keynes's adherence to the liquidity-preference principle preserve him from any neo-classical taint but it also exonerates him on the indeterminacy charge, *in the sense that* he had failed to allow for the effects of changing income on the rate of interest. On the question of a formal proof of determinacy, however, the position is somewhat different. In developing Hicks's original *IS–LL* formulation, Hansen argued that Keynes's interest theory, like the classical and loanable-funds theories which preceded it, was indeterminate. However, Hansen tempered his criticism by pointing out that Keynes, unlike his predecessors, had all the elements in his theory to produce a determinate solution but that he never brought them together in a way which showed that he had anything more than an *LM* curve.[22]

Clearly, the relevance of the Hicks–Hansen formulation to Keynes's work depends very much on correct interpretation. It has become fashionable to deride the stable curves of the *IS–LM* model as misrepresenting Keynes's true message, but it does provide a useful summation of some central ideas.

For example, in his reply to Hicks, Keynes pointed out that the inducement to invest depends predominantly on expected income for the period of the investment and that this is reflected in the marginal efficiency of capital, so that 'as soon as the prospective yields have been determined, account has been implicitly taken of income, actual and expected'.[23]

Therefore, notwithstanding our remarks earlier concerning the instability of the marginal efficiency of capital, if we have regard to Keynes's method of 'taming the real world', a given state of long-period expectations will give the quantity of investment appropriate to each level of the rate of interest. There is thus a justification for the apparently stable *IS* curve, on the assumption that long-period expectations do not change.

Moreover, because the *IS* curve shows points of equilibrium, with saving equal to investment for each rate of interest and corresponding level of income, it usefully encapsulates the Keynesian notion of the rate of saving being entirely determined by the rate of investment. For if expectations change and the curve shifts we are again in equilibrium with saving equal to investment at a new level of income. The rate of saving thus plays no further part in the analysis and we concentrate on changes in income and employment.[24]

If, on the other hand, there is a change in the propensity to save (consume), the *IS* curve will again shift as income changes but there will be no change in the rate of saving, which will still be equal to investment.

Similar considerations apply to the *LM* curve, which shows various (equilibrium) levels of the rate of interest as determined by (i) a given stock of money and (ii) different levels of the demand for money corresponding to different income levels and states of expectations regarding the future course of the rate of interest. With long-period expectations given, the curve will be stable.

However, only when the *IS* curve is superimposed on the *LM* curve, so that the actual level of transactions demand for money is known, is a determinate solution for the rate of interest possible. And here the final position of equilibrium will depend upon the *slope* of the *LM* curve, for this will show by how much the rate of interest must change so as to reconcile the level of *aggregate* demand for money to the available supply.

For example, with a given state of long-period expectations, the *LM* curve will flatten out as the rate of interest falls relative to some notional 'safe' rate. The demand for money due to the speculative motive will therefore be highly elastic with respect to changes in the rate of interest, so that within this range an increased demand for transactions balances due to a rise in the level of income can be accommodated with little disturbance to the market rate.

Conversely, as the rate of interest rises relative to the safe rate, the demand for money becomes increasingly inelastic, so that an increased transactions demand can only be accommodated from the given stock at the expense of a significant change in the market rate.

Note here that a change in long-period expectations will shift the structure of relative interest rates up or down, so that there is notionally a different *LM* curve with liquidity-trap region for each state of long-period expectations.

Note also, therefore, that with respect to the productivity and thrift argument it is perfectly possible for the rate of interest to change due to a change in long-period expectations *independently* of any shift in the *IS* curve. This is the intangible but highly potent element in the process that can render 'real' changes useless. Keynes argued that free-market influences could so condition expectations that the rate of interest might for long periods be held at a level too high for full employment. This point will be developed below.

Note finally that a stable *LM* curve due to a fixed money stock is entirely appropriate because, as we shall argue below, it was Keynes's contention that the peculiarity of money lies in the fact that in the absence of intervention by the monetary authorities, the supply is highly inelastic with respect to market forces alone.

THE SIGNIFICANCE OF $LP = LF$

Does the formal equivalence of the liquidity-preference and loanable-funds theories imply that the theories are simply alternative approaches to the same truth, so that they can be employed indifferently depending upon the type of analysis required?

The formal equivalence is usually demonstrated within a Walrasian general equilibrium system. General equilibrium implies that if $n - 1$ markets are in equilibrium, the nth market must also be in equilibrium by definition. Now, it is assumed that by the liquidity-preference theory the rate of interest is determined in the money market and by the loanable-funds theory in the bond market. Consequently, with an economy consisting of three markets – for goods, bonds and money – equilibrium in the market for goods and money, or goods and bonds, will also imply equilibrium in the markets for bonds and money respectively.

Therefore, at this theoretical level there is nothing to distinguish the theories. However, the model does not inform us as to the nature of the variables involved and therefore says nothing about causality. In particular, if the supply of bonds is determined by investment and the demand for bonds by saving, the all-important question of the nature of saving and its relationship to investment is left out of account. And this is especially relevant, as Keynes was able to demonstrate that Ohlin's 'credit' or 'loan' approach to the theory of interest, which typified the line of approach of neo-classical economists, was essentially the same as the classical theory with the supply and demand for credit equivalent to saving and investment respectively.[25]

For a more particular case, we have seen that the supply of loanable funds consists of prior saving, plus dishoarding and credit expansion. Many years ago Hansen pointed out that in an article published subsequent to the *General Theory*, Keynes agreed that the funds available for current investment could be stated in these terms and in doing so recognised the formal accuracy of the Robertsonian definitions.[26]

However, we have argued that formal equivalence based on these grounds reduces the loanable-funds theory to an account of sources and channels devoid of operational significance.

A KEYNESIAN CONCLUSION ON LOANABLE FUNDS

The fundamental weakness of the loanable-funds theory lies in its treatment of saving, for to state that prior saving is a source of finance from a flow-of-funds point of view (that is, 'tagging' and tracing the progress of a particular unit of bank deposits) does not imply that the way to prepare for increased investment is to 'save more' at a prior date.

Nevertheless, because investment and saving are equal by definition it is possible to go on thinking that an increased propensity to save is equivalent to an increased demand for securities. It may also act as an excuse for *not* believing that this is *not* the case. In commenting on Robertson's criticism of Keynes's view of investment and saving, Joan Robinson wrote to Keynes:

> I believe he has now got as far as seeing that you say that an increase in [the] propensity to save does not, in general, raise the demand for securities. Of course he will never grant the point, because the fact that $S=I$ is a truism absolves him from believing that it is true.[27]

Consequently, on a Keynesian view, the loanable-funds theory is either wrong and dangerously misleading, or an entirely innocuous account of the channels through which money flows. Moreover, the implication is that there can be no 'reconciliation' between the two theories in a valid 'composite' approach when one of the constitutents is fundamentally in error.

11 A Monetary Theory of the Rate of Interest

INTRODUCTION

In approaching Keynes's own theory of the rate of interest, there are four points to be kept in mind. The first is that Keynes was driven to seek a new explanation of interest once he realised that classically based theories were involved in logical error and had to be replaced. The second is that in a monetary economy the rate of interest is a monetary phenomenon and derives from the uniqueness of money. The third is that because of its monetary nature the rate of interest exerts a powerful regulatory influence on the level of economic activity. The fourth is that while on a purely mechanical level the interest rate is proximately determined by the available stock of money and the aggregate demand for money, this is so only on the understanding that 'all influences other than the amount of money are portmanteaued in the liquidity function'.[1]

THE SEARCH FOR A NEW EXPLANATION

We begin with the point of departure from classically based theories. Keynes had established that the necessary equality between saving and investment is ensured by changes in the level of income rather than the rate of interest. But the effect was to deprive him of a theory of interest: 'if the rate of interest is not determined by saving and investment in the same way in which price is determined by supply and demand, how is it determined?'[2] For it was obvious, to put it another way, that given the causal relationship between investment and saving it was 'impossible to name a rate of interest at which the amount of saving and the amount of investment could be unequal. Whatever determines the one, determines the other at the same time.'[3]

Keynes's understanding of interest as being the meaning of liquidity preference came only subsequently – 'appreciably later' – by way of an intuitive flash;[4] and only after his discovery that the well-trodden paths led nowhere:

> One naturally began by supposing that the rate of interest must be determined in some sense by productivity – that it was, perhaps, simply the monetary equivalent of the marginal efficiency of capital, the latter being independently fixed by physical and technical considerations in conjunction with the expected demand. It was only when this line of approach led repeatedly to what seemed to be circular reasoning, that I hit on what I now think to be the true explanation.[5]

THE RATE OF INTEREST AND THE MARGINAL EFFICIENCY OF CAPITAL

The problem was that since saving is wholly determined by investment, we need to know what determines investment. Keynes rejected extant explanations based upon the productivity of capital, both because of the ambiguities they contained and for other reasons which we shall come to shortly.[6] Instead, he made use of a concept based upon Irving Fisher's 'rate of return over cost' and which he called the marginal efficiency of capital.[7] Though formally identical to Fisher's formulation, it was Keynes's contribution to provide a rigorous definition and to stress that the returns to capital investment encompassed the *entire* stream of prospective returns.

The returns were 'prospective' in that they could not be known but only estimated, so that central to Keynes's outlook was the unknowability of the future – the uncertainty present in a monetary economy (the real world) – and the importance, therefore, of expectations, of entrepreneurial confidence, as an influence on economic activity. For Keynes,

> The schedule of the marginal efficiency of capital is of fundamental importance because it is mainly through this factor (much more than through the rate of interest) that the expectation of the future influences the present. The mistake of regarding the marginal efficiency of capital primarily in terms of the current yield of capital equipment, which would be correct only in the static state where there is no changing future to influence the present, has had

the result of breaking the theoretical link between today and tomorrow.[8]

However, the important point for present purposes is that the m.e.c. cannot be the determinant of the rate of interest for the simple reason that knowledge of the current rate of interest is a necessary ingredient of the investment decision.[9] Either (a) we must use the market rate of interest to capitalise the series of prospective annual returns to obtain a present value or demand price of capital which can then be set against the supply price, or (b) we can work out the rate of discount (the m.e.c.) which makes the stream of prospective returns just equal to the supply price and compare it to the market rate of interest.

Consequently, if the Fisher–Keynes formulation is accepted, an attempt to derive the rate of interest from the marginal efficiency of capital must involve a circular argument and a logical error;[10] a conclusion which had, Keynes noted, been sensed by Alfred Marshall.[11]

It would demonstrate, moreover, the indeterminacy of the classical system. That is, while the two systems have it in common that in equilibrium the m.e.c. will be equal to the rate of interest – due to the equalisation of the advantages of holding assets and loans – the classically based economists give causal priority to the m.e.c. But this cannot be right, because the m.e.c. depends upon the price of capital assets (as compared with their costs of production), and it is movements in this which will determine the rate of new investment and therefore the level of income. Consequently, in equilibrium this price will be consistent with only one given level of income; at which level the m.e.c. will be equal to the rate of interest. Therefore, the m.e.c. is not determined unless the level of income is given.

There are two implications. The first is that it is the rate of interest which determines the m.e.c. rather than vice versa.[12] The second is that the classical theory cannot apply to economic systems in which the level of income is capable of fluctuation.[13]

THE RATE OF INTEREST

We have argued that in equilibrium the m.e.c. will be equal to the market rate of interest, and this for the simple reason of equalisation of advantage in the choice between holding assets and loans. We should also be clear that Keynes meant 'the' rate of interest to refer to 'the rate of interest on a loan of given quality and maturity';[14] and that he was well aware that this was done for the sake of simplicity, and that we are in reality 'dealing with complexes of rates of interest and discount corresponding to different lengths of time which will elapse before the various prospective returns from the asset are realised'.[15]

What has not so far been explained is, what the rate of interest is and why it plays the part it does. We have simply introduced a given rate of interest into the calculation of the m.e.c. and as a standard relative to the m.e.c. as part of the investment decision. The omissions can be made good under three headings: (i) a further consideration of the implications of 'thrift' or saving; (ii) the nature of capital; (iii) the rate of interest as a monetary phenomenon.

THE EFFECTS OF SAVING

We have already noticed the depressing effect of saving on economic activity. Not only does it reduce present consumption without at the same time implying any commitment to specific consumption at a specified future date; but also, because entrepreneurs' expectations of future consumption are strongly influenced by their observation of present consumption, a reduction in present consumption may reduce the prospective yield of planned investments and so reduce the demand for capital goods as well.[16]

Two new elements now enter. First, suppose it were possible to combine an act of abstention from present consumption with a specific order for consumption goods in the future. This would obviously help to sustain entrepreneurs' expectations, so that they would seek to switch resources unemployed through the diminution of present consumption, to production intended to satisfy future consumption. However, there may not be a complete offset to the reduction in present demand and present employment – because of the nature of the forward order.

If, for example, the specified future consumption demanded a process of production which involved the devising of new techniques and methods and the production and introduction of new types of capital equipment, the supply price relative to prospective yield might be such that the marginal efficiency might be *below* the current rate of interest. In other words, the means of preparation for the planned consumption might be so inconveniently 'roundabout' that it would be postponed in the hope of more favourable financial conditions in the future, so that the effect on current employment would still be adverse. We shall return to this important point below.

The second new element is to stress that the act of saving in fact involves no specific order for future consumption but, rather, results in the accumulation of wealth: 'a potentiality for consuming an unspecified article at an unspecified time'.[17] The rate at which wealth is accumulated will be governed by the rate of saving and hence by the rate of investment; whereas the distribution of wealth will depend upon the consumption–saving behaviour of individuals.

But does not the accumulation of wealth nevertheless maintain employment through the wealth-owner's desire to hold investments which will in turn act as stimulus to the production of capital goods? Two considerations are relevant. First, Keynes would argue that what the wealth-owner desires is not a capital asset as such but rather its prospective yield, so that to the extent that saving does not enhance prospective yield it will not stimulate investment.

The second consideration is that in order to increase one's wealth-holding it is not *necessary* to purchase a new capital asset, for the *individual's* stock of assets will grow ineluctably through the very act of saving. The accumulation will in the first instance consist of money received as income and not spent on consumption, but thereafter the wealth-holder is faced with the choice between purchasing real capital assets or debts (bonds), or simply holding money.

Nevertheless, *new* wealth can only be created by new investment and this will depend on the desire of wealth-holders to purchase new capital assets. In this they will be guided by an asset's prospective yield (given the rate of interest), which will in turn depend on a prediction of a future demand for a particular good at a specific date.[18]

Now we begin to see why wealth-holders do not satisfy an increased desire to hold wealth by purchasing new capital assets *in any case*, simply being content with whatever prospective yield their expectations throw up.

It will be recalled that Keynes justified wealth-holders' desire to hold money rather than bonds by reference to their expectations of future bond prices in the face of uncertainty. The resulting speculative demand for money taken in conjunction with that part of the money stock left over from the demands of the active circulation will determine the market rate of interest. It is this market rate of interest on debts which will compete with the marginal efficiency of new capital assets for the wealth-holder's attention, and so set a standard below which the marginal efficiency of capital assets cannot fall if they are to be newly produced.

Therefore, in order for wealth-holders to seek to purchase new capital assets and so stimulate investment and employment, the prospective yield on capital assets and hence their marginal efficiency will have to be in excess of the market rate of interest.

THE NATURE OF CAPITAL

Keynes's discussion of the nature of capital in chapter 16 of the *General Theory* is either glossed over or omitted in many accounts, yet it contains his justification for a rejection of the productivity theory of interest. Having in the previous section dwelt on the demand side, in stressing the importance of prospective yield, we must now look more closely at the process of production itself and the role of capital within it.

Much of the discussion in chapter 16 is unintelligible until placed against its proper background. That background is the Austrian theory of capital, and in particular the capital theory of E. von Böhm-Bawerk. Böhm-Bawerk's main conclusion was that the more 'indirect' or 'roundabout' the method of production employed, the greater would be the output produced. The characteristic feature of roundaboutness is the *time* spent on the production process; the more time spent in developing and improving the techniques and equipments employed the more *efficient* will the process be and the greater the output they will produce.

The reference Keynes gives to Marshall's *Principles* makes clear Böhm-Bawerk's great stress on this doctrine, arguing that: 'methods of production which take time are more productive'; and that 'every lengthening of a roundabout process is accompanied by a further increase in the technical result'.[19]

The relevance of this influential doctrine for present purposes is that the more roundabout the production process and hence the type of capital employed, the greater would be the demand for resources and hence the higher the rate of interest. The higher the productivity of capital, therefore, the higher the rate of interest would be.

Keynes disputed that the physical efficiency of a production process depended on its length: some lengthy processes were efficient as were some short processes. Lengthy processes might be very inefficient due to 'such things as spoiling or wasting with time'.[20] Moreover, if we regard labour as the sole factor of production, with capital as past labour embodied in assets,[21] then, with a given labour force, there must be some optimal relation between the proportion of workers employed in making machines and those employed in working them. In other words, it will not follow that as the roundaboutness of the process used increases, the value of output will continue to increase in proportion to the number of workers employed, even if its physical efficiency continues to increase.

In fact, Keynes would maintain that 'in the case of the great majority of articles it would involve great technical *in*efficiency to start up their input more than a very modest length of time ahead of their prospective consumption'.[22] Therefore, in the more general case, 'those long and roundabout methods, which involve much locking up of capital'[23] are to be avoided in favour of shorter and more efficient processes.

On this view, then, *lengthiness* is one among several special cases in which production takes place (labour is employed) in 'less agreeable attendant circumstances'.[24] Other examples are processes involving unpleasant ('smelly') and risky working conditions. But there is no productivity theory of smelly or risky processes as such, so why should there be a special one for roundaboutness?

Keynes rejects the productivity approach and instead argues that because of their 'less agreeable attendant circumstances', these processes will only be undertaken in anticipation of a higher reward. Therefore, these processes would have to be kept sufficiently *scarce* so as to command a higher price.

It is the concept of *scarcity* that Keynes puts in the place of productivity as the factor determining the return on capital. By keeping a capital asset sufficiently scarce, the capitalised value of its prospective yield can be kept sufficiently high in relation to supply price so as to produce a rate of reward high enough for the special-case processes to be undertaken.[25]

But Keynes's approach is completely general, for it can deal with the case in which, due to the strength of the desire to postpone consumption, lengthiness becomes an 'agreeable attendant circumstance' so that physically *inefficient* processes would be employed 'provided they were sufficiently lengthy for the gain from postponement to outweigh their inefficiency'. The corollary of this is, of course, that *short* processes would be less suitable so that they 'would have to be kept sufficiently scarce for their physical efficiency to outweigh the disadvantage of their early delivery of their product'.[26]

We mentioned earlier that the calculation of prospective yield would, in the absence of a firm order for future consumption of a specified kind, have to be based on entrepreneurs' expectations of these. Consequently, it is not the case that some ideal production process will set the date at which consumption should take place; but, rather, that expectations as to the date at which consumers' demand will become effective will determine the optimum roundaboutness of the process to be used.

It follows that the most efficient process consistent with the time-period available will be chosen. However, for every good in consumption there will be a time-interval for which the production process will be optimal. If the interval were shorter, the process would be less efficient physically; while if it were longer, storage costs and deterioration would reduce efficiency.[27]

But we have not yet taken into account the rate of interest. If the rate of interest is greater than zero it will introduce a new element of cost which will increase with the length of the production process. Thus, the optimum length of the process will be reduced and production will be postponed until the value of prospective returns has risen sufficiently to cover the higher costs to be borne. These higher costs will reflect both the interest charges incurred and the lower efficiency of the reduced period of production. Consequently, we see that:

> capital has to be kept scarce enough in the long period to have a marginal efficiency which is at least equal to the rate of interest for a period equal to the life of the capital, as determined by psychological and institutional conditions.[28]

It is, therefore, clear that the rate of interest, by regulating the rate of production of capital goods, will set a limit to the level of employment. Moreover, Keynes emphasises that it is the *rate of interest on money* which plays this key role, and we must now ask why this should be the case and what are the psychological and institutional factors which determine its level.

THE RATE OF INTEREST AS A MONETARY PHENOMENON

One of the most striking things about Keynes's approach to interest theory is his insistence that he starts from the *definition* of interest itself; that he takes what the rate of interest actually *is* and then explains why this should be the case and why it should be of significance in a developed economy.

We begin with a definition of interest, which 'is, in itself, nothing more than the inverse proportion between a sum of money and what can be obtained for parting with control over the money in exchange for a debt for a stated period of time'.[29] Keynes believed his definition to be the definition familiar from common usage and would be recognised as such; it is, we might say, what every schoolboy knows. Moreover it is a starting-point which exists independently of and predates the various *theories* of interest; and in taking as his own approach an explanation based on ordinary experience he is simply rationalising what *is*:

> To speak of the 'liquidity-preference theory' of the rate of interest is, indeed, to dignify it too much. It is like speaking of the 'professorship theory' of Ohlin or the 'civil servant theory' of Hawtrey. I am simply stating what it is, the significant theories on the subject being subsequent. And in stating what it is, I follow the books on arithmetic and accept the accuracy of what is taught in preparatory schools.[30]

The clue to Keynes's approach to an explanation of what is common usage is provided by the following:

> the rate of interest (as we call it for short) is, strictly speaking, a *monetary* phenomenon in the special sense that it is the *own rate* ... on money itself, i.e. that it equalises the advantages of holding actual cash and a deferred claim on cash.[31]

This leads on to the 'notion of interest as being the meaning of liquidity preference';[32] so that, 'it is precisely the liquidity premium on cash ruling in the market which determines the rate of interest at which finance is available'.[33]

Clearly it is money's special attribute, deriving from its peculiar role in a monetary economy and the demand for money (liquidity preference) to which it gives rise, that in turn determines the premium on money and therefore the rate at which loans can be obtained. Therefore the interest on money is:

> simply the premium obtainable on current cash over deferred cash, so that it measures the marginal preference (for the community as a whole) for holding cash in hand over cash for deferred delivery. No one would pay this premium unless the possession of cash served some purpose, i.e. had some efficiency. Thus we can conveniently say that interest on money measures the marginal efficiency of money measured in terms of itself as a unit.[34]

Keynes's explanation of the special position occupied by the rate of interest *on money* is given in chapter 17 of the *General Theory*, another chapter which is either ignored, glossed over or heavily criticised and condemned. His thesis is as follows.

THE MONEY RATE OF INTEREST AND ITS ECONOMIC SIGNIFICANCE

Given that the money rate of interest is simply the difference between a sum of money and the sum that can be obtained by parting with it for a specified period, say, one year, expressed in percentage terms, Keynes reasoned that there must be an analogue of the rate of interest on money which applies to every kind of durable commodity. For example, in the case of wheat:

> there is a definite quantity of ... wheat to be delivered a year hence which has the same exchange value today as 100 quarters of wheat for 'spot' delivery. If the former quantity is 105 quarters, we may say that the wheat-rate of interest is 5 per cent per annum; and if it is 95 quarters, that it is *minus* 5 per cent per annum.[35]

For every durable commodity, therefore, there will be a rate of interest in terms of itself – an *own rate* of interest; so that we could envisage there being, apart from the money rate of interest, a wheat rate of interest, or a house or steel-mill rate of interest, etc.

Each of these commodities is *exactly equivalent* to money in the sense that it can be used as a standard wherewith to measure the marginal efficiency of capital. For example, the marginal efficiency of a capital asset in terms of wheat can be obtained by finding the rate of discount which makes the asset's prospective yield, calculated as the present value of a series of wheat annuities, equal to its supply price in terms of wheat.

The same result will be obtained by using any commodity, since the relative magnitudes of the prospective yield and supply price will be the same whatever terms they are measured in.[36]

As a basis for making a *distinction* between money and other types of assets, the next step is to see how an own-rate of interest might be calculated for each asset, measured in terms of itself as standard. Keynes suggested three attributes which are possessed by all assets, though in different degrees. These are: (i) yield, q: obtained 'by assisting some process of production or supplying services to a consumer'; (ii) carrying cost, c: wastage suffered or cost incurred merely by holding an asset through time; (iii) liquidity premium, l: some assets are more easily disposed of (exchanged for other assets) than others, depending on the mode of exchange employed in the economy in question. Liquidity premium is the amount people are willing to pay to own assets which possess this quality, because of the sense of security or convenience it assures them.

The own-rate of interest on any commodity can now be stated as being equal to $q - c + l$. In other words, the total return to be expected from ownership of the asset in question over a period will be equal to its yield *minus* its carrying cost *plus* its liquidity premium. The values that will be fitted into the equation will clearly be different for different assets, but Keynes finds an important point of distinction which sets money apart from other assets: namely, that whereas the carrying costs in respect of money are negligible, it has a substantial liquidity premium, so that:

> it is an essential difference between money and all (or most) other assets that in the case of money its liquidity-premium much exceeds its carrying cost, whereas in the case of other assets their carrying cost much exceeds their liquidity-premium.[37]

However, in equilibrium the expected returns from holding different assets will be equalised, so that we must take into account expected changes in relative values over the relevant period. Take own-rates as follows, noting how own-rates reflect the relevant strengths of the various attributes for each asset:

Houses: $q-c+l = q_1$
Wheat: $q-c+l = -c_2$
Money: $q-c+l = l_3$

Because we shall need to compare the results, the appreciation or depreciation of the various assets over the period must be measured by a common standard. Any commodity could be used for this purpose but we shall use money, as a unit of account.

Let the expected percentage change in value of houses in terms of money be a_1; and of wheat in terms of money a_2. Wealth-holders may now choose between assets according to the rates of return they offer as measured in terms of money, as follows:

Houses: $a_1 + q_1$ = house-rate of money-interest
Wheat: $a_2 - c_2$ = wheat-rate of money-interest
Money: l_3 = money-rate of money-interest

By observing relative rates of interest, wealth-holders will purchase assets for which expected returns are highest.

Understand now that the own-rates we calculated earlier were, in fact, marginal efficiencies, being rates of return over cost. We have now rendered these marginal efficiencies into money terms, just as earlier we gave an example using wheat as the standard.

From our earlier discussion we recall that when for any asset the demand price exceeds supply price, the asset will be newly produced. In other words, for these assets marginal efficiency will exceed the rate of interest. As production continues the marginal efficiencies of the assets will fall, due both to a fall in prospective yield as the supply of the particular type of asset is increased, and because supply price will rise with increasing pressure on production facilities. When the marginal efficiency is equal to the rate of interest, production will cease, unless, of course, the rate of interest is able to fall in line with the marginal efficiency.

Returning to our example, therefore, if we now assume that the own-rate of interest on one of the assets, say, money, is either fixed or falls more slowly than own-rates on other assets as output increases, the implications are as follows.

Equalisation of advantage will ensure that in equilibrium, $a_1+q_1 = a_2-c_2 = l_3$. With all rates equal but with l_3 fixed or falling more slowly than q_1 or $-c_2$ are falling, it must be the case that a_1 and a_2 will be rising. What this means is that because the rates of interest we have calculated take account of expected changes in value, the fall in the present money price of houses and wheat *relative to their expected future price* will ensure that production of these assets will be postponed until prices are more favourable and production again becomes profitable. In other words, the inability of the marginal efficiency of money to fall in line with the marginal efficiency of houses and wheat will choke off production of these latter commodities.[38]

Production will only continue at the present time where future production costs are expected to rise relative to current production costs, to an extent which will cover the carrying costs of currently produced assets for the period up to the date of the expected higher prices.

Notice that though we have, rather suggestively, used the own-rate of interest on money to set the limit to the rate of output, we have not shown that this must necessarily be the case; and at this stage of the argument it would not help matters to substitute houses or wheat as the standard of value. It, is rather,

> that asset's rate of interest which declines most slowly as the stock of assets in general increases, which eventually knocks out the profitable production of each of the others, – except in the contingency...[mentioned above] of a special relationship between the present and prospective costs of production.[39]

Nevertheless, Keynes brought forward powerful arguments in support of his belief that money does indeed possess:

> special characteristics which lead to its own rate of interest in terms of itself as standard being more reluctant to fall as output increases than the own-rates of interest of any other assets in terms of themselves.[40]

The characteristics of money which *in combination* produce this result are given as follows.

THE MONEY RATE AND THE CHARACTERISTICS OF MONEY

(a) Inelasticity of supply

In comparison with most other assets which enter into our calculations, money is, both in the short and long run, very highly inelastic in supply with respect to its value. As the quantity of resources which a unit of money can command increases, there is no automatic mechanism inherent in a free-enterprise economy which can increase supply in line with demand and so reduce money's value in terms of other goods.

Recall that in the case of assets which are capable of being newly produced, a rise in their market price will stimulate production so that their stock will rise and their marginal efficiencies will fall. But, short of action by the monetary authority, or other special effects we shall introduce below, money's own rate cannot be reduced in this way. If on the other hand,

> money could be grown like a crop or manufactured like a motor-car, depressions would be avoided or mitigated because, if the price of other assets was tending to fall in terms of money, more labour would be diverted into the production of money.[41]

Notice that the conclusion holds good absolutely in the case of an inconvertible paper-money governed by laws of legal tender. It would seem to be contradicted, however, in the case of a traditional commodity-money like gold, as money's higher price would stimulate increased output in gold-producing countries. But short of an entirely fortuitous event like a major gold-strike, the effect must be limited. Indeed the textbooks tell us that one of gold's chief characteristics, which makes it suitable as a standard of value, is its inelasticity of supply.[42] But this quality is, of course, the source of the difficulty we are considering.

In modern terms, money is principally bank money, a secondary money created on the basis of holdings of cash, or primary money. However, given that bankers' reserves at the Bank of England, which are the equivalent of currency, can be controlled by the monetary authority, this should present little disturbance to the conclusion. It is interesting that Keynes does actually speak of a 'managed' currency.[43]

(b) Zero elasticity of substitution

However, money is not unique in being inelastic in supply in the face of a rise in demand. All 'pure-rent factors' have the same characteristic. Where money differs from them and from other assets is that 'it has an elasticity of substitution equal, or nearly equal, to zero'. What this means is that because money is demanded for its special characteristics as money, an intensified desire for the command of those characteristics which leads to a rise in the exchange value of money, cannot as a matter of definition lead to the substitution for money of other assets which do not possess those characteristics. The implication is that as the demand for money increases, there is no value at which people will begin to substitute other assets such that demand is diverted elsewhere; with the consequence that money becomes 'a bottomless sink for purchasing power'.[44]

Where a commodity-money is dominant, it is possible, as we noted in Chapter 1, that a change in the relative monetary and commodity values will lead to an increased minting of coin, but this is not a consideration in modern circumstances.

(c) Stability of the effective quantity of money

The third characteristic of money is that not only is there no market mechanism for increasing its nominal supply when its exchange value increases, but also there is no satisfactory method whereby its real, or effective, supply can be increased to meet the same circumstance, so as to produce a sufficient decline in the money rate of interest.

The effective quantity of money can be increased through a reduction in the money wage. In order to speak generally, the reduction is measured in terms of the *wage-unit*, which is the money wage of a standard labour unit. The reduction has its effect in two ways. Not only is the level of money income reduced so that the fall in transactions-demand increases the quantity of money available to satisfy the speculative motive, but also, as the level of money income falls the real value of the money stock will be increased.

The first problem, however, arises from uncertainty as to the expectations that will be aroused by a fall in the wage unit. If, on the one hand, the fall is such as to engender expectations that it will rise in the future, the effect will be beneficial, in as much as expectations of more-favourable economic conditions will raise the prospective yields of assets other than money, so that their marginal efficiencies will rise relative to that of money. This, of course, produces the same result as a fall in the money rate of interest, so that the initial effect is reinforced. If, on the other hand, a fall in the wage unit leads to expectations of further falls, the depressing effect on the marginal efficiency of capital may offset the fall in the money rate of interest.

The second problem is that the money wage may be reluctant to fall in the first place, due to the 'stickiness' of wage rates in terms of money. The stability of the money wage as compared with the real-wage rate plays a central part in Keynes's employment theory (see below, Chapters 12, 22), and derives from the fact that wages are fixed in terms of money rather than some other commodity.

(d) The yield from liquidity

Finally, and most fundamentally, money's peculiar ability to satisfy the desire for liquidity preference means that even a substantial increase in the effective quantity of money may not produce a corresponding decline in the money rate of interest:

> beyond a certain point money's yield from liquidity does not fall in response to an increase in its quantity *to anything approaching the extent* to which the yield from other types of assets falls when their quantity is comparably increased.[45]

This, we may say again, is the key point: money's own-rate falls *more slowly* than own-rates on other commodities.

A principal reason why money is able to satisfy so completely the urge towards liquidity is that, as against virtually all other assets, money's liquidity premium is greatly in excess of its carrying costs. This means that there will be no significant offset to the subjectively perceived advantages of holding wealth in money form. Consequently, subject to the qualification introduced below (Chapter 12), money will continue to be held because its 'spendability' does not deteriorate with time. It was for this reason that unorthodox economists had suggested introducing artificial carrying costs as a way of discouraging money-holding.[46]

12 The Conditions for Money as the Standard

We can now bring the argument of the previous chapter together and develop some of its aspects further.

THE SIGNIFICANCE OF THE MONEY RATE OF INTEREST

As output increases the forces which operate to reduce the own-rates of interest of assets in production will be inoperative or weak in the case of one or more assets. The asset whose own-rate declines *most* slowly will thus become the greatest of the own-rates and set a limit to the growth of output and employment.[1] The greatest of the own-rates will be the money rate of interest; its significance deriving from the peculiarity of money.

The peculiarity of money depends on its having a high liquidity premium *relative* to its carrying-cost. That is, both liquidity and carrying-costs on most commodities – apart from gold, silver and bank notes – are at least as high as the liquidity premium on money; so that even if a wheat standard were to inherit money's liquidity premium its own-rate would be unlikely to rise above zero. It is central to Keynes's argument that the money rate of interest will remain significantly above zero.[2]
Keynes's argument that the money rate of interest will remain significantly above zero.[2]

LIQUIDITY

Liquidity, then, is not to be measured by an absolute standard. Notions of what makes assets liquid will vary with time, place and the organisation of society. Nevertheless, wealth-owners will have a subjectively determined order of preferences – a scale of liquidity – which will find expression in the varying liquidity premiums that they attach to assets.[3]

Keynes notes that in the estimation of the public, money is '*par excellence*' liquid. This is, of course, as it should be, in an orderly society in which methods of payment and settling debts are well established and understood and which develop naturally over time. Nevertheless, we can distinguish certain qualities which in the minds of wealth-owners will be associated with the liquidity of assets in general and money in particular.

A liquid asset is one for which the supply is highly inelastic rather than easily increased by private initiative, and we have mentioned crops and cars as being unsuitable in this respect. The corollary of this is that money itself will cease to be regarded as liquid 'if its future supply is expected to undergo sharp changes'.[4] If, for example, money wages were to be highly flexible in terms of money, the effective supply of money would by the same token be subject to violent change.

In addition, the implications of this conclusion for government-directed economic policy measures must not go unremarked. Undue reliance by the authorities on an active monetary policy as a principal means of short-term economic control could undermine faith in the ability of money to perform its main function, of satisfying liquidity preference on both active and inactive account. Therefore, *on the basis of his theoretical analysis* Keynes would be opposed to a policy which could only serve to increase rather than decrease uncertainty in this way.

Another test of liquidity is whether an asset has a high or low elasticity of substitution. Assets for which the demand can be easily satisfied by a change in relative prices, so that demand is diverted to other assets, will not be considered highly liquid.

For assets with close substitutes there is the problem of identity: of setting some limit so as to obtain an identifiable quantity which can be labelled 'money'. This is a question familiar to present-day monetary economists and has been the subject of considerable debate.[5] If no unequivocal definition of money can be established, the quality of 'scarcity' is lost so that a query will arise as to 'money's' elasticity of supply. For money to attract to itself the very high liquidity premium ascribed by Keynes it must be such that no other asset can step into its shoes to satisfy liquidity preferences. Given that its liquidity premium must be *relatively* very high, it is possible to justify, both on theoretical and empirical grounds, a definition of money which is 'co-extensive with bank deposits', as suggested by Keynes.[6]

THE STABILITY OF MONEY WAGES

The 'qualification' referred to in the previous chapter (p. 152) is really a condition of money's liquidity which has not so far been fully brought out.

We have already taken note of Keynes's assertion that wages tend to be sticky in terms of money. We have also argued that if this were not the case, the (effective) quantity of money could be subject to violent fluctuation, with adverse consequences for the perceived liquidity of money. It follows as one of Keynes's most important conclusions that for money to retain its pre-eminent position on the scale of liquidity *the stability of the money wage must be maintained.*

At the same time Keynes saw this very stickiness of wages as stemming from their being fixed in terms of money, for:

> the expectation of a relative stickiness of wages in terms of money is a corollary of the excess of liquidity-premium over carrying costs being greater for money than for any other asset.[7]

It is clear, therefore, that each quality exists as a condition of the other and to breach one or other of the conditions would destroy both qualities.

This is a most important point. It means, for example, that in conditions of 'over-full' employment (such as obtained during the quarter-century after 1945), the upward tendency of the money wage could lead to changes in the price level, which would, in turn, produce expectations of future movements in the value of money which would feed back into changes in money wages. Carried to excess it could undermine confidence in the efficacy of the monetary mode of exchange itself; an outcome the significance of which will become apparent later (Chapter 21).

Consequently, it is those characteristics which make money liquid which will raise the expectation that wages fixed in terms of money will be relatively stable. If, therefore, wages are sticky in terms of money the normal expectation will be 'that the value of output will be more stable in terms of money than in terms of any other commodity'.[8] It follows that this expectation would *not* be held with confidence if wages were fixed in terms of a commodity standard with a high elasticity of production, like wheat.

In turn, it is the expectation of relative stability in money wages and the value of output that so greatly enhances the liquidity premium on money:[9] a conclusion, we should note, that says much about the level of capacity at which the economy can safely be run in the absence of external restraint on the price level; and about the notion of 'full employment' in the context of Keynesian economics.

THE IMPLICATIONS OF REAL-WAGE STABILITY

This conclusion also begs the question of what would happen if a policy were pursued of stabilising real wages rather than money wages? It would mean that an attempt would be made to maintain the purchasing power of wages, so that incomes would be calculated in terms of the goods and services that workers typically consume. By fixing wages in terms of these 'wage-goods', by reference to price indices, the real wage would be stabilised but the money wage would be subject to frequent adjustment, as would firms' money costs and, therefore, prices.

The effect would be exacerbated by changes in the proportions in which workers divide their income between consumption and saving (the propensity to consume) and by changes in entrepreneurs' propensity to invest. Both of these would directly increase demands on resources (complicated by 'bottlenecks' in production) and the resulting price signals would feed back into the real-wage calculation and therefore money wages and prices.

It will be recalled that the 'stickiness' of wages fixed in money terms depended on the qualities that made money liquid. If, therefore, wages are fixed in terms of wage-goods, which have a high elasticity of supply and which have many close substitutes, we are choosing commodities as the standard which have a relatively low liquidity premium. In addition, wage-goods typically have high carrying-costs,[10] so that whatever yield from liquidity could be obtained from holding wealth in this form would be offset by costs of storage, wastage and so on. Wages fixed in terms of such a standard are most unlikely to be sticky and there would be no 'expectation of relative stability in the future money cost of output'.

Such a policy is, therefore, likely to produce violent fluctuations of money prices. These in turn would give rise to uncertainty as to the exchange value of money and therefore the role of money and the stability of the monetary order itself.

In any case, a policy based on the presumption that the real wage should be more stable than the money wage is appropriate only to an economy characterised by stability of employment. That is, only in a (classical) fully adjusted, full-employment economy, in which the money wage is a residual product of the real wage and the price level determined in accordance with the quantity theory, would it be correct to pursue policies designed to facilitate maintenance of the status quo. And even this would only be a policy of ensuring the maintenance of the real wage appropriate to full employment. If the real wage was *not to change*, so that employment would be assumed not to need to change, the assumptions relating to such a hypothetical economy would be even more restrictive.

In an economy of the type envisaged by Keynes, on the other hand, in which the level of employment is subject to wide variation, Keynes's view – at least in the *General Theory* – was that a move towards full employment could only occur if the real wage was more variable than the money wage.[11] This then left the way open for a policy of stabilising the money wage which, because it promoted the stability of money prices and enhanced the liquidity of money and its role as the standard, became 'a condition of the system possessing inherent stability'.[12]

REDUCING THE OWN-RATE ON MONEY

We can now see clearly why a policy aimed at reducing the own-rate on money by increasing the effective quantity of money would have such deleterious effects. Not only might the flexibility of money wages have adverse effects on the prospective yield of investments, but the concomitant changes in the value of money could undermine the stability of the monetary economy itself. It is also clear, therefore, why any policy aimed at reducing the own-rate of interest on money should concentrate *not* on the erosion of liquidity premium but on the raising of carrying-costs.

13 The Market Rate of Interest and its Economic Significance

INTRODUCTION

An important conclusion follows from Keynes's view of interest as a monetary phenomenon. That is, because the carrying-costs on money are negligible, the (nominal) rate of interest cannot in practice be negative.[1] Or, as Hicks expressed it: 'If the costs of holding money can be neglected, it will always be profitable to hold money rather than lend it out, if the rate of interest is not greater than zero.'[2] In addition, however, 'institutional and psychological factors are present which set a limit much above zero to the practicable decline in the rate of interest'.[3]

THE 'PURE RATE' OF INTEREST

We have already met the 'psychological factors' – as the determinants of individual wealth-owners' liquidity preference. The measure of liquidity preference is the liquidity premium on money; or the money rate of interest.

But this statement is, strictly, only true because money's own-rate is, uniquely, composed almost entirely of liquidity premium; there being zero yield and negligible carrying-costs to take into account. In turn, we have seen that the high liquidity premium obtaining on money stems from the expectation of a reasonable stability of money wages and prices; while this stability is itself a function of money having low elasticities of production and substitution.

It is, of course, these characteristics of money which help to ensure the *maintenance* of a high liquidity premium on money and, therefore, a high money rate of interest, in the face of a rise in the exchange value of money. There is, uniquely in the case of money, no increase in the stock of money in response to market forces alone to force the marginal efficiency of money down towards zero. Nevertheless, our previous analysis of the psychology of liquidity preference indicates that it is always open to the monetary authority to increase the available money stock by way of open-market operations. But even here the very characteristics that enable money to satisfy liquidity preference on inactive account will set a limit to the efficacy of monetary policy in reducing the rate of interest.

The money rate of interest is, given the level of income and transactions and a fixed money stock, explained by expectations as to the future of the rate of interest. As the market rate of interest falls, it falls *relative to* the 'safe' rate, so that the risk of illiquidity resulting from a subsequent *rise* is increased. In addition, however, the *absolute* fall progressively reduces the 'current earnings from illiquidity, which are available as a sort of insurance premium to offset the risk of loss on capital account, by an amount equal to the difference between the *squares* of the old rate of interest and the new'.[4]

The implications of this can be graphically illustrated by showing that, whereas at 4 per cent it is worth holding a long-term bond unless the rate is expected to rise by more than 4 per cent of 4 per cent (that is, by more than 0.16 per cent per annum), at 2 per cent the rise will have to be only 0.04 per cent per annum to offset the running yield on the debt. As the risk of loss is progressive as the market rate falls, there will be an increasing tendency to prefer money to bonds so that open-market operations will produce ever-smaller decreases in the rate of interest for given changes in the quantity of money; purchases of debt by the authorities will take place at a virtually unchanging price.

In the limit, 'liquidity preference may become virtually absolute in the sense that almost everyone prefers cash to holding a debt'.[5] This limiting case is the famous 'liquidity trap' which Keynes regarded as a logical possibility – a possibility nevertheless – rather than a frequent occurrence. For the moment it will be best to think of this case as one of increasing resistance to further change as the rate of interest falls to *an absolutely low level*, for, conceptually, there will be a separate liquidity trap for each given state of long-period expectations.

MONETARY POLICY AND THE PURE RATE

It is evident in what sense the money rate of interest – the liquidity premium ruling on money in the market – is governed by psychological factors, in that nothing more 'tangible' than expectations as to its future level can set a limit to the speed of its decline. This conclusion has important implications for the conduct of monetary policy, in that:

> at a level *above* the rate which corresponds to full employment, the long-term market rate of interest will depend, not only on the current policy of the monetary authority, but also on market expectations concerning its future policy. The short-term rate of interest is easily controlled by the monetary authority, both because it is not difficult to produce a conviction that its policy will not greatly change in the very near future, and also because the possible loss is small compared with the running yield (unless it is approaching vanishing point). But the long-term rate may be more recalcitrant when once it has fallen to a level which on the basis of past experience and present expectations of *future* monetary policy, is considered 'unsafe' by representative opinion.[6]

Perhaps the best-known example of an official interest-rate policy which failed because the market had no faith that it could succeed, was Chancellor Hugh Dalton's drive for ultra-cheap, long-term money between 1945 and 1947. Whatever other factors contributed to the frustration of Dalton's policy, there was a widespread conviction that cheap money, as exemplified by the issue of 2½ per cent Treasury Stock 1975 or after – the 'Daltons' – could not be sustained.[7]

Here was a monetary policy which failed because it struck market opinion as being 'experimental in character', whereas the rate of interest is, perhaps, more:

> a highly conventional, rather than a highly psychological phenomenon. For its actual value is largely governed by the prevailing view as to what its value is expected to be. Any level of interest which is accepted with sufficient conviction as *likely* to be durable *will* be durable.[8]

There will, of course, be fluctuations of the actual market rate about the expected normal level as circumstances change; and, in particular for present purposes, a change in the level of activity that causes the quantity of money required to satisfy transactions-demand to grow faster than the money stock, will force a rise in the market rate. But the real problem lies with the expected normal rate, which may be by convention at a level 'chronically too high for full employment'.

That interest is a highly conventional phenomenon is both a weakness and a strength. On the one hand, the problem becomes intractable if the role of convention is overlooked and the ruling rate of interest is believed to be the product of more tangible 'free-market' forces. This, of course, was the point of Keynes's attack on the classical and classically based theories of interest, and in this he was anticipated by Gesell, who cited:

> the comparative stability of the rate of interest throughout the ages as evidence that it cannot depend on purely physical characters, in as much as the variation of the [m.e.c.] ... from one epoch to another must have been incalculably greater than the observed changes in the rate of interest.

What this means in terms of Keynes's thesis is that:

> the rate of interest, which depends on constant psychological characters, has remained stable, whilst the widely fluctuating characters, which primarily determine the schedule of the marginal efficiency of capital, have determined not the rate of interest but the rate at which the (more or less) given rate of interest allows the stock of real capital to grow.[9]

If, on the other hand, the malady is correctly diagnosed, attention can be directed to modifying the conventional view, which by its very nature should be amenable to a degree of 'persistence and consistency of purpose by the monetary authority'. Here the touchstone of success will clearly be the pursuit of policies which appear to the market to be reasonable, appropriate and sustainable.

THE EFFECTIVE RATE OF INTEREST

We have so far been dealing with the determination of the rate of interest as the determination of the liquidity premium on money, or, as we might now term it, the 'pure rate' of interest. But to find the 'effective rate' of interest – the rate which will actually appear in the market to set a limit to the expansion of output and employment – we must introduce further considerations, which arise from the estimation of expected return from an investment project and from the process of financing investment. We begin with the elements entering into the entrepreneur's investment decision.

Given supply price, the higher is the rate of interest the higher will prospective yield have to be to produce a rate of discount at least equal to the market rate of interest. Other considerations apart, the appropriate rate of discount will have to be at least equal to the pure rate of interest.

However, other considerations do enter. The first is 'entrepreneur's risk'. That is, in planning investment in conditions of uncertainty, the state of long-term expectations upon which the investment decision is based will depend not only on the entrepreneur's most probable forecast of future conditions but also on the *confidence* with which he makes the forecast.[10]

Entrepreneur's risk, therefore, reflects the doubts in the entrepreneur's mind 'as to the probability of his actually earning the prospective yield for which he hopes'.[11] Keynes identifies this as a 'real social cost', for the 'riskier' the entrepreneur perceives his venture to be the wider the margin he will require between the yield he expects and the rate of interest obtaining on debts in the market. It is the margin of safety required for the entrepreneur to commit his funds to the purchase of capital assets rather than to the purchase of existing securities in the market. It has the effect of setting a limit above the pure rate of interest below which prospective yield must not fall if the investment is to take place.

We have so far tacitly assumed that the entrepreneur will be employing his own funds, but where external finance is required there will have to be an allowance for the costs (transactions costs) of bringing borrower and lender together.[12]

In addition, we must take account of the risks incurred by the lender in making the loan. These arise from the possibility both of voluntary default (moral hazard), and involuntary default due to the failure of the project to produce the expected return and to the failure of the entrepreneur to make sufficient allowance for risk.

Note that this addition to the cost of investment only arises because of the use of external finance. If funds were provided internally, lender's risk would clearly not exist. It must presumably be regarded as a necessary part of a developed financial system, which is characterised by not only external finance but also *indirect* external finance, with the use of intermediaries, so that costs enter at several stages.

The significant aspect of lender's risk that Keynes emphasises is that it 'involves in part a duplication of a proportion of the entrepreneur's risk which is added *twice* to the pure rate of interest to give the minimum prospective yield which will induce the investment'.[13] This is because the immediate lender (who may or may not be the ultimate lender) will make an allowance for the riskiness of the venture, in the same way as the entrepreneur, which will be reflected in the margin between the pure rate and the rate which he actually charges.

Of course, the entrepreneur does not make his allowance for risk on the basis of the pure rate but, rather, on the basis of the rate he is actually quoted in the market (the effective rate), which will already include the lender's allowances for moral hazard and the riskiness of the prospective investment; hence the duplication. All-in-all, a limit is set significantly above the pure rate of interest below which prospective yield must not decline if investment is to proceed.

Note that while this duplication of allowance for risk is important in a time of low investment and high unemployment, it can be seen as of equal importance in the euphoric atmosphere of a boom, when the allowances for risk made by both borrower and lender may be 'unusually and imprudently low'.

Once we take into account allowances for risk and the psychological factors which determine them, it becomes clear that even where efforts to reduce the pure rate have some success, the effective rate may not decline at the same speed and may become irreducible within a conventional framework of monetary and financial arrangements below a certain minimum figure. If, for example, the lender's allowance for moral risk adds appreciably to the cost of borrowing, there is little the prospective borrower can do to disabuse the lender of his beliefs and so bring down the effective rate.

THE ECONOMIC CONSEQUENCES OF A 'STICKY' MARKET RATE

In order to understand the implications for a society of a rate of interest which reaches its lower limit much above zero, we must first consider what would happen if the rate were free to fall towards zero in step with the marginal efficiency of capital.[14]

Assume that the society reaches full employment with a stock of capital so abundant that its marginal efficiency falls to zero. All then depends on whether the society's desire to accumulate wealth – to make provision for the future – is satisfied by the amount of wealth represented by the existing capital stock, given that there is full employment and that the zero rate of interest yields a nil return to wealth-holding. If so, an equilibrium would be reached.

If, however, the desire to accumulate wealth is not satisfied, so that the propensity to save is still positive, the outlook for society is bleak. The capital stock cannot be further increased because if investment were to continue the marginal efficiency of capital would fall below zero; and we have already argued that the (nominal) rate of interest cannot be negative. Therefore, with no further net investment, equilibrium will demand a zero rate of saving, so that the level of income must fall until aggregate saving becomes zero.

The actual mechanism of adjustment will be via a reduction of the capital stock and employment by entrepreneurs, who, if they continued to provide a level of employment appropriate to the existing capital stock, would make losses, as the desire to save reduced the level of expenditure and income.

Around the long-run equilibrium, designated by a zero marginal efficiency of capital and a zero rate of saving, economic activity would follow a short-run cyclical pattern, with revived expectations leading to a boom and an increased capital stock (and lower marginal efficiency of capital); followed by a slump with a reduced capital stock (and higher marginal efficiency of capital).

Consequently, a long-run state of underemployment equilibrium is the fate of any society in which the marginal efficiency of capital reaches the lower limit of its decline before the desire to accumulate wealth is satisfied. If, therefore, the rate of interest becomes 'sticky' at a level appreciably above zero, the marginal efficiency of capital will cease to fall at a point corresponding to a smaller capital stock, so that the likelihood of the desire to save having become satisfied is diminished.

Therefore, Keynes saw the dire consequences outlined above as being more than a logical and distant possibility:

> The post-war [after 1918] experiences of Great Britain and the United States are, indeed, actual examples of how an accumula-

> tion of wealth, so large that its marginal efficiency has fallen more rapidly than the rate of interest can fall in the face of the prevailing institutional and psychological factors, can interfere, in conditions mainly of *laissez faire*, with a reasonable level of employment and with a standard of life which the technical conditions of production are capable of furnishing.[15]

Given, therefore, the circumstances surrounding the rate of interest, we are dealing with the consequences of an unsatisfied desire for wealth on the part of the *rich*. A society that is poorer, in the sense of possessing similar technical expertise but a smaller stock of capital, will be better placed to experience prosperity, since the exploitation of investment opportunities will provide continuing expansion of output and employment. Ineluctably, however, the day will arrive when the 'abundance of capital will interfere with the abundance of output' and that society, too, will 'suffer the fate of Midas'.[16]

KEYNES'S VISION: A PREVIEW

What, then, is to be done with economies whose free-market fate is to cycle dismally about a long-run underemployment equilibrium? One pointer lies in Keynes's conclusion that the unsatisfied desire to accumulate wealth, resulting in the expenditure of savings on assets 'which will in fact yield no economic fruits whatever, will increase economic well-being'. That is, in the prevailing circumstances, such apparently (economically) useless projects as the building of mansions by the rich, or for that matter the construction of pyramids or cathedrals, will not only increase employment but also the 'real national dividend of useful goods and services'.[17]

But can it be thought satisfactory to base the economic salvation of society on piecemeal and wasteful expedients when the very same principles of effective demand might be harnessed for schemes of social betterment?

Keynes's conclusion was that, left to itself, the unregulated economy would not except briefly and exceptionally be capable of rising out of its chronically underemployed state. His radical and thoroughgoing solution of the problem envisaged an unprecedented extension of state involvement in the organisation of economic activity. By this means he meant to create a long-run, full-employment economy which, by being purged of the more objectionable features of capitalism, would by the same token be a safeguard for the future of individual liberty.

Predictably, a solution which involved the simultaneous strengthening of the role of the state and of personal freedom, contained a seeming paradox which was to excite the fears of Keynes's libertarian critics, as we shall see.

It appeared indeed a radical solution – though not, perhaps, egregiously so when set beside the prospects for the unregulated alternative. It contained, moreover, a message of hope where other economists, and notably Robertson, saw full employment as an 'impracticable ideal' and envisaged only a stabilising of employment at a level a little higher than that experienced in the 1930s.

In the next chapter we shall account for the characteristic features of a modern 'old–rich' economy as Keynes saw them; elaborate on the relative roles of the marginal efficiency of capital and the rate of interest; and, finally, examine the theoretical basis of Keynes's proposed solution and his preferred strategy for achieving it.

14 The Keynesian Economic Problem and its Solution

INTRODUCTION

Keynes regarded the post-1918 experiences of Great Britain and the USA as actual examples of his thesis that technically advanced, capital-rich economies could suffer depression and privation where they might reasonably expect full employment and prosperity. The factors common to both, which for Keynes explained the apparent anomaly, were that the level of economic activity was dependent almost entirely on the free play of market forces, and that the rate of interest and the marginal efficiency of capital had come into a special relationship with each other such that, in the absence of any purposive management of investment and consumption behaviour, full employment could not be achieved.

THE STABILITY OF THE MONETARY PRODUCTION ECONOMY

As to the actual course of events in a modern, monetary-production economy, Keynes's conclusion from theory would be that because the determinants of investment depended on judgements about the future which in the nature of things could not be based on any 'adequate and secure foundation', the volume of investment could be expected to 'fluctuate widely from time to time'. And, indeed, actual, real-world economies did experience 'severe fluctuations of output and employment'. However, it was also clear from the facts of experience that the modern economic system was not violently unstable:

> Indeed it seems capable of remaining in a chronic condition of sub-normal activity for a considerable period without any marked tendency either towards recovery or towards complete collapse.[1]

Economic activity followed, rather, a cyclical pattern, with upward or downward movements fading and becoming reversed before they could proceed to extremes, so that 'an intermediate situation which is neither desperate nor satisfactory is our normal lot'.[2]

These characteristics could not follow of logical necessity but must be due to the actual circumstances and behavioural propensities of the modern condition. In particular, Keynes ascribed the stability of the economic system to several factors including, the limited response of investment to changes in the prospective yield of capital or of the rate of interest; and to a positive but relatively modest (and certainly finite) value for the multiplier. In addition, the stability of the money wage in the face of moderate changes in employment ensured the stability of the price level.[3]

As well as the conditions for the *stability* of the economy, Keynes offers an explanation, deriving from his basic theory, of why it follows a pattern of alternate recession and recovery.

EXPLAINING THE TRADE CYCLE: THE RATE OF INTEREST AND THE M.E.C.

The actual course of the trade cycle is a very complex phenomenon, but it is possible by concentrating on essential characteristics to come to conclusions concerning the relative roles of the marginal efficiency of capital and the rate of interest that will be applicable in a wider context. We shall get the relationship right if we bear in mind that (a) the rate of interest might 'fluctuate for decades about a level which is chronically too high for full employment',[4] and (b) full employment is difficult to achieve because of 'the association of a conventional and fairly stable long-term rate of interest with a fickle and highly unstable marginal efficiency of capital'.[5]

Two aspects of the trade cycle are of particular interest here: the *cyclical* nature of fluctuations, and the phenomenon of the *crisis*. Both are to be explained primarily by reference to changes in the marginal efficiency of capital.

THE REGULARITY OF FLUCTUATIONS

The regularity of the boom–slump sequence derives from the fact that 'capital assets are of various ages, wear out with time and are not all very long lived'.[6] Thus, a fall in the rate of investment below some minimum level will in time be followed by a reduction in the size of the capital stock and a rise in the marginal efficiency of capital sufficient to stimulate recovery with a rise in investment above the minimum.

Similarly, the period of time which must elapse before recovery begins is determined by the speed of recovery of the marginal efficiency of capital. This, in turn, is governed by two stable time-factors which thus operate to produce a cycle of predictable length. First, the time it takes for capital to become sufficiently scarce to produce a rise in the marginal efficiency of capital 'may be a somewhat stable function of the average durability of capital in a given epoch'.[7] And second, the burden of carrying-costs on accumulated stocks of unfinished goods will ensure that these stocks are absorbed as quickly as possible. Thus the depressing influence of the disinvestment which the absorption of stocks represents will be removed within a certain period which Keynes estimated at between three and five years. Once recovery gets under way it will become self-generating and so cumulate into the boom, which will in due course be brought to a halt by the 'crisis'.

THE CRISIS: COLLAPSE OF THE M.E.C.

The crisis is an important element in the cycle, in as much as it brings about the substitution of a downward for an upward tendency in a manner that is both sudden and violent and from which, after an interval, recovery only gradually gathers.[8] It is relevant here because it is to be explained by a sudden collapse in the marginal efficiency of capital which is, in turn, a product of the way in which capital assets are valued on an organised stock market.

In the later stages of the boom, a characteristic mood of optimism will sustain expectations of prospective yield at a level that will outweigh the depressing effects of a growing capital stock on marginal efficiency. But due to the precariousness of the basis of expectations and to the existence of an organised capital market highly sensitive to shifts of opinion, the sudden onset of doubt concerning prospective yield – perhaps caused by a perceptible reduction of current yield – can lead to a massive revaluation of capital assets and a collapse in the marginal efficiency of capital.[9]

THE MARKET VALUATION OF CAPITAL ASSETS

For it was Keynes's view that the market valuation of capital assets is governed by short-run considerations unrelated to the actual worth of investment projects. This was essentially a modern phenomenon, a product of the state of evolution of business organisation. In times when the ownership and management of business undertakings lay in the same hands, an investor would be committed to his project throughout its life and would value it accordingly.

But when, as a means of widening the basis of financing enterprise, ownership became separated from control, it also became necessary to reconcile the possibly divergent interests of passive and active investors. This was accomplished by the establishment of a secondary, resale, market for equities and debts, which gave the passive investor the opportunity periodically to review his commitments as between one firm and another and as between illiquidity and liquidity.

The effect, however, was to produce a situation in which capital assets were subject to frequent revaluation, and to create a class of purchasers ignorant of and indifferent to the ultimate outcome of investments. Stock-holders would make their redispositions on the basis of their expectations of short-run changes in market valuation; these expectations taking the form of a simple rule of thumb that, over the near future, present trends would continue unless there were definite indications to the contrary.

The 'conventional' valuation, having no basis in actual knowledge of investment projects, was thus extremely precarious and could be influenced by such insubstantial factors as short-run changes in the profitability of existing investments and by successive moods of optimism and pessimism.

Moreover, it was against this background that the professional dealers had their effect on market prices; not, however, by attempting to forecast prospective yield but by 'foreseeing changes in the conventional basis of valuation a short time ahead of the general public'.[10] This was the business of *speculation*, the battle of wits which Keynes characterised in his oft-quoted remarks about 'beating the gun' and of playing games of 'Snap, of Old Maid, of Musical Chairs'.[11]

It is still a moot point whether speculation exerts a stabilising or destabilising influence on stock-market prices, and there is a significant body of opinion which would argue that speculators operate to reduce fluctuations.[12] However, given the precariousness of the 'conventional view', and given that the object of speculation is to 'guess better than the crowd how the crowd will behave',[13] it cannot be said that speculation does anything to reconcile market valuation with the estimation of prospective yield, which was Keynes's point. It would be more accurate to say that speculation merely makes stock-market prices respond more sensitively to changes in factors which actually influence stock-market prices. We shall return to this topic in Chapter 18.

Much thus depends on whether the market is governed by *enterprise*, which concerns itself with the forecasting of prospective yield, or by *speculation*, and it was Keynes's view that as markets become better organised the risk of their being dominated by *speculative* influences would increase.

That capital assets are subject to frequent revaluation is thus of great significance, for while the original purpose of this was to 'make a market' in existing investments and so maintain the confidence of purchasers, they:

> inevitably exert a decisive influence on the rate of current investment. For there is no sense in building up a new enterprise at a cost greater than that at which a similar existing enterprise can be purchased; whilst there is an inducement to spend on a new project what may seem an extravagant sum, if it can be floated off on the Stock Exchange at an immediate profit.[14]

Notwithstanding the above line of argument, however, it should be borne in mind that even in the absence of a resale market for existing investments and the instability caused by frequent revaluation, unregulated *enterprise* would still constitute an unreliable means for securing a satisfactory rate of investment. For it is too strongly dependent on what Keynes referred to as 'animal spirits – of a spontaneous urge to action rather than inaction', or on the presence or absence of spontaneous optimism, than on a precise calculation of prospective returns. It is a circumstance which increases the severity of slumps and depressions, and which makes the attainment of a satisfactory state of activity and employment conditional on the climate for investment being just right for the average entrepreneur.

THE SLUMP AND THE RATE OF INTEREST

We can now see why, when disillusion replaces overblown optimism, the boom will come to an end suddenly and comprehensively with a collapse in the marginal efficiency of capital. Moreover, while it would be possible for changes in the propensity to consume to constitute an offset to the failure of investment, it is more likely that, left to itself, consumption would compound the problem, as a 'stock-minded public' reduced their consumption in line with the fall in stock-market valuations.

Furthermore, while we have been concentrating on factors influencing the marginal efficiency of capital, we must also take into account possible changes in the rate of interest.

We should first note that the general failure of confidence which surrounds the collapse of the marginal efficiency of capital will increase liquidity preferences so that the rate of interest will rise. The initial effect will be to strengthen the negative influences on investment, and it is unlikely at this stage that any reduction in the rate of interest which could practicably be achieved would serve to offset the collapse in the marginal efficiency of capital.[15] As the slump proceeds, however, a reduction in the rate of interest will be an increasingly beneficial aid to recovery and, Keynes argues, 'probably a necessary condition of it'.[16]

THE RELATIVE ROLES OF THE M.E.C. AND THE RATE OF INTEREST

The proper relationship between the marginal efficiency of capital and the rate of interest is now clear. At the beginning of the slump it is the collapse of the marginal efficiency of capital which has causal precedence; for 'liquidity preference, except those manifestations of it which are associated with increasing trade and speculation, does not increase until *after* the collapse in the marginal efficiency of capital';[17] while later on, a reduction in the rate of interest becomes a necessary but not sufficient condition for recovery.

IMPLICATIONS FOR POLICY

Because the marginal efficiency of capital has precedence,[18] Keynes saw priority in policy moving away from the purely monetary (by way of influencing the rate of interest), and towards the control of factors influencing the marginal efficiency of capital.[19]

But how was this to be done when in a largely unregulated economy the marginal efficiency of capital is governed by the 'uncontrollable and disobedient psychology of the business world'?[20] Keynes's answer was that it could not be done in the prevailing conditions, and he concluded that a lasting improvement in the level of output and employment could only be achieved by far-reaching changes in the organisation of economic life:

> In conditions of *laissez faire* the avoidance of wide fluctuations in employment may, therefore, prove impossible without a far-reaching change in the psychology of investment markets such as there is no reason to expect. I conclude that the duty of ordering the current volume of investment cannot safely be left in private hands.[21]

By implication, responsibility for determining investment would to a significant extent pass into public hands. But as this element is central to Keynes's wider strategy for dealing with the problems of depressed, capital-rich economies, a fuller treatment must wait until we have dealt with the other element in the investment equation: the rate of interest.

THE CASE IN FAVOUR OF A LOW RATE OF INTEREST

Keynes's ultimate economic solution involved extraordinary measures for the regulation of the rate of interest, as it did for the rate of investment. In 'normal circumstances', however, Keynes saw the rate of interest as exercising 'a great, though not a decisive, influence on the rate of investment'.[22] In general terms, the *problems* to which Keynes addressed himself involved the rate of interest being held at too high a level, and in the following paragraphs we shall examine the arguments in favour of the rate of interest being low rather than high.

(a) The trade cycle

First, if we return briefly to the problems of the trade cycle,[23] we recall that in the slump no practicable reduction in the rate of interest would be sufficient to offset the effects of a collapse in the marginal efficiency of capital. But Keynes's explanation of the slump was different from the classical view, which saw the problem as one of over-investment in the preceding boom. On this view, therefore, the classical remedy against slumps would depend on the avoidance of over-investment, by means of a rise in the rate of interest.

Much, however, turns on the definition of over-investment that is being used. Keynes argues that the term should properly be applied to a situation in which there is such an abundance of capital goods that society could find no reasonable use for any more. But even if a boom were normally to produce this state of affairs the imposition of a high rate of interest would not be appropriate, in that it might discourage useful investments and have an adverse influence on the propensity to consume. Rather, the proper course would be to stimulate consumption by the most effective means available.

In Keynes's sense, however, over-investment would properly refer to a situation in which a high rate of interest would, in the over-optimistic mood of the boom, fail to deter investments *that in normal times would be seen to be doomed to disappointment.* With disappointment there would follow an over-pessimistic marking-down of expected returns and a resulting collapse in the marginal efficiency of capital. If, therefore, in the circumstances of the boom a high rate of interest does not deter 'over-investment', the correct remedy is not to raise interest rates but to lower them. For a low rate of interest will not only mitigate the extent of disappointment but also act as a positive incentive to investment.

Thus, while the classical solution would abolish booms and relegate the economy to a permanent state of semi-slump, Keynes's solution would abolish slumps and inaugurate a permanent state of quasi-boom.

(b) International trade and payments

Next, in the sphere of international trade and payments, the argument is in favour of national autonomy in interest-rate determination so that a rate consistent with a full-employment level of investment for each economy can be chosen.[24] But this, note, is not an argument in favour of giving priority to stability at home at the expense of stability abroad; for in Keynes's view the simultaneous pursuit of full-employment policies by all countries together would, in fact, promote international stability by removing the principal source of conflict.

The conflict which Keynes had in mind was that which sprang from the struggles for competitive advantage under the international gold standard. Under a system in which a country's exchange rate is fixed and its money stock and interest rates are largely determined by external factors, the only means available to deal with unemployment is to achieve a trade surplus; for then gold can be imported, the money stock increased and the rate of interest reduced. In other words, a rate of interest standing at too high a level for full employment cannot be reduced by an expansionary monetary policy unless such a policy is justified under the rules of the gold standard.

Because, however, the international balance of payments must sum to zero, the gaining of a competitive advantage by one economy can only be at the expense of another, which will be forced to export gold and follow a restrictionary monetary policy. Thus the unemployment is transferred from the one to the other; the system generates conflict.

Moreover, for the type of economy with which we are centrally concerned, that of which the capital stock is so great that the marginal efficiency of capital is tending to fall faster than the rate of interest will allow, the international economic system in which it is forced to operate is of great significance. For on Keynes's view a solution to its problem is dependent on autonomy in economic policy, whereas under the gold standard its options are greatly reduced; and

> those statesmen were moved by common sense and a correct apprehension of the true course of events, who believed that if a rich, old country were to neglect the struggle for markets its prosperity would droop and fail.[25]

If, on the other hand, all countries were free to pursue investment and interest-rate policies designed to achieve full employment at home, its special problem of chronic unemployment equilibrium could be alleviated as part of the solution to the global economic problem. And as individual economies were freed from the necessity of gaining a competitive advantage so as to export unemployment, international trade would become 'a willing and unimpeded exchange of goods and services in conditions of mutual advantage'.[26]

(c) The usury laws

Keynes's analysis also provides a cogent economic explanation for legislation that in earlier times imposed restrictions on the rise in interest rates. In predominantly agricultural economies, wealth-owners may have attributed a high liquidity premium to the possession of land; for land, like money, may have very low elasticities of production and substitution. It is thus possible that in certain periods 'the desire to hold land has played the same role in keeping up the rate of interest at too high a level which money has played in recent times'.[27]

The parallel is not exact but Keynes suggests that, at times, the high rates of interest on mortgages on land may have had a depressing effect on the demand for investment in newly produced capital good, in just the same way as *the competition from high yields on long-term bonds* has depressed investment in modern economies.

Because, moreover, attempts were made to control rates of interest on mortgages by means of the *usury laws*, these can now be seen as being much more than an irrelevant manifestation of ecclesiastical prejudice. Amid the insecurities of a life which was generally hostile to investment, the attempts of the medieval church to distinguish between the return from loans of money and the return from active investment are seen in a new light. Keynes saw them as:

> an honest intellectual effort to keep separate what the classical theory has inextricably confused together, namely the rate of interest and the marginal efficiency of capital. For it now seems clear that the disquisitions of the schoolmen were directed towards the elucidation of a formula which would allow the schedule of the marginal efficiency of capital to be high, whilst using rule and custom and the moral law to keep down the rate of interest.[28]

This leads us directly to our final point, which is concerned with the rate of return expected by wealth-holders.

(d) Expectations of the rentier

Keynes believed that by comparison with the situation obtaining in the nineteenth century, there had been an adverse change in the relationship between the marginal efficiency of capital and the money rate of interest, such that the relatively high rate of interest was a disincentive to active investment. The change, however, had come not from a rise in the rate of interest but, as might be expected from our argument in the preceding chapter, a fall in the marginal efficiency of capital.

In the more advantageous situation of the nineteenth century, a variety of influences[29] had combined:

> to establish a schedule of the marginal efficiency of capital which allowed a reasonably satisfactory average level of employment to be compatible with a rate of interest high enough to be psychologically acceptable to wealth-owners [whereas]...The acuteness and the peculiarity of our contemporary problem arises ... out of the possibility that the average rate of interest which will allow a reasonable average level of employment is one so unacceptable to wealth-owners that it cannot be readily established merely by manipulating the quantity of money.[30]

Consequently, Keynes saw the removal of the impediment to full employment, represented by the attitudes of the *rentier* class, as a major concern of his overall strategy.[31]

Thus a fall in the rate of interest is a necessary condition for the establishment of economic prosperity. Furthermore, for the full implementation of Keynes's solution the fall must involve fundamental change; for it must overcome all the resistance to a further fall which is concentrated at the bottom end of the interest-rate range.

BRINGING DOWN THE RATE OF INTEREST

It is also clear that orthodox methods of influencing the rate of interest will not be equal to the task.[32] In particular, monetary policy will become increasingly impotent as the rate of interest falls, as liquidity preference tends towards the absolute. At a very low level of the long-term rate (say 2 per cent) there is 'more to fear than to hope' on capital account while the running yield offers little in the way of compensation. The passive investor will prefer to hold money.[33]

There is, of course, the possibility that the public might be conditioned to the acceptance of lower rates simply because the conventional rate has no firm foundation in 'secure knowledge'. The reduction would be accomplished in a series of stages so that expectations might adjust to the acceptance of a permanently lower level of rates. But again, this will only be effective 'up to a point'. As the price of long-term bonds rises, the passive investor, by seeking to avoid capital losses from illiquidity – that is, by holding money – will at the same time be indicating the minimum acceptable rate of return on wealth-holding. The rate of interest will fall no further.

Consequently, if othodox means would not serve, Keynes was ready to use the unorthodox, and he envisaged the authorities taking direct control to set interest rates at the appropriate level.[34]

THE STATE AS ENTREPRENEUR

We can now see that the state will assume a dual responsibility. While on the one hand it must reduce the rate of interest to a level consistent with a full-employment rate of investment, its primary concern will be to regulate the rate of investment and the size of the capital stock by other means. Given the inherent difficulties of influencing the marginal efficiency of capital in an economy of individualistic capitalism, the state itself would have to take responsibility for '*directly organising* investment'.[35]

The state indeed would become the majority entrepreneur, for Keynes envisaged a 'somewhat comprehensive socialisation of investment'.[36] This did *not*, however, imply state socialism, with public ownership of the means of production, distribution and exchange; for to achieve its ends it was only necessary that the state should 'determine the aggregate amount of resources devoted to augmenting the instruments and the basic rate of reward to those who own them'.[37]

Keynes justified this greatly enhanced role for the state on the grounds that, as compared with the individual entrepreneur, the state was uniquely placed 'to calculate the marginal efficiency of capital-goods on *long views* and on the basis of the general social advantage'.[38]

In other words, even though the state would draw its economic advisors from the same pool of talent as was available to private industry, it would set them objectives based on different criteria. In particular, it would not have to be bound by narrowly commercial considerations. Also, it would be free of the influences of short-term fluctuations in the secondary-market valuation of investments. Finally, it would not have to await a burgeoning of the urge to action' or an access of 'spontaneous optimism' before initiating investment.

KEYNES'S SOLUTION: THE SHORT RUN AND THE LONG RUN

The solution to the Keynesian economic problem has two aspects. The first is short-run and deals with the achievement and maintenance of full employment. The second is long-run and concerns Keynes's objective of depriving capital of its scarcity value. While the first would be universally recognised as a desirable goal, in respect of which others might differ from Keynes only in the manner of its achievement, the second is a 'practical judgement' rather than a 'theoretical imperative' and is justified by the social advantages which Keynes believed would follow.[39]

The two aspects, though distinct, are intimately related, for each is in part implied by the other. The drive towards full employment will involve both an increase in the rate of investment and a reduction in the rate of interest. But an increase in the level of effective demand can come either from an increase in investment *or* consumption, and the fall in the rate of interest may so stimulate the propensity to consume that full employment could become a reality 'with a *rate of accumulation* not much greater than at present'.[40]

However, the rate of accumulation will obviously determine the rate of growth of the capital stock,[41] so that in planning the strategy for full employment we must have regard for the achievement of Keynes's second objective, whereby the marginal efficiency of capital would approach zero, within one, or at most two, generations.[42]

In the short run, of course, investment and consumption can both increase to serve the same ends, and in tandem with a socially controlled rate of investment Keynes envisaged the encouragement by all means of an increase in the propensity to consume, for 'it is unlikely that full employment can be maintained, whatever we may do about investment, with the existing propensity to consume'.[43]

However, when full employment is reached and output becomes completely inelastic, a larger share for investment *must* imply a lower propensity to consume.[44] It is thus to the long run that the question of the burden to be borne by the present generation, so as to benefit a future generation, properly belongs. For the rapidity with which a state of *full investment* can be reached will depend on the extent to which the present generation is prepared to restrict its own consumption.[45]

The resolution of this problem is clearly a matter for the expression of the political will; while the implementation of the chosen policy should present no insuperable difficulties, given that the state will directly control investment and can influence consumption through the tax system and the rate of interest.[46]

It is also important to understand the mechanism of adjustment to long-run equilibrium. We have already argued that if full employment is to be achieved the rate of interest must be set to correspond to the appropriate point on the schedule of the marginal efficiency of capital. The rate of investment thus determined will, in turn, govern the rate of growth of the capital stock. However, as the capital stock increases, the schedule of the marginal efficiency of capital will shift downward, so that, if equilibrium is to be maintained continuously during the period of transition, the rate of interest will have to decline in step.

THE NEW ORDER

When the process comes to an end the economic positions of the principal actors will have changed dramatically. Capital will now be so abundant that its marginal efficiency will have fallen to 'a very low figure'.[47] Consequently, owners of capital will no longer enjoy a return derived solely from its scarcity value. Keynes justified this deprivation on the grounds that, as compared perhaps with land, there is no intrinsic reason why capital should be scarce. Only in a situation in which the long-run (full-employment) desire to accumulate wealth faded before the capital stock had reached its optimal level would there be a genuine scarcity, signified by the offer of interest to reward an actual sacrifice of present consumption. And even here the role of the state in managing both investment and consumption should smooth the path.

There would, however, still be a return to the ownership of capital, derived from the forecasting of returns on risky projects, for 'there would still be room...for enterprise and skill in the estimation of prospective yields about which opinions could differ'.[48] Indeed, Keynes envisaged a tax system devised to encourage the active investor to continue his useful function, though for a lower level of reward than previously. For, with the pure rate of interest driven to zero, the return from the use of capital assets

> would have to cover little more than their exhaustion by wastage and obsolescence together with some margin to cover risk and the exercise of skill and judgement. In short, the aggregate return from durable goods in the course of their life would, as in the case of short-lived goods, just cover their labour-costs of production *plus* an allowance for risk and the costs of skill and supervision.[49]

As much as the scarcity value of capital, Keynes regarded the existence of a class of functionless investors, the *rentiers*, as one of the 'objectionable features of capitalism'. It was, moreover, the minimum acceptable rate of return on accumulated wealth which, in a *laissez-faire* system, formed the chief obstacle to a fall in the rate of interest to a very low level. Consequently, there could be no mere modification of the position of the *rentier* class; it would have to disappear completely.

People would, of course, still be free to accumulate wealth but their accumulation would not grow, because in long-run equilibrium the pure rate of interest would decline to zero. For, whereas the marginal efficiency of capital would largely consist of a premium in respect of entrepreneur's risk, the return to the provision of finance for investment would largely consist of premiums in respect of lender's risk. The 'euthanasia of the rentier' would follow as a matter of course.[50]

The economy would thus enter a quasi-stationary state in which 'change and progress would result only from changes in techniques, taste, population and institutions'.[51] And, with the establishment of a long-run, full-employment level of output the classical theory would come into its own, with self-interest determining the composition of final output, the mode of combination of the factors of production and the distribution of the value of the final product.[52]

For it was *not* Keynes's intention to show that the free-market system misallocated those factors of production that it actually employed, but only that it was incapable of guaranteeing their employment in sufficient volume. And, in seeking to remedy the defects of the system, Keynes was by the same token attempting to preserve its positive features, of individual liberty and enterprise, for,

> the result of filling the gaps in the classical theory is not to dispose of the 'Manchester System', but to indicate the nature of the environment which the free play of economic forces requires if it is to realise the full potentialities of its production.[53]

While the ends that Keynes envisaged might have received general approbation, the means by which he proposed to achieve them did not. By providing a theoretical justification for state intervention in the economy – based, moreover, on the alleged superiority of the public over the private view – Keynes seemed to some critics to be opening a Pandora's Box, from which would issue fundamentally destructive forces.

Part III
The Keynesian Revolution and its Critics

2: Monetarists and Austrians

15 The Consequences of Mr Keynes?

INTRODUCTION

The Keynesian Revolution was essentially a revolution of economic principles rather than, say, of policy prescriptions. As a consequence, the criticism of the *General Theory* which followed its publication in 1936 – and which, as we have seen, found its most telling expression in the work of D.H. Robertson – was directed primarily at the fundamentals of Keynes's theory. Nevertheless, the conclusions that Keynes derived from his theory were clearly intended to have important implications for policy, and it was on the question of the consequences that were said to flow from the application of Keynes's ideas that the Keynesian Revolution was ultimately to face its greatest challenge.

THE KEYNESIAN REVOLUTION: THE REASON WHY

The circumstance which prompted Keynes to write the *General Theory* was the period of continuous mass unemployment which the United Kingdom experienced during the 1920s and 1930s. It was written in revolt against the established economic orthodoxy which, Keynes perceived, provided no basis for the policy measures that were being recommended by the majority of contemporary economists – on grounds which must, therefore, have been *ad hoc* and intuitive. It is the lack of correspondence between contemporary theory and policy which answers the criticism of the Keynesian Revolution, that there already existed theory sufficient to supply an explanation of events.[1]

It was, thus, in attempting to produce an economic theory which would explain the facts of experience, that Keynes was impelled, late on in his professional career, to set about re-examining the main ideas of his existing *magnum opus*, the *Treatise on Mondey*, published in 1930.[2] The revolutionary thesis he produced stood classical economics on its head and provided the theoretical basis for economic policy for much of the following forty years.

THE OBJECTIVES OF THE *GENERAL THEORY*

We must remind ourselves that in the *General Theory* Keynes sought to do three things. The first was to show that the existing orthodoxy was inappropriate for dealing with any economic situation other than the special case of the full employment of resources. This was because the assumptions upon which this highly logical system of thought was based led to the conclusion that the system would tend automatically to equilibrium at full employment. Policy implications would therefore relate to attempts to remove obstacles to free adjustment.

Second, he aimed to provide an alternative theory of the working of a monetary production economy which would be *general*, in the sense that it would demonstrate that the system could be in equilibrium at any level of employment, and that the special case of full-employment equilibrium would require the components of aggregate demand, consumption plus investment, to stand in a particular relationship to each other. Because Keynes believed this to be an unlikely occurrence, government intervention would normally be required in modern circumstances. Notice that the fundamental change-about here is that government intervention, which had hitherto been regarded as an obstacle to the achievement of full employment, was now to be a necessary condition of it. That is, the state is explicitly written into the economic equation.

Third, he sought to apply the principles of his general analysis to the elucidation of the particular problem faced by developed, capital-rich, economies such as the UK and the USA. This Keynes saw as the failure of investment due to the conjunction of a low and falling marginal efficiency of capital and a rate of interest which failed to fall in step, so that the economy was forced to cycle about an underemployment equilibrium.

That the chronic-stagnation outcome and the manner in which the problem must be tackled, is the ultimate point of Keynes's thesis, is demonstrated, as intimated earlier, by the fact that Keynes confined his analysis largely to the internal economy. For the new way of analysing the working of the economy and the way in which this knowledge could be used to defeat stagnation, was intended to apply *to all governments*, so that, pursuing full-employment policies, international trade could be carried on with a view to mutual advantage rather than competition to export unemployment.

These points must be borne very clearly in mind, because although the framework of analysis Keynes produced was first applied in the exceptional circumstances of the war economy, with the restoration of peace after 1945 economic policy was avowedly 'Keynesian' and was directed to the simultaneous achievement of favourable outcomes for employment, growth, balance-of-payments and price-level objectives.

THE TAMING OF THE KEYNESIAN REVOLUTION

So long as success in large measure attended these endeavours, the actual relation that the stylised 'Keynesian' policies, based on the finely tuned management of aggregate demand by way of the government's annual budget (with monetary policy and direct controls in a subordinate role), bore to Keynes's own thesis, went largely unquestioned. And when these policies seemed no longer to work and the objectives could no longer be achieved, Keynes's critics old and new were quick to see in the discomfiture of the 'Keynesians' the long-predicted failure of the Keynesian Revolution itself.

In dismissing 'Keynesian' economics Keynes's critics were happy to see the baby thrown out along with the bath-water – though their implied rejection of Keynes's own work could only be sustained by caricaturing it in terms of textbook 'Keynesianism'. The reasons which prompted these tactics are not hard to find.

On the one hand, Keynes himself was recognised to be intellectually superlative and with one foot as firmly planted in the money-making purlieus of the real world as the other was set in the choicest corner of the garden of academe. Consequently any theory or cause he espoused would have to be given every serious consideration.

On the other hand, it is indisputable that Keynes was the fountainhead of an influential modern stream of thought which provided explicit justification for substantial state participation in the economy. To those opposed to state intervention, the free-marketeers and libertarians, the advent of Keynes was a serious challenge – in particular as the objectives of his strategy seemed to make 'good economic sense' and had, moreover, appealing humanitarian overtones.

Salvation for the critics came in the usual way, in as much as the *General Theory* was made accessible in the form of a stylised model. Thereafter the critics were aided by the working of the natural process whereby, over time, original works become classics, and therefore unread, while attention is concentrated exclusively on the stylised model which takes on the persona of the parent work, so that the two stand or fall together accordingly as the model appears to perform well or badly.

In the following eight chapters we shall reply to the attack on Keynes based on the supposed consequences of Keynesian economics, in the same way as we dealt with the attack on the fundamentals of Keynes's theory itself; that is, by dealing individually with the specific criticisms made by his opponents. By examining and answering these criticisms we shall find that Keynes's thesis emerges largely undiminished by the facts of the British economic experience since 1945, and that it contains some enduring principles to aid us in tackling the economic problems of the 1980s and beyond.

Because our concern is with the specific criticisms on which the attack on Keynes is based, it follows that we shall have only a secondary interest in the actual turn of economic events which brought disillusionment with 'Keynesian' economics and provoked the revolt against the Keynesian Revolution itself. Though an interpretation of events in the light of Keynes's thesis will be hinted at below, for the moment an outline of the events themselves will suffice.

ECONOMIC SUCCESS IN THE AGE OF KEYNES

We must begin by noting the extraordinary contrast in the levels of employment achieved by the British economy as between the inter-war decades of the 1920s and 1930s and the quarter-century after 1945. The era of mass unemployment in the United Kingdom began with the slump of 1920–21. The problem was exacerbated by the world slump of 1929 and reached its peak in 1932. The subsequent recovery received a set-back from the recession of 1937 and it was not until 1941 – the third year of war – that full employment was attained. Over the period 1921–39 unemployment averaged almost 10 per cent.[3]

By contrast, for a period of two-and-a-half decades after 1945 the UK economy enjoyed continuous full employment, sustained at levels of unemployment far below expectations of what could possibly be achieved. In his study of post-war employment prospects published in 1944, Sir William (Lord) Beveridge had suggested that as a 'conservative rather than an unduly hopeful, aim', after allowing for short-term unemployment due to seasonal, frictional, and fluctuations-of-trade factors, the economy might be expected to reach full employment, with 3 per cent of the workforce unemployed.[4] Keynes, however, had intimated that he regarded this figure as over-optimistic, in the light of his own earlier estimate of 5 per cent unemployment as an *average* to be aimed for.[5]

Nevertheless, in the outcome, Beveridge's figure of 3 per cent does indeed appear 'conservative', while Keynes's 5 per cent seems unduly pessimistic; though it should be noted that Keynes had an abiding fear of inflation as a result of over-stimulation from the centre. Not until the beginning of the 1970s did unemployment reach 3 per cent, and typically during the 1950s and 1960s the figure was within the range 1.3 per cent to 2.3 per cent. Although a slight upward trend in unemployment is discernible during the 1960s, it is only at the end of that decade that the first of a series of significant upward shifts occurs, bringing a trend which was to culminate in the mass unemployment of the 1980s.[6]

This, of course, was a quite remarkable achievement; but with the economy running so close to capacity there was perennial concern about inflation. In fact, the British economy was inflationary over the whole of the quarter-century from 1945, though the rates of inflation actually experienced were modest by later standards. It is interesting to note that there is a small but distinct upward trend in inflation during the 1960s, in parallel with the movement upward in unemployment during the same period. Similarly, it is from the end of that decade that the significant changes are observable, with annual rates of inflation in each year above the average for the previous twenty years. With the exception of 1972 and 1973, inflation accelerated in each year from 1968 to 1975, to unprecedented levels for the United Kingdom in peacetime, after which the trend was reversed.[7]

We should also notice that the period of 'Keynesian' prosperity was roughly coterminous with the Bretton Woods system, with its obligation to maintain a predetermined pattern of exchange rates. The balance of payments was thus regarded throughout as a major constraint on any sustained policy of expansion. Nevertheless, the British economy grew, and although the rate of growth was disappointing by international standards, it was historically high. In the

1970s, however, in keeping with the British economy's deteriorating performance in employment and prices, the rate of growth of Gross Domestic Product fell sharply.

THE SYSTEM IN CRISIS

Judged on the criterion of adherence to broadly 'Keynesian' demand management policies (howsoever modified through pressure from the IMF), the Age of Keynes persisted until 1979, only coming to an end with the election in that year of a government which explicitly rejected 'Keynesian' economics. Judged, however, by the standard of apparent success of 'Keynesian' policies, the 1970s had already inaugurated the post-Keynesian era, as established economic relationships crumbled and inflation climbed in a time of mounting unemployment.

There followed the 'crisis in macroeconomics', as 'Keynesian' economists, who now constituted the established orthodoxy, sought to explain the coexistence of inflation, the textbook 'Keynesian' symptom of an 'overheated' economy, with unemployment at record levels for the post-war period. To account for this emergent 'stagflation' they were forced to appeal to the intervention of extra-market forces such as sociological factors, the monopoly power of trade unions to raise wages and the advent of large autonomous increases in world commodity prices.[8]

But if the events of the 1970s had produced a crisis of confidence in 'Keynesian' economics, there were other schools of thought ready to compete for attention with alternative sets of analysis, diagnosis and policy recommendations.

ALTERNATIVE VIEWS

To the monetarists, for example, a school founded by Professor Milton Friedman and his collaborators at the University of Chicago in the 1950s, the configuration of macroeconomic variables so confusing to 'Keynesians' was easily explicable in terms of a theory which accorded central importance to the money supply. Monetarists distinguished carefully between real and monetary influences on the economy and, in opposition to the established 'Keynesian' economics, emphasised the powerful and pervasive effects of changes in the quantity of money, analysed as between the short run and the long run. In particular, by arguing that the level of employment was determined by real forces acting on the labour market, the monetarists could show that monetary stimulus applied to relieve unemployment could bring only a temporary benefit before manifesting itself in rising prices. By this means they were able to suggest that the unemployment–inflation trade-off of the Phillips curve relation[9] (a relation thought to be quintessentially 'Keynesian') was at best a short-run phenomenon. They could also argue that with unemployment fixed at its 'natural' equilibrium rate, inflationary pressure would be minimised by the imposition of a policy rule which would keep the rate of growth of the money stock in line with the underlying growth rate of the economy.

It followed that the 'Keynesian' preoccupation with demand management was entirely misplaced and monetarists argued that attention should instead be directed towards the supply side; to helping, that is, in true classical fashion the real market economy to adjust freely to 'full employment' equilibrium.

Benefiting from the disarray of the Keynesians, the monetarists gained greatly in support during this period, and attracted such influential attention that their views underpinned the official economic policy of the Conservative government elected in 1979.

But there was another group of Keynesian critics who from the British point of view had been brooding in the wings since the 1930s, and who were similarly to find favour with a Conservative government committed to the restoration of the market economy. This was the Vienna School of economists, or Austrians, who were quite clear that the inflation and unemployment of the 1970s were a direct, if unduly delayed, result of the Keynesian adventure; the consequences of which were entirely predictable when interpreted in terms of pre-Keynesian monetary theory.

We should also mention here, in connection with the Austrian School, the group of British 'liberal' economists, who attacked Keynesianism in its various forms on the grounds that it justified and promoted state intervention in the economy and so encouraged the spread of *collective choice* at the expense of individual liberty. In warning against the dangers of collectivism in a society very different from that of Keynes's day, liberals proposed measures to safeguard personal freedom which went beyond the purely economic and envisaged reform of the constitution itself.

In dealing in turn with these schools of thought, we shall primarily be concerned to assess the validity of the arguments they employed to attack the Keynesian Revolution, rather than with the intrinsic worth of the monetarist and Austrian doctrines respectively. In addition, however, a critical assessment of monetarist and Austrian doctrines will provide a valuable additional form of defence against Keynes's critics.

16 Monetarism
I: The Counter-Revolution

INTRODUCTION

Monetarists can be thought of as constituting the majority party among those ranged in opposition to Keynes; as against the Austrians as minority party, whose work is generally less well known. In addition, the monetarist framework of analysis so closely parallels that of Keynes that points of potential conflict are easily identified, and the interesting questions concern the validity of the monetarists' interpretation of Keynes's propositions in relation to their own and the provenance of the monetarist model itself, in terms of the relative importance of pre-Keynesian and Keynesian influences.

This is to be contrasted with the Austrian-school approach, which operates at a different (micro-economic) level of aggregation and which in its structure more closely resembles the Robertsonian theory discussed earlier. Nevertheless we should also notice that the espousal by some monetarists of the rational-expectations hypothesis (see Chapter 18, below) has had the effect of incorporating elements of Austrian-school business-cycle theory into at least one version of the monetarist model, and that this somewhat blurs the distinction made above.

MILTON FRIEDMAN AND THE COUNTER-REVOLUTION

Furthermore, though monetarists are united as members of a broad school of thought by their adherence to a set of commonly accepted empirical propositions,[1] it is nowadays possible to identify several distinct varieties or sub-schools of monetarism, each of which specifies a particular version of the monetarist model. It is possible, for example, to distinguish between Friedmanite monetarism, sticky-wages monetarism, and rational-expectations monetarism.[2] But it was not always so, and for present purposes we shall largely confine our attention to the work of the 'founding father' and foremost exponent of monetarism, Milton Friedman. For it was Friedman who developed monetarism specifically as a critique of Keynesian economics in order to produce a 'counter-revolution' in monetary theory which would displace and supersede the Keynesian Revolution.

Under Friedman's hand the counter-revolution was to be a coolly scientific affair based on the precepts of positive economics[3] and free of the heat that has to some extent marked the Austrian school attack on Keynes. Friedman intended that his counter-revolution should succeed on the very same basis as that on which, he argued, the Keynesian Revolution had been shown to fail: namely, by its ability to meet the criterion of empirical verification. Though Friedman, after some prompting, was careful to acknowledge his debt to Keynes and to pay fulsome tribute to his stature as an economist, his final verdict was to award Keynes an E-for-Effort for a Good Try:

> I believe that Keynes's theory is the right kind of theory in its simplicity, its concentration on a few key magnitudes, its potential fruitfulness. I have been led to reject it, not on these grounds, but because I believe that it has been contradicted by evidence: its predictions have not been confirmed by experience. This failure suggests that it has not isolated what are 'really' the key factors in short-run economic change.[4]

But what, according to Friedman, was the perceived weakness in Keynes's theory which had been exposed by the turn of events and so left the way open for a legitimate challenge? The nub of the answer to this question is that whereas the economic problem of the post-war world was increasingly that of inflation, rather than the persistent unemployment of the inter-war period, Keynes had deprived himself of a theory of the absolute price level in his attempts both to discredit the quantity theory and to construct a mechanism of adjustment to monetary disturbance which would support his assertion of the possibility of underemployment equilibrium. Thus flawed, it was simply a question of time before Keynesian economics would be seen to fail in the face of the inflationary conditions with which it was not equipped to deal.

On the other hand, the quantity theory of money, in whichever particular form it was expressed, was essentially a theory of the general price level; and it was Friedman's substantive contribution to monetary economics to restate the quantity theory in an exact, empirically testable form that would provide a means for analysing the effects of changes in the quantity of money on the economy. This, note, was its specific, scientific, politically neutral purpose, and on these grounds it stands independently of Friedman's well-publicised libertarian views.

Nevertheless, there remains the question of the quantity theory as the theoretical basis of the monetarist counter-revolution; and it is here, used as a framework within which Friedman conducted his critique of Keynesian monetary theory, that the quantity-theory concept has wider implications, as we shall see.

The restated quantity theory, with its emphasis on the stability of the demand for money and of the lagged relationship between monetary change and (nominal) income change, clearly carried implications for the conduct of monetary policy in the control of inflation. But claimed technical superiority in dealing with a problem of continuing concern to policy-makers was not of itself sufficient to ensure the substitution of monetarist for Keynesian economics as the predominant view within the profession.

A STRATEGY FOR COUNTER-REVOLUTION

H. G. Johnson has argued, on the 'as if' principle, that if Friedman had consciously set out to displace Keynesian economics, success for his counter-revolution would have been dependent upon his being able to reproduce the conditions which had enabled the Keynesian Revolution to succeed against the established orthodoxy of Keynes's day.

Circumstances became increasingly favourable to Friedman from the mid-1950s onwards, as Keynes's followers (the profession at large) 'elaborated his history-bound analysis into a timeless and spaceless set of universal principles ... and so established Keynesianism as an orthodoxy ripe for counter-attack'.[5]

The characteristic features of the 'Keynesian' orthodoxy included a belief that mass unemployment was endemic in unmanaged capitalist economies and that unemployment is always the problem of overriding concern for policy-makers, with a consequent tendency to understate the dangers of inflation. In addition, the profession had become oppressively top-heavy with economists who had been borne to prominence on the flood of the Keynesian tide, and who 'continued to trade on their foresight, to the academic detriment of their juniors'.[6] Finally, the enormous interest in model-building and econometric testing which Keynes's work had stimulated, had begun to wane.

Thus the Keynesian orthodoxy had become vulnerable to attack on the same grounds as had the classical orthodoxy. These were: the existence of an important economic and social problem with which the established orthodoxy could not deal (unemployment for Keynes; inflation for Friedman); together with a central proposition of the orthodoxy which was patently inapt (the automatic adjustment of the economy to full-employment equilibrium, for Keynes; a belief that 'money doesn't matter', for Friedman).

Success for the would-be revolutionary/counter-revolutionary would then depend upon being able to formulate an alternative theory, in a way which would exploit the dynamic within the profession of the ambitious but frustrated young against the established elders. This would involve judgements as to its general level of difficulty, the appeal of its methodological approach and the opportunities it presented for empirical testing. For the counter-revolutionary, however, there was the additional problem of having to demonstrate that the problem of inflation should be given a higher priority than unemployment – and it is this factor which accounts for the less rapid encroachment of monetarist ideas, from the mid-1950s, than was the case with Keynesian economics after 1936.

Considerations of strategy apart, therefore, the basis of Friedman's attack on Keynes was the 'Keynesian' proposition that 'money doesn't matter'; and the case in favour of a counter-revolution in monetary theory was made to depend upon the prior question of the stability of the demand for money.

Friedman's argument is summarised in the following paragraphs. Notice that it takes the form of a reply by Friedman to the Keynesian Revolution *interpreted as* an attack on the quantity theory of money. It does not, therefore, deal ostensibly with matters which have occupied us importantly in previous chapters, though it does imply a view as to the role they play. Indeed we shall find that it is in the *implications* that the real challenge to Keynes is contained.

FRIEDMAN'S THESIS

Friedman has argued that before, say, 1930 the quantity theory was the accepted monetary orthodoxy and monetary policy was seen as the principal means for stabilising the economy. Analysed in terms of

Irving Fisher's quantity equation ($MV = PT$) this implied that:

> the term for velocity could be regarded as highly stable, that it could be taken as determined independently of the other terms in the equation, and that as a result changes in the quantity of money would be reflected either in prices or in output. It was also widely taken for granted that short-term fluctuations in the economy reflected changes in the quantity of money, or in the terms and conditions under which credit was available. It was taken for granted that the trend of prices over any considerable period reflected the behaviour of the quantity of money over that period.[7]

However, the experience of the Depression (which Friedman sees as stemming in the UK from the contraction produced by the restored gold standard 1925–31; and in the USA from the Great Crash of 1929) destroyed faith in the quantity theory due to a misinterpretation of money's role in events. The reality was, argues Friedman, that in the USA the size of the money stock had declined sharply over the relevant period as a result of official action – and the effect of this had been reinforced by a concomitant fall in velocity. But, misled by official pronouncements, Keynes and others believed that expansionary monetary policy had been tried and found to be ineffective.

Keynes, therefore, produced an alternative theory in which output and employment were determined by autonomous and induced expenditures, and which accounted for the Depression in terms of a failure of investment brought on by a collapse of investment opportunities. In this theory the money–income relation was largely ignored, because Keynes had interpreted the apparent impotence of monetary policy as being due to the fact that velocity, instead of being highly stable, *is highly adaptable*, adjusting passively to accommodate changes in money or income.

Given the historical context of his theory, Keynes believed that changes in expenditure would result in changes in output rather than prices and, deprived of a theory of the absolute price level via the quantity theory, he postulated that prices are determined largely by wages and that wages are themselves historically determined. It was by this means that Keynes was able to support his assumption that 'in the modern world prices are highly rigid'.[8]

The consequences of Keynes's (supposed) misinterpretation of the Depression were therefore far-reaching. Henceforth the main instrument of economic stabilisation would be the government's budget, with monetary policy used only in a subordinate role, to provide cheap money. Moreover, while wages remained stable, prices would be stable; but *by implication* incipient inflation would be due to the cost-push of wages which would, therefore, have to be controlled via incomes policy.

Though there was general acceptance of this approach to macroeconomics after the Second World War, Friedman argues that, from early on, several factors combined to produce a reaction against Keynesianism. For example, the predicted post-war slump failed to materialise, and this cast doubt on Keynes's belief in the increasing scarcity of investment opportunities. Also, attempted cheap-money policies, such as that of Dr Dalton in Britain, had to be abandoned because of their inflationary effects.

In addition, new historical research indicated that monetary policy had exerted a powerful, albeit negative, influence on the course of the Depression. Furthermore, empirical studies brought renewed faith in the stability of the money–income relation and comparative studies of the monetary and budgetary effects of government policy showed monetary influences to be the more powerful.

Finally, the inverse relationship between expansionary monetary policy and falling interest rates postulated by Keynes, was shown to exist only in the short run. In the longer run, money, prices and interest rates all rise together, implying that the quantity of money rather than the rate of interest provides the better indicator of monetary conditions.

THE QUESTION OF VELOCITY AND ITS SIGNIFICANCE

Whatever implications they may have for 'Keynesian' economics, however, these points are not necessarily hostile to Keynes. They will for the most part be dealt with below, but one is of central and immediate interest. This is Friedman's assertion that Keynes misinterpreted the role of monetary policy in the Depression and sought to account for its impotence by postulating that velocity is unstable, adapting passively to offset changes in the quantity of money.

This point is clearly of great importance for Friedman's case and he describes it as 'an essential element of the Keynesian doctrine'.[9] It stands, of course, in stark contrast to the monetarist view that the demand for money is highly stable – and seems, therefore, destined to play the part of Aunt Sally.

But apart from its obvious implications for monetary policy, the passivity of velocity has a deeper significance due to the nature of the condition required to make it so: namely, that the demand for money is perfectly elastic at some given level of the rate of interest. In other words, for Keynes to claim that velocity is adaptable and monetary policy is therefore useless, his economy must be assumed to be operating in the liquidity trap.

On this interpretation, the significance of the liquidity trap is two-fold. It *presumes* both a transmission mechanism linking monetary change to economic activity which is not that of the classical quantity theory,[10] and, moreover, a transmission mechanism which can be completely blocked off. Therefore, by means of the liquidity trap, Keynes was able both (i) to deny the classical quantity theory as the major theory of short-run fluctuations and long-run prices – and therefore as the proper framework for stabilisation policy, and (ii) to provide a way of preventing the economy from reaching full employment through monetary influences (of whatever kind) alone, so that government spending and taxing would become necessary constituents of economic management.

But there is clearly more to this interpretation than the substitution by Keynes of one form of economic regulation for another, and a clue to Friedman's real intentions can be derived from the account he gives of the reasoning behind the Keynesian transmission mechanism.

FRIEDMAN AND THE 'LIQUIDITY TRAP'

We begin with the liquidity trap itself, which Friedman saw as being of crucian importance for Keynes. He speaks of:

> my interpretation of Keynes's views ... particularly with respect to the key role that Keynes assigns to the liquidity trap.[11]

Also:

> In my interpretation of Keynes, I put great emphasis on highly elastic liquidity preference, calling this his 'special twist' and 'a key element' in his proposition about long run equilibrium.[12]

And:

> my view that absolute liquidity preference plays a key role. Time and again when Keynes must face up to precisely what it is that prevents a full-employment equilibrium, his final line of defence is absolute liquidity preference.[13]

Moreover, although absolute liquidity preference is clearly a limiting case of a range of possibilities, it is for Keynes's purposes the one to be regarded as typical; for Keynes 'treated velocity as if in practice its behaviour frequently approximated that which would prevail in this limiting case'.[14]

The strategic importance of absolute liquidity preference stems from the 'narrowness' of the Keynesian transmission mechanism relative to that of the classical quantity theorists and monetarists:

> The difference between us and the Keynesians is less in the nature of the process than in the range of assets considered. The Keynesians tend to concentrate on a narrow range of marketable assets and recorded interest rates. We insist that a far wider range of assets and interest rates must be taken into account – such assets as durable and semi-durable consumer goods, structures and real property. As a result we regard the market rates stressed by the Keynesians as only a small part of the total spectrum of rates that are relevant.[15]

In turn, 'this difference in the assumed transmission mechanism is largely a by-product of the different assumptions about price'.[16] That is, 'because the Keynesians take the price level as an institutional datum, they regard a change in the interest rate as the means whereby people are induced to hold a larger or smaller quantity of money'.[17] In other words, it is by means of his assumptions regarding the general price level that Keynes forces the economy to adjust to monetary change via a narrow range of market interest rates. However, we must be clear that:

> Treating the price level or the wage level as an institutional datum, or, as Keynes did, as a 'numeraire', is not equivalent to asserting that wages or prices are constant. It means rather, that the theory in question has nothing to say about what determines the wage

> level; that the forces determining the wage level are forces abstracted from in the theory.[18]

That is, 'Keynes's formal theory ... has nothing to say about what determines the absolute price or wage level, though it does have some implications for the behaviour of prices relative to wages'.[19]

It will be recalled that wages were the major determinant of prices, because for Keynes:

> when there was no full-employment equilibrium, there was also no equilibrium nominal price level; something had to be brought in from outside to fix the price level; it might as well be institutional wage rigidity.[20]

Thus what Friedman regards as 'Keynes's critical assumption'[21] is to be seen as 'arbitrary' and having 'no theoretical underpinning' and that chapter 19 of the *General Theory* ('Changes in Money-Wages'),

> adds nothing important to the rest of the Keynesian apparatus; it rather illustrates how that apparatus can be applied to a particular problem and gives a basis for regarding rigid wages as not only an observable phenomenon but also a desirable policy.[22]

Friedman argues that the claimed desirability of rigid wages and prices in the *General Theory* is not based on a belief that flexible wages and prices must perforce be unstable in a free labour market under uncertainty; rather, that flexible wages and prices would in practice be highly unstable because of their 'role in bringing a highly unstable m.e.c. schedule and a highly elastic liquidity preference schedule into the relation which maintains investment at the full employment level'.[23]

The reason why Friedman attributes critical importance to the Keynesian assumption that the price level is an institutional datum, will now become clear. For, if prices are not flexible, then at a stroke: (i) the transmission mechanism implied by the classical quantity theory is denied and instead monetary effects on the economy can be channelled through a narrow range of market interest rates; (ii) these effects can be made nugatory by the absolute liquidity preference to which a rigid price level gives prominence.

Taking these in reverse order, Friedman argues that 'the importance attached to "absolute liquidity preference" or a high interest-elasticity of the demand for money ... can be regarded as a direct consequence of his assumption about the relative speed of adjustment of price and quantity'.[24] Also, Friedman quotes Keynes's proposition that 'the fact that contracts are fixed, and wages are usually somewhat stable, in terms of money unquestionably plays a large part in attracting to money so high a liquidity premium'.[25]

It is, however, on the question of the role of inflexible prices in denying the classical quantity theory that Friedman's ultimate purpose is revealed, for here the assumed relative speed of adjustment of price and quantity is opposite to that claimed by Keynes:

> The quantity theorists (including Keynes in *Monetary Reform*) found it natural to regard changes in the quantity of money as affecting prices in the first instance, and to regard the interest rate as determined by saving and investment or lending and borrowing. Monetary changes affected the interest rate by producing inflation (or deflation), which shifted the saving and investment functions by leading lenders to demand higher (or lower) nominal rates.[26]

Thus monetary changes affect only the nominal values of saving, investment and the rate of interest; a proposition which is very familiar from our previous discussion of the classical theory; as is the implied relationship between saving and investment and their role in determining the real rate of interest.

FRIEDMAN'S CLASSICAL ASSUMPTIONS

It has always been Friedman's contention that the origins of monetarism lay in his reformulation of the classical quantity theory as a theory of the demand for money; a reformulation (acknowledged to be) much influenced by Keynes's liquidity-preference theory. And in his reply to D. Patinkin's charge that his famous 'Restatement'[27] was merely an elaboration of Keynes without any substantive reference to the classical quantity theory, Friedman reveals his true allegiance to the classical transmission mechanism and, therefore, to the wider classical assumptions which are its concomitants:

> a final and decisive, piece of evidence against Patinkin's claim that my 'analytical framework is Keynesian'. For in this respect the

> treatment in my 'Restatement' and in my 'Theoretical Framework' (except where I am discussing the Keynesian theory) is the quantity theory treatment. I too pay no attention to 'the effects on the rate of interest' of shifts in the demand function for money. I too tend to minimise changes in market interest rates as the primary channel through which changes in the quantity of money affect spending, output and prices.[28]

What we are suggesting is that by his development of the classical quantity-theory transmission mechanism, under the influence of Keynes, in terms of a very wide range of own-rates, Friedman is also expressing sympathy for other vitally important aspects of classical theory which lie outside his immediate and explicit preoccupation with the stability of the demand for money and the money–income relation. In particular, he would affirm the classical belief in the long-run tendency of the economy towards full employment; a tendency that Keynes would categorically deny.

That this is, in fact, the case is confirmed by the following explicit statement:

> The long-run equilibrium in which, as I put it, 'all anticipations are realised' and that is determined by 'the earlier quantity theory plus the Walrasian equations of general equilibrium' is not a state that is assumed ever to be attained in practice. It is a logical construct that defines *the norm or trend from which the actual world is always deviating but to which it is tending to return or about which it tends to fluctuate*. The hypothesis that the logical construct does specify the norm or trend in this sense is entirely compatible with the existence of uncertainty, just as the hypothesis that $s = \frac{1}{2}gt^2$ specifies the law of falling bodies is entirely compatible with the existence of air.[29]

In other words, Friedman's view is entirely in accord with the classical assumption that the economy will unaided tend towards equilibrium at full employment.[30] This, taken together with his postulated stability of the demand for money and a transmission mechanism which relates monetary change to income change through a prior effect on a wide range of existing assets and prices/interest rates, suggests that the counter-revolution in monetary theory consists of a careful, empirically testable, restatement of Say's Equality via the 'direct mechanism' of the quantity theory.[31] But it is not the specific antecedents of Friedman's monetary theory[32] that concern us here but rather the implications for his attack on Keynes of his classical assumptions.

KEYNES IN MANAGEABLE TERMS

Friedman makes Keynes's denial of the classical quantity theory, together with the associated relationship between saving, investment and the rate of interest, to depend on his crucial assumption regarding the rigidity of prices, which in turn leads to the liquidity trap and the instability of the demand for money as the typical case. By claiming that the counter-revolution was based on a restatement of the quantity theory as a theory of the demand for money, Friedman was able to reduce Keynes's revolutionary hypothesis to the simple empirical question of the stability of the demand for money and the money–income relation. By adducing evidence of such stability Friedman was thus able to defeat the Keynesian challenge and by the same token reinstate classical economics.

On this view, therefore, whatever refinements Keynes may have made to previously existing monetary theory, his major contribution actually boils down to an analysis of the possible consequences of the observation that in modern economies money wages and prices are rigid or adjust more slowly than quantities; together with the claim that this observation and analysis explains persistent unemployment and provides the basis for an underemployment equilibrium.

But if on this view rigid wages and prices produce Keynesian economics, flexible prices betoken the quantity-theory transmission mechanism and we are back in a world of Say's Law, of saving giving rise to investment and of the rate of interest determined by productivity and thrift.

By concentrating attention on the question of the rigidity of wages and prices and the instability of the demand for money as an attack on the classical quantity theory, Friedman was able to sidestep the issue of Says Law, the unstated assumption which Keynes believed underlay neo-classical economics. Instead, he preferred to 'regard the saving–investment sector as unfinished business';[33] and his restated version of the quantity theory obscured the issue with its wide-ranging transmission mechanism based on a multiplicity of (flexible) prices and interest rates, covering both consumer and producer goods.

A REPLY TO FRIEDMAN

(a) Investment and saving

But in Keynes's view the relationship between investment and saving was of fundamental importance and constituted a touchstone of his ultimate beliefs about the way in which the economy worked. Saving was only a creature of investment, while investment itself played the key role in the theory of effective demand which was Keynes's answer to Say's Law. For it was, of course, Say's Law that chiefly occupied Keynes's thoughts, and not the classical quantity theory, which was destroyed only incidentally in the process of defeating Say's Law.

(b) Say's Law

It was this preoccupation with Say's Law, dealt with by following through the causal sequence of the classical economics, which explains why Keynes introduced liquidity preference and the quantity of money so late on in the *General Theory*. It also nullifies Friedman's attempt to use this point to argue that Keynes regarded monetary policy as of little importance.[34] It is simply that there was the prior and more fundamental question of Say's Law and the investment–saving relationship to be resolved first.

(c) Monetary policy

And here we should be clear that Keynes did not believe monetary policy to be useless, but only that the causal nexus through which monetary change influenced the economy was so much less direct than that postulated by the quantity theory that monetary policy was too imprecise for use as a principal tool of economic management; and, indeed, that its inexpert use could have a deleterious effect on expectations. It was for this reason that Keynes envisaged a direct role for the state in organising investment.

(d) Velocity

On the other hand, there is no basis for the belief that in normal conditions Keynes's demand for money is wildly unstable, as Keynes's own account of the model of adjustment to an exogenous change in the money stock which accrues as someone's income, makes clear.[35] Rather, the establishment of such a belief among those opposed to Keynes owes much to Friedman's careful preparation of the ground for his counter-revolution. H. G. Johnson has argued:

> A stable demand function for money is by no means inconsistent with the Keynesian macro-economic general equilibrium model and indeed is presumed to exist in the construction of the standard *IS–LM* diagram. But the empirical finding of the existence of the function has been widely adduced in support of the quantity theory as against the rival Keynesian theory, a procedure justified only by the identification of the Keynesian orthodoxy with the proposition that money does not matter and that velocity is *either* highly unstable *or* infinitely interest elastic.[36]

It is only in the 'liquidity trap' case of absolute liquidity preference that velocity will adapt passively to changes in the quantity of money. It is this case which Friedman generalises for his instability charge – a charge which raises questions about the meaning of the term 'instability'. It is clear from the above quotation that Johnson distinguishes 'instability' from the mere technical movement of velocity inherent in the unique 'liquidity trap' case. The term is often used loosely, even by Keynes himself, simply to denote variability. Professor Laidler has described as instability the variability of the demand for money which results from changing expectations of future interest rates – in as much as changes in the value of what is regarded as the *normal* level of the rate of interest will bring about changes in the demand for money at any particular level of the market rate.[37] Because, that is, the demand for money changes on account of variables which are not directly observable, the difficulty of predicting the effects of monetary policy is due to the 'instability' of the demand for money.

This is certainly a problem for econometricians and policy-makers, but for present purposes the important point is that variability is not due to 'irrational' behaviour. Demand changes on account of changes in long-period expectations as well as endogenous variables, and for Keynes there is no reason to believe that long-period expectations will allow the *market* rate to fall to the full-employment level. The breakdown in the 1970s of the previously observed short-run stability of the demand for money is entirely compatible with Keynes's view.

(e) Liquidity trap: I

In assessing the relevance of the liquidity trap itself we should distinguish between two cases: the general case, and the special case.

In the more general case, Keynes would accept that discretionary monetary policy would have a discernible but difficult-to-predict effect on output and employment in an otherwise unmanaged underemployment economy. The important question, however, would be whether the authorities could, by pursuing a policy of monetary expansion *à outrance*, push the economy to full employment by driving down the rate of interest.

It is here that the question of market expectations as to the 'appropriateness' of any given level of interest rates becomes relevant (the rate of interest, we recall, being a 'highly conventional' phenomenon); in that the market may refuse to acquiesce in the consequences of any monetary policy which it deems inappropriate in any given set of economic circumstances influencing market conditions. The range within which the actual market rate will move will be determined by the state of long-period expectations. If monetary policy attempts to force the market rate below the limit of the range, market opinion will view the falling rate as increasingly unsafe so that liquidity preference will increase.[38] Moreover, though market expectations may be judiciously manipulated so as to make monetary policy more effective, the market will resist officially inspired adventures. Keynes would appear to envisage the need for the market's acceptance of the viability of the underlying economic policy, if success is to be achieved.[39]

On this view, the failure of Dr Dalton's ultra-cheap money experiment during the period 1945–7, which Friedman cited as evidence against Keynes, does in fact support Keynes's as well as Friedman's case, in that both market expectations and money supply elements play a part. Recall that Dalton attempted to 'talk down' the long-term rate of interest by a progressive policy of refinancing government debt at lower rates so as to condition the market 'psychologically' to the acceptance of a long-term rate of 2.5 per cent – without the inflationary effects of an undue rise in bank credit.

But while the effect of expectations is explicit – manifested in the adverse statements of the clearing-bank chairmen – the influence of monetary change is less certain and depends on the view taken of 'the slower rate of growth of bank deposits after 1946'.[40]

We should also notice that in citing the Great Contraction in the USA, 1929–33, as the event which convinced Keynes that monetary policy was ineffective, Friedman is in fact giving an illustration of the powerful *contractionary* effect of a *restrictive* monetary policy; which is not at all the same thing as saying that an *expansionary* monetary policy would have commensurately powerful effects in *increasing* output and employment. For Friedman's own argument is that the 'Great Depression ... was widely interpreted as demonstrating that monetary policy was ineffective, *at least against a decline in business*'.[41]

In addition, the fact that 'the monetary authorities proclaimed that they were pursuing easy money policies when in fact they were not',[42] is beside the point and says nothing about the effectiveness of a counter-depression monetary policy.

(f) Liquidity trap: II

The second case involving the liquidity trap is Keynes's special case of a capital-rich economy in which the marginal efficiency of capital is falling faster than the long-term rate of interest so that investment fades away. We have already examined at some length the reasons for the stiffening of resistance to successive falls of the rate of interest when it has already fallen to an historically low level; again it is chiefly market expectations as to the appropriate level for the long-term rate which will, in Keynes's view, defeat monetary policy.

(g) Transmission mechanism

Notice that it is the long-term market rate which is relevant for Keynes. Although he envisaged a wide spectrum of own-rates of interest, Keynes singled out the own-rate on money because, as the rate appropriate to financing decisions, it was affected by the high liquidity premium on money – hence the attention directed to the long-term market rate as the rate *relevant to the finance of investment*. Consequently, the narrowness of his transmission mechanism compared with that of the quantity theory was not the result of a deliberate attempt by Keynes to create a convenient 'choke point' in his desire to establish the conditions for underemployment equilibrium; but was simply a reflection of his attempt to isolate the factors which entered into the determination of his key variable – the rate of investment.

(h) Price flexibility

It follows, therefore, that acceptance of the monetarist assumption that prices are flexible upwards would not in itself imply acceptance of the classical model; for the relevant transmission mechanism would still be that which emphasises the rates appropriate to the investment decision. For Keynes, the relative speed of adjustment of prices and output would depend on the level of employment, with the tendency for prices to rise as the result of a change in the quantity of money, increasing with the level of employment.

Overall, therefore, and given his preoccupation with a transmission mechanism relevant to the determination of the rate of investment, Keynes does offer a clearly defined route by which monetary change will have its effect on the economy. But Keynes's attack on the quantity theory is predicated on his belief that in classical economics monetary theory is essentially a theory of the absolute price level, with output and employment determined independently by real forces. Keynes's causal nexus argues both that monetary change can have 'real' effects, and that due to the nature of a monetary economy the extent of such effects is uncertain. That is, except at full employment monetary theory is no longer unequivocally a theory of the price level, and in underemployment states the outcome of monetary change is unclear.[43]

Because of his concentration on the need to deny the quantity theory as a theory *only of prices in a classical full employment economy*, Keynes did not deal at length with the question of the precise relationship between money and prices in an underemployment economy. It was Friedman's valuable contribution to investigate empirically the effects of monetary change; though until his adaptation of the Phillips curve in an expectations-augmented form, the best he could offer was an empirical proposition relating monetary change to changes in nominal income.

IN CONCLUSION

To sum up, the final objective of the counter-revolution was not *only* a wholly useful and commendable attempt to direct attention to the monetary analysis which 'Keynesian' economics neglected; but was also intended to foist upon Keynes a basically classical model hamstrung by 'real world' constraints which could then be refuted empirically.

But, as we have seen, Keynes envisaged no long-run tendency for the economy to move towards full employment. It is not simply that the 'air' in Friedman's analogy of the law of falling bodies prevents the falling apple from reaching the ground in the manner prescribed by the formula. It is, rather, that the apple is subject to no such compulsion. Instead, Keynes's *laissez-faire* economy plunges on in shifting equilibrium with no more tendency to gravitate to equilibrium at full employment than at any other level of income.

17 Monetarism II: Monetarism, Keynes and the 'Keynesians'

INTRODUCTION

Though the real challenge to Keynes lay in the 'invisible' elements of Friedman's counter-revolution, the subsequent monetarist–Keynesian' debate has been conducted entirely in terms of the 'visible' elements, which are alternative formulations of empirical relationships that have their counterpart in the 'Keynesian' model.

A RESTATEMENT OF THE QUANTITY THEORY?

Indeed, the centrepiece of Friedman's model has been interpreted by some commentators as a generalisation of Keynes's liquidity-preference theory; as against Friedman's claim that its origins lie in pre-Keynesian monetary theory *via* the 'oral tradition' of the University of Chicago. The outcome of this particular debate is unclear – and is of secondary importance for present purposes – though the following provides guidance as to a possible conclusion.

First, though Friedman's work represents a *development* of a 'fundamentally Keynesian capital theoretic approach to monetary theory' and is, therefore, 'Keynesian', it is 'no more *Keynes*' model than Keynes' "Marshallian" theory of income determination is Marshall's theory'.[1]

Second, both Keynes's and Friedman's theories can be regarded as having a common root in the Cambridge cash-balances version of the quantity theory, of which they emphasise and develop different aspects: for Keynes a closer analysis of the motives for holding money; for Friedman, the demand for money as a 'particular application of the general theory of demand'.[2]

Third, the degree of influence of Keynes's own formulation on Friedman depends on the extent to which liquidity-preference theory can be interpreted as a distinct break with previous theory.[3]

But aside from the merely technical aspects of its construction, there is a deeper sense in which Friedman's theory is a development of the quantity theory, in that, as argued earlier, Friedman used the term 'quantity theory' as synonymous with classical economics, so that Friedman's monetarism, in its wider ramifications, is underpinned with classical assumptions. And while, in constructing his demand for money function and transmission mechanism, Friedman explicity recognises that his work 'has been strongly influenced by the Keynesian analysis of liquidity preference'[4] and incorporates the 'liquidity effect stressed by Keynes',[5] his intention is to produce a wide-ranging channel through which money will influence economic activity so as to retain the price-flexibility aspect of the quantity theory[6] – in contrast to Keynes's 'artificially restricted' transmission mechanism.

Finally, we might notice that the version of the quantity theory cited by Friedman as providing the rationale for monetary policy in pre-Keynesian times, is that of Irving Fisher. But Fisher's views cannot be regarded as typical. For, while 'Irving Fisher's empirical work on the relationship between money and prices ... is not far removed from modern monetarism', other earlier quantity theorists did not share Friedman's belief in the stability of the demand for money but, rather, 'spent much of their time contemplating the empirical possibility of autonomous shifts in velocity'.[7]

THEORETICAL AND EMPIRICAL CONCLUSIONS ON FRIEDMAN, KEYNES AND THE 'KEYNESIANS'

But despite its classical foundations, Friedman's monetarism contains several features which we should associate with Keynes; and the broad professional consensus which has developed in respect of some key monetary relationships is antipathetic to modern 'Keynesian' ideas rather than to the economics of the *General Theory*.

(a) Macroeconomic equilibrium

As to common features, both Keynesians and monetarists believe in the efficacy of aggregate (macroeconomic) analysis; a belief which is not shared by the Austrian school. Similarly, Friedman, like Keynes, recognises the existence of uncertainty; though in Friedman's case, while individual uncertainty is said to justify the holding of real-money balances,[8] its implicit inclusion in the model is not held to disqualify an assumption that the long-run tendency of the economy is towards equilibrium at full employment.[9] Consequently, while both Friedman and Keynes view the economy as being inherently stable, in the sense that it tends naturally towards or fluctuates about equilibrium, Keynes's theory of effective demand precludes any possibility that this equilibrium can relate to a unique (full-employment) level of output and employment.

Analytically this is the most important distinction between Keynesian and neo-classical economics, and for the monetarists implies a belief that the unimpeded working of the market economy will produce the optimal outcome.[10] It is also consistent with the (un-Keynesian) prescription of a monetary policy rule; for with employment tending to settle at the natural (full-employment) rate of unemployment, inflation can be avoided by allowing the money stock to grow in line with the underlying growth rate of real output.

(b) The causal nexus

When we turn to the transmission mechanism, we find that though monetarists are sensitive about the charge that, as against Keynes's formulation, they are held to believe in 'some mysterious "direct" influence of money on expenditure',[11] 'direct' and 'indirect' are precisely the terms used by Friedman to characterise the monetarist and Keynesian positions respectively.[12] Nevertheless, despite the monetarist stress on 'a much broader and more "direct" impact on spending', and notwithstanding the wider connotations of Friedman's approach, there is *in practice* 'no essential difference between it [the transmission mechanism of Friedman and his followers] and that analysed, for example, by [the Keynesian] James Tobin and his associates'.[13]

(c) The demand for money

Similar conclusions follow with respect to the demand for money; for notwithstanding the elaborate original specification of Friedman's function and his inability to discover any significant influence of the rate of interest, empirical studies of the demand for money, both by monetarists and Keynesians, have typically and simply been cast in terms of alternative measures of money and income and market interest rates. It is, moreover, now generally accepted that the demand for money is interest-elastic.

Furthermore, in seeking to distinguish Friedman's work from that of Keynes, commentators have pointed to Friedman's inclusion of inflation as an own-rate of return on money: a relationship said to be explicitly denied by Keynes.[14] However, Friedman, in the course of justifying his own approach, has reminded us that Keynes, in his *Tract on Monetary Reform*, 1923, 'has an excellent and explicit discussion of inflation as a tax and of the effect of the tax on the quantity of real balances demanded'.[15] The point was not, of course, relevant at the time the *General Theory* was written.

(d) Deficit spending, money and inflation

There is, next, the question of the effect of different methods of financing government budget deficits. For the monetarists, inflation is always a monetary phenomenon, so that a budget deficit will only have a significant effect on inflation if it gives rise to an increase in the quantity of money.

This proposition is important on two counts. First, it can be used to explain how Keynes's followers were able to continue 'to regard prices and wages as an institutional datum and to neglect the effects of price flexibility'. Second, it serves to reconcile the apparent contradictions in criticisms made of post-war Keynesianism: namely, that on the one hand 'Keynesians' are claimed to argue that 'money doesn't matter' and to advocate instead an active budgetary policy; while on the other hand are held responsible for creating inflation – at the same time as inflation is said to be everywhere a monetary phenomenon.

A reconciliation can be effected by arguing that 'Keynesians' restrict their analysis to the 'first-round effect of a budget deficit financed by creating money and neglect the cumulative effect'. The principle can be explained in terms of an *IS–LM* model.

For example,[16] a budget deficit created, say, for one year to expand income will cause the *IS* curve to shift to the right and then back again as real and nominal incomes rise for the set period and then fall again. This is the first-round effect. If, however, the deficit is financed by new money, the *LM* curve will also shift to the right and will remain at its new position *after* the *IS* curve has shifted back, on account of the permanently higher money stock. Consequently, even if real income falls back to its initial level, *nominal* income will continue at the new higher level, due to the effect of the increase in the quantity of money on the price level. This is the cumulative effect. Its neglect by 'Keynesians' led to an emphasis on wages as the determinant of prices and the advocacy of incomes policy as the way to control inflation.

But this is not all. Monetarist analysis puts 'Keynesian' deficit spenders on the horns of a dilemma. If, to avoid the inflationary effects of a change in the money stock, the government deficit is financed by borrowing from the non-bank public, the excess demand for money will raise interest rates and so 'crowd out' private-sector investment expenditure.

It can, of course, be argued that it is important to 'distinguish cases in which real output is supply constrained from those in which it is merely money constrained'.[17] For present purposes, we need only note that Keynes analysed the question of finance in some detail (as we saw in Chapters 9 and 10), in terms partially similar to Friedman.[18] In particular, he was clear that a deficit (or any form of increased expenditure) financed from the existing money stock would cause interest rates to rise and a transfer of funds from idle to active balances, so that velocity would rise to accommodate the increased spending.

However, Keynes also dealt specifically with the case of the government 'printing money where-with to meet its current expenditure'. The new money accrues as income, but because only a fraction will be required to finance transactions, the balance will spill over into the purchase of:

> securities or other assets until r has fallen so as to bring about an increase in the magnitude of M_2 and at the same time to stimulate a rise in Y to such an extent that the new money is absorbed either in M_2 or in the M_1 which corresponds to the rise in Y caused by a fall in r.[19]

Thus Keynes, as against the 'Keynesians', does acknowledge possible cumulative effects as emphasised by Friedman. But although the monetary effects of a budget deficit can be the same for Keynes and Friedman, Friedman's more 'direct' mechanism would predict an earlier and more certain effect on prices of a change in the quantity of money than would be the case for Keynes.

(e) Empirical evidence

The picture is the same when we turn to areas in which there is now a broad professional consensus on empirical grounds. For example:

> the demand for money does seem to be more stable over time than the early critics of monetarism suggested, while shifts in it have been neither new phenomena, nor of sufficient magnitude seriously to undermine long-run relationships between money and income.[20]

They do, however, cast doubt on the wisdom of restricting monetary policy to the observance of monetary rules, when shifts in the demand for money due to institutional change would indicate the need to retain some discretion.

In addition, these results and the 'evidence for the existence of a causative relationship that has run primarily from money to money income rather than vice versa',[21] would indicate a greater degree of divergence between monetarists and 'Keynesians' than between monetarists and Keynes.

For Keynes, as for the monetarists, causality ran from money to income – though for Keynes in the conditions of the 1930s there was clearly a greater concern with changes in output rather than prices. Money enters the system either via the operation of the gold standard, or as a policy variable, via official open-market operations; while shifts in velocity occur due to perfectly 'rational' changes in expectations.

This is to be contrasted with an extreme 'Keynesian' viewpoint such as that expressed by N. Kaldor,[22] whereby changes in the quantity of money are endogenously determined; and velocity varies to offset any exogenous change in the quantity of money, through the activities of non-bank financial intermediaries.

Here the reverse causality implied by the first proposition can be explained historically as belonging to the era of fixed exchange rates (1945–72) and the relative openness of the British economy. Similarly, the second proposition derives from British experience prior to the Competition and Credit Control reforms of 1971, when key interest rates were administered, and the growth of disintermediation to satisfy the demands of borrowers unsatisfied through officially controlled sources of lending, was thereby encouraged. Once interest rates are market determined, an equilibrium price for credit will be established and the incentives for disintermediation decline.

In the same vein, the monetarist finding that *ceteris paribus* there is overwhelming evidence that inflation varies directly with the level of aggregate demand,[23] only becomes remarkable when set beside the extreme 'Keynesian' claim that inflation is always a cost-push phenomenon. Conversely such a finding is quite in accord with Keynes's own explanation of changes in the absolute price level; an explanation examined in Chapters 8 and 22.

18 Monetarism III: Rational Expectations

Having replied at some length to the criticisms of Keynes, both explicit and implicit, contained in the monetarist counter-revolution, we can now look for further support for Keynes in the weaknesses of the monetarist position itself.

MONETARISM, SMALL AND BIG

There are two constituents of 'visible' monetarism. The first is 'small' monetarism, which covers the purely technical or scientific elements and is politically neutral. Its positive contribution has been to stimulate serious work on the effects of money on the economy during the period of the 'Keynesian' hegemony. The empirical propositions of which it consists are not necessarily hostile to Keynes; though the grounds upon which its advocacy of a monetary policy rule is based, would be.

The second constituent is 'big' monetarism, which has wider economic, social and political concerns. It favours individual freedom of choice and small government, and is based on a belief in the benign working of market processes. Though essentially hostile to Keynes it has weak theoretical and empirical underpinnings. 'Big' monetarism is of interest here because its advocacy of the defeat of inflation as a principal goal of government economic policy finds no support in the theoretical analysis of the economic effects of inflation produced by 'small' monetarism. Furthermore, this tension between 'big' and 'small' monetarism has been exacerbated by important theoretical developments intended to overcome the technical inadequacies of 'small' monetarism.

MONETARISM TRANSFORMED AND RESCUED

The inadequacies of monetarism were pointed out a decade-and-a-half ago by H. G. Johnson.[1] Johnson predicted that the monetarist challenge would 'peter out', for two reasons: first, because the economic problem with which monetarism felt itself best equipped to deal – inflation – would never be accorded the same priority as the Keynesians' unemployment; second, because of deficiencies in its analytical apparatus, as exemplified by its failure to specify the price–output response of the economy to monetary change, and its reliance on the 'black-box' methodology of positive economics. Because of these deficiencies, monetarism would lose its identity through inevitable synthesis with Keynesian economics.

Johnson's prediction failed on both counts. The events of the 1970s gave the ascendancy to inflation in popular and professional opinion and brought to power a government whose main economic priority was the defeat of inflation. Also, in terms of its analytical apparatus, monetarism has been rescued from the doldrums by the development of the rational-expectations hypothesis, which has enabled the deficiencies noted by Johnson to be bypassed. At the same time, however, the advent of rational expectations has for monetarists widened still further the discrepancy between the analytical and policy significance accorded to inflation.

To explain why this is so, we begin with the Phillips curve, which for 'Keynesians' seemed to provide evidence of a stable functional relationship between inflation and unemployment. To monetarists, however, the very notion of such a trade-off was implausible; their classical assumptions instead leading them to believe that 'the system tends in and of itself to operate at or near "full employment", regardless of the inflation rate, if policy makers do not upset matters'.[2] Consequently, it was only when the Phillips relationship was modified to allow for a distinction between real and monetary magnitudes – its expectations-augmented form – that it was able to illustrate the monetarist case. In this form it provided Friedman with his 'missing equation' relating output and price responses to a change in the quantity of money, and rendered money as a long-run theory of the price level.

As to the crucial question of the theory behind the curve, Friedman originally pursued the idea that excess supply or demand in the labour market would exert downward or upward pressure on the *real* wage so as to restore equilibrium. Consequently, workers would seek to make adjustments to the *money* wage in the light of movements in the general price level. In other words, workers would be motivated to adjust the price of their labour in response to 'quantity signals' (unemployment!).

Later, however, Friedman adopted the much more radical approach now dominant among monetarists, of interpreting the expectations-augmented Phillips curve as an *aggregate supply curve*, whereby workers freely adjust labour supplied in response to changes in the price level, and so make changes in output and employment a supply response to inflation.

Consequently, if expectations are fulfilled, employment and the real wage will be at the natural, equilibrium ('full employment'), level; while deviations away from equilibrium will be due to the non-fulfilment of expectations. Since workers will be motivated to maximise utility, failure to achieve equilibrium must be due to a failure of information upon which expectations are formed: that is, due to random 'shocks'.

THE RATIONAL-EXPECTATIONS HYPOTHESIS

The view that, subject to random and unpredictable shocks to the system, output and employment levels obtaining will represent the outcome of voluntary choices made by individuals on the basis of available information, is one part of the rational-expectations hypothesis.[3] The distinctive and crucial twist, however, is that in making their choices individuals will form their expectations 'rationally', as '(statistically) optimal predictions based on the available information'. This implies that they 'will not make continuous and systematic errors in forming their expectations of inflation, as the adaptive expectations hypothesis implies'.[4]

Therefore, on one, innocuous, interpretation, the rational-expectations hypothesis performs the useful function of directing attention to the question of how individuals form their expectations, and makes the wholly reasonable assertion that they will be motivated to equate the marginal returns of expected outcomes with the marginal costs of obtaining information. On this view, the hypothesis is only remarkable when set beside the alternative, adaptive-expectations, approach, and simply asserts that by learning from their experiences individuals will choose among alternative learning rules and discard those which systematically lead them into error and real losses of utility.

On this interpretation, rational expectations poses no threat to Keynes, in whose vision firms and individuals – whether in the money market, capital market or labour market – will act rationally to optimise their respective positions.

RATIONAL BEHAVIOUR AND THE STOCK EXCHANGE: TWO VIEWS?

L. M. Lachmann has described the Stock Exchange as a market in 'continuous futures', which has consequently:

> always been regarded by economists as the central market of the economic system and a most valuable economic barometer, a market, that is, which in its relative valuation of the various yield streams reflects, in a suitably 'objectified' form, the articulate expectations of all those who wish to express them. All this may sound rather platitudinous and might hardly be worth mentioning were it not for the fact that it differs from the Keynesian theory of the Stock Exchange which is now so much *en vogue*.[5]

That the interpretation of Keynes's view of the Stock Exchange is a matter of the profoundest importance, is illustrated by B. Kantor, who, in his attempt to draw out the positive and beneficial implications of the rational-expectations approach, states that 'Keynes's fundamental attack on classical economics was directed at the supposed irrationality of stock markets and so investment decisions'.[6]

But we must be careful, for as we saw in Chapter 14 Keynes was concerned that the existence of a secondary, resale, market for securities allowed prices to fluctuate in the short run for reasons wholly unrelated to the ultimate viability of the investment project which originally gave rise to the securities; and that these short-run fluctuations could have a deleterious effect on the outlook of potential investors in new capital equipment.

In this regard, operators on the Stock Exchange would be acting irrationally if, on detecting a developing mood of pessimism in the market (based upon whatever grounds), they did *not* make their positions consistent with a fall in security prices. This would be so even though their expectations of the ultimate outcome of the project were of the soundest; though in the more likely case their portfolio itself would be chosen not on this basis but on grounds of expected short-term price fluctuations. Or as Lachmann himself argues, in words strangely reminiscent of Keynes:

> while the future will always remain uncertain, it is possible for the individual *to acquire knowledge about other people's expectations and to adjust his own accordingly.*[7]

Thus, for Lachmann, expectations are reconciled and made consistent by trading in futures markets; such trading being a stabilising influence on the market. But this does not, of course, answer Keynes's point, which is based on the distinction between long-term and short-term considerations. G. L. S. Shackle has argued:

> Futures markets? They can reconcile, just conceivably, our present ideas, based on our present knowledge. What of tomorrow's new knowledge, destroying the old or rendering it obsolete, what of tomorrow's choices and decisions, tomorrow's discoveries, tomorrow's inventions, work of imagination, tomorrow's output from the Cosmic Computer which may, after all, not be a computer but an ERNIE?[8]

For Keynes, as well as Lachmann, a (short-term) market view is formed by individuals adjusting their expectations to the expectations of others:

> Knowing that our own individual judgement is worthless, we endeavour to fall back on the judgement of the rest of the world which is perhaps better informed. That is, we endeavour to conform with the behaviour of the majority or the average. The psychology of a society of individuals each of whom is endeavouring to copy the others leads to what we may strictly term a *conventional* judgement.[9]

A view so formed can be subject to fluctuations due to accessions of optimism and pessimism, and though such behaviour is influenced by 'vague panic fears and equally vague and unreasoned hopes',[10] it is nevertheless 'rational' if it is based on, and follows from, all available information relevant to individual market operators seeking to forecast short-term movements in securities prices, including information about the expectations of other operators.

RATIONAL EXPECTATIONS, RISK AND UNCERTAINTY

That expectations in such markets are rational has been established by reference to tests of the efficient-markets hypothesis. The efficient use of information in markets produces efficient prices, which are 'equilibrium prices conditional on all information available when prices are established'. If prices are efficient, price changes should be random, since ruling prices will have been formed on the basis of all relevant information, and price changes will flow only from new information. Evidence in support of the hypothesis is claimed to be very strong.[11]

However, simply to establish that behaviour is 'rational' in this sense is not at the same time necessarily to give the conclusion empirical content. For, as Lucas has argued:

> Without some way of inferring what an agent's subjective view of the future is, this hypothesis is of no help in understanding his behaviour. Even psychotic behaviour can be (and today is) understood as 'rational', given a sufficiently abnormal view of relevant probabilities.[12]

Indeed, rational expectations assumes the coincidence of subjective and true probabilities, and given the importance for Keynes of the distinction between uncertainty and risk, the direct challenge of rational expectations to Keynes's main thesis fades away once it is acknowledged that the hypothesis does not apply in situations that F. H. Knight called 'uncertainty'; situations, that is, in which it is not possible to guess which, if any, observable frequencies are relevant. In other words, though expectations theory can hypothesise about the way in which we may arrive at decisions concerning the future, it cannot make the future *knowable*; for as Shackle has so graphically expressed it, 'time-to-come is the void, waiting to be filled by enterprise, by action which manifests originative acts of mind. *Expectation* names almost the whole business of pragmatic thought.'[13]

Lucas himself suggests that the rational-expectations approach will be most useful:

> in situations in which the probabilities of interest concern a fairly well-defined recurrent event, situations of risk in Knight's termi-

nology. In situations of risk, the hypothesis of rational behaviour on the part of agents will have usable content, so that behaviour may be explainable in terms of economic theory. In such situations, expectations are rational in Muth's sense. *In cases of uncertainty, economic reasoning will be of no value.*[14]

RATIONAL EXPECTATIONS AND THE LABOUR MARKET

The case in which the rational-expectations approach truly opposes Keynes is in its application to the labour market, in which, as we have seen, it reinforces the aggregate-supply-curve interpretation of the expectations-augmented Phillips curve. We shall pass over the attempts of the rational-expectations monetarists to account for the fact that the labour market is notoriously a quantity-adjusting rather than a price-adjusting market, in terms, for example, of the voluntary inter-temporal substitution by workers of work and leisure over the business cycle.[15]

Instead we shall direct attention to the basic assumption from which such attempted explanations begin, which is to proceed 'as if' the labour market, like the securities market, clears continuously and only departs from market-clearing equilibrium because of random and unpredictable shocks. That is, that the bargaining behaviour of workers and unions is such as to ensure that wages and prices will adjust 'as if' the labour market is governed by a Walrasian-style apparatus; so that, for example, wages will always be reduced to offset an excess supply of labour and restore (voluntary) full-employment equilibrium.

The notion that workers can create employment by adjusting money wages relative to the price level is quite contrary to Keynes's view.[16] Nor is the Keynesian reassured by Laidler's suggestion that the labour market should be treated as a Hicksian 'fixprice' market, so that 'the interaction of inflation and unemployment is best analysed on the premise that the Phillips curve represents the disequilibrium response of prices to a mismatching of supply and demand';[17] for the implication is that if prices were somehow made flexible (a one-time Hayekian strategy: see below, Chapter 20), the system would adjust to equilibrium at full employment.

This is, of course, a very classical idea and rational-expectations monetarists are aptly known as new-classical school. In their basic model we 'begin' in the labour market with the determination of employment and the real wage; find the level of output by reference to the production function; and introduce the quantity of money to determine the absolute price level and the money wage. The system is again dichotomised between real and monetary sectors.

Under rational expectations there is no longer a short-run trade-off between unemployment and inflation such as could be exploited by policy-makers under adaptive expectations; and monetary policy can make an impact on employment and output only by being applied in a random and unpredictable fashion. Because the system can be in equilibrium at any level of absolute prices, and inflation is irrelevant to output and employment, money is 'super-neutral', and we are, in effect, back in the world of Say's Identity, the strictest version of the classical quantity theory.

RATIONAL EXPECTATIONS AND THE MONETARIST VIEW OF INFLATION

While the rational-expectations hypothesis has given new life to the monetarist counter-revolution and enabled it to survive the pitfalls forecast by Johnson, it has at the same time accentuated a contradiction which was always present in the monetarist case:

> There has always been tension between ideological monetarism, which promises to rescue us from inflation, and theoretical monetarism, which says that inflation has little or no effect on the real performance of the economy. The tension is accentuated in monetarism mark II, which relies heavily on the neutrality of money, even on super neutrality, and applies the 'classical dichotomy' to continuously moving equilibrium.[18]

The way in which inflation will affect the economy under monetarist assumptions will depend on whether it is anticipated or unanticipated. In neither case does monetarist theory justify giving priority to inflation as a goal of macroeconomic policy; though perhaps we should add that on monetarist assumptions there is relatively little else to which policy might give priority.

If inflation is fully anticipated, nominal contracts such as wage rates, interest rates and government taxes will incorporate the expected (equals actual) rate of inflation. Here inflation has two effects, both minor.

The first is known as the 'shoe-leather' effect because it involves people making more frequent trips to the bank. Because inflation raises nominal interest rates it also increases the cost of holding non-interest-bearing forms of money, such as currency and current-account deposits. To economise on these holdings people will visit the bank more often to cash more but smaller cheques. The second effect is the 'menu cost' of inflation, so-called because of the need frequently to revise advertised prices. The shoe-leather cost is the more theoretically significant effect of inflation but it is empirically small.[19] For rational-expectations monetarists concerned with policy, however, it must assume a disproportionate importance, as, for example, Hahn has noted.[20]

It is where inflation is *unanticipated* that on some monetarist views it can have 'real' effects.

For the rational-expectations school, of course, transitory deviations of employment and output from their natural levels can only occur if the monetary authorities are prepared to vary money and prices in a random and unpredictable manner; an unlikely occurrence. However, monetarists who choose not to follow the rational-expectations path will to a degree avoid thereby the theory/policy conflict over inflation. But by the same token they will deprive themselves of its relatively strong methodology and so be left with models which are weaker theoretically. For example, Higham and Tomlinson have drawn attention to the uncertain basis for Friedman's assertion that inflation can have real effects – and in particular that high inflation will be associated with high unemployment.[21] This view is of particular importance because it has influenced the government in its designation of inflation as the primary economic problem.

On Friedman's view, inflation causes unemployment because as inflation rises it becomes more volatile. Increased volatility of inflation affects the economic system in two ways. The first is that because market arrangements adjust imperfectly to inflation they become subject to increased uncertainty. However, Friedman can only conclude that this 'may contribute to the recorded increase in unemployment'.[22] The second is that it causes the market pricing system to become a less efficient co-ordinator of economic activity, because changes in the absolute price level are mistaken for changes in the relative prices which guide behaviour. Again, however, Friedman is only able to assert that 'it seems plausible that the average level of unemployment would be raised by the increased amount of noise in market signals, at least during the period when institutional arrangements are not yet adapted to the new situation'.[23] Finally, Friedman adds that high inflation may lead to the imposition of wage and price controls which will reduce economic efficiency and so cause unemployment.

Higham and Tomlinson extended Friedman's cross-country study but found 'no general support for the proposition that inflation and unemployment move in the same direction'.[24]

VIEWS OF INFLATION AND THE CONCEPT OF MONEY

However, our main point here is theoretical. The reason why monetarist theorists find it difficult to attribute to inflation the importance they instinctively feel it should deserve as a concern of economic policy, is to be found in their theoretical conception of money itself. This conception is shared by all modern mainstream monetary economists. Laidler and Rowe have pointed out that:

> In modern monetary theory, money, or more precisely 'real balances', is simply another durable good available to be held by the utility maximising individual or profit maximising firm. The tools of supply and demand analysis may be applied to it as to any other durable good.[25]

They argue that while the adoption of this approach has proved useful as the basis of empirical investigations into the workings of the monetary system over the last two decades or so, it provides a misleading guide to the 'social consequences of variations in the purchasing power of money'.

For it is from treating money as a private durable good that the 'shoe-leather' theory of the cost of inflation naturally flows. Similarly, though unanticipated changes in the price level will cause mistakes to be made about relative prices, it can still be assumed that markets will continue to clear, for nothing has happened to prevent individuals from exploiting all opportunities for 'mutually beneficial and consciously desired acts of exchange'. On this basis the notion of involuntary unemployment is meaningless.

However, by following an alternative approach to the concept of money, one that treats money not as a private good but as a public good, a social institution among a complex of social institutions, the treatment of changes in the value of money in mainstream monetary theory can be seen to be inadequate. For,

> if monetary theory is best approached along Austrian lines, then we must conclude that mainstream monetary theory, for all its considerable accomplishments, not only trivialises the social consequences of inflation in particular ... but that it grossly underestimates the destructiveness of monetary instability in general.[26]

It is to this alternative approach that we now turn.

19 The Austrians I: Tenets of the Faith

AUSTRIANS AND MONETARISTS

Superficially at least, the Austrians have much in common with the monetarists and the two schools are popularly regarded as being synonymous.

Both, for example, subscribe to the essential veracity of the quantity theory and regard inflation as a monetary phenomenon caused by a too rapid increase in the money supply. Similarly, because both schools regard the quantity of employment as being determined by real forces, it follows that for both any attempt to reduce unemployment below its equilibrium level by a policy of monetary expansion can lead only to inflation. In addition, both schools argue the merits of the free-market economy and provide analyses ascribing poor economic performance to the effects of state intervention.

There, however, the resemblance ends, except that the strengthening of theoretical monetarism in recent years, in particular in the development of the rational-expectations approach, owes much to Austrian influence. Otherwise, the differences are quite marked.

For example, in contrast to all other schools, the Austrian approach is *a priori* and deductive and eschews any reliance on quantitative functional relationships and statistical techniques of verification.[1] Macroeconomic aggregative concepts are regarded as meaningless and analysis is resolutely conducted at the microeconomic level.

Also, in place of the purposeful 'economy', Austrians substitute the essentially purposeless '*catallaxy*', which can be seen as producing the harmonious outcome of a multitude of individually determined goals through the process of free voluntary exchange. It is this notion which for Austrians replaces the timeless theoretical paradigm of the classical economics as the basis for theorising.

Most important of all, however, is that for Austrians money is not neutral. By contrast with the monetarists, Austrian *theory* allows monetary change to have real effects, in producing the trade cycle and causing inflation and unemployment. There is, therefore, no conflict, no tension, between Austrian theory and Austrian policy proposals.

Furthermore, the Austrians accord money not only technical functions but also a wider social role, in which trust in money as a social institution guarantees a stable value for the monetary commodity; while the confidence engendered by monetary stability helps to maximise the extent of voluntary exchange and therefore of economic welfare and individual freedom of choice. It follows that inflation, in producing changes in the value of money, will tend to restrict its use so that voluntary exchange and economic welfare decline and with them personal freedom.

For the Austrians, therefore, a policy of monetary stability is justified both on narrowly economic grounds and on the basis of their broader economic and social philosophy.

THE AUSTRIAN CHALLENGE TO KEYNES

Both because the Austrian approach has at its centre the notion of catallaxy, rather than the full-information, barter-type, theoretical construct which Keynes attacked as the invalid basis of the classical economics, and because it successfully integrates the technical functions of money (money as a private durable good) into a wider view of its economic and social role, it presents in some ways a more formidable challenge to Keynes than that posed by monetarism. It is nevertheless a challenge (we shall argue) that ultimately fails.

The Austrian attack on Keynes will be dealt with in two parts, divided along the lines indicated above. That is, we shall deal first with Hayek's charge that Keynesian policies, by leading to over-expansion of the money supply, produced inflation and unemployment. We shall deal second with the broader economic, social and political effects of inflation and, therefore, with the consequences of Keynes's alleged plan to use inflation as a way of increasing employment by way of deliberate deceit in the labour market.

As a preliminary we shall look more closely at the distinctive features of Austrian economics.

THE AUSTRIAN SCHOOL OF THOUGHT

The Austrian school of economics was founded in the late nineteenth century by Carl Menger, at the University of Vienna. Other members of interest for present purposes were E. von Böhm-Bawerk, who devised the Austrian theory of capital and interest; and L. von Mises for his own work on money, and as the teacher of the present leader of the school and doyen of Austrian economics, Professor F. A. von Hayek. We must also introduce at this juncture the nineteenth-century German sociologist Georg Simmel, whose work ran parallel to that of the Austrian school proper. Simmel's analysis of money as a social institution forms a basis for the second part of the Austrian attack on Keynes, dealt with below.

The origins of the school lay in the development of opposition to the established German historical school, which stressed the 'historical' or inductive approach to the study of economics. The main point of contention between the schools was one of methodology, with Menger emphasising the deductive approach, whereby economic theories are derived deductively fron axiomatic premises, in opposition to the established inductive approach rooted in economic history.

ECONOMY AND *CATALLAXY*

The methodological distinctiveness of the Austrian approach has endured. At the present day it is *sui generis* rejecting both the empirically based 'positive' economics, on the one hand, while at the same time avoiding the restrictive assumptions of Walrasian general equilibrium economics, on the other.

Instead, Austrians adopt what they see as a more realistic, disaggregative, approach in which all economic activity is undertaken by individual employers, producers, consumers, savers and investors. Also, because aggregative analysis relies on essentially artificial theoretical and empirical constructs to sustain a 'macroeconomic' view, Austrians have developed alternative concepts for organising and analysing ideas about economic phenomena.

Because the unit of analysis is now the *individual* consumer or producer, the perception of economic events and expectations is by nature subjective rather than objective. Consequently, it is not possible to comprehend economic activity as a macroeconomic entity ('the economy as a whole') with its attendant notions of macroeconomic goals which can be specified and achieved or not achieved.

This is because the concept of the *economy* is properly reserved for entities that have a perceivable purpose and objective which guides their behaviour, such as the firm. Separate parts of the firm are aware of the way in which their activities combine for a specified *purpose*, which is to organise factors of production in order to achieve output of a marketable good or service, with the explicit intention of achieving a specified *objective*, such as to maximise profits.

By contrast, this cannot be true taking all individual consumers and producers together. Rather, individuals come together in society voluntarily to take advantage of the opportunities which free association provides, through the process of exchange, for the achievement of individually determined ends and the reconciliation of divergent interests for mutual benefit. Consequently, the spontaneously created market order, or *catallaxy*,[2] is different from the economy in that it can have no common purpose beyond that of being an end in itself. It is, therefore, essentially without goals except as these pertain to the individual participants.

The idea of the market being guided or managed in the interests of all participants taken together is consequently a nonsense. It is, rather, an article of faith that the *catallaxy* will allow the production of a greater quantity of desired goods and services than would become available under any alternative system, though their distribution must *consequently* be the outcome of a process which is essentially a game of skill and chance.[3]

Because it has no aggregate objectives the *catallaxy* cannot be comprehended in aggregate terms, so that information regarding the whole cannot be known. Instead, the information required for the individual components to achieve their subjectively determined goals is only obtainable through the system of relative prices. That is, relative prices provide the only source of (empirical) information relevant to the activities of consumers and producers. Therefore, welfare will be maximised if prices are freely determined and correctly reflect states of supply and demand for factors, goods and services.

This analysis also has implications for the concept of 'equilibrium'. In the orthodox model, general equilibrium can be perceived to exist because all the information required to make plans consistent can be specified as inputs into the model. With given endowments and behavioural assumptions the outcome is logically determined and genuine freedom of choice is excluded.

On the Austrian view, however, equilibrium of the orthodox kind relates only to the individual participant and means only that his plans are realised. But there can be no objectively determined equilibrium for the *catallaxy* since it is subject to true uncertainty and allows for the exercise of genuine choice.

That is, because individual behaviour is guided by subjectively determined goals and a subjective perception of the costs involved, it is not possible to *know* whether an observed outcome is optimal by observing measurable prices and costs. The knowledge required to produce equilibrium is not therefore available to the central planner but is a function of the operation of the free market itself. Consequently, we may merely assume a *tendency towards* equilibrium and can assist in its achievement by allowing the competitive process to work unimpeded.[4]

This approach is clearly the antithesis of Keynesian economics, with its identification of 'macroeconomic problems' and the requirement of significant state intervention for their solution. For modern *macroeconomics*, of whatever persuasion, is essentially Keynes's creation, and the Austrian attack on Keynes begins with Keynes's implicit confusion of the *catallaxy* with an *economy* and therefore over the question of the possibility of identifying and achieving *macroeconomic* goals.

More particularly it depends on Keynes's belief that central government can identify macroeconomic goals and achieve them through its power to vary the quantity of money. For ignorance of traditional analysis led Keynes, against the accumulated wisdom of economic science but in agreement with a long line of recognised cranks, to advocate discretionary monetary policy as a way of stimulating output and employment.

20 The Austrians
II: Hayek and the Trade Cycle

INTRODUCTION

From the Austrian point of view, Keynesian policies provided temporary stimulation of output and employment, but the longer-term effects have been to produce serious inflation and unemployment. The only curious feature is that the predicted consequences were so long delayed. The only solution to the problem is a painful period of readjustment before full employment and stable prices can be achieved through the operation of free-market forces.

We associate this criticism of Keynes with F. A. Hayek, whose views suddenly came into prominence and fashion again in the 1970s after a long period of comparative neglect. It was a late call for a theory eclipsed by the Keynesian Revolution but recalled to life by the inability of the 'Keynesians' to explain the stagflation of the 1970s.

It is a criticism based upon Hayek's development of Böhm-Bawerkian capital theory, in conjunction with the Wicksell restatement of the quantity theory to produce a monetary theory of the trade cycle.

A MONETARY THEORY OF THE TRADE CYCLE

We have already been introduced to Böhm-Bawerk's theory (Chapter 11, above), which directly associates the degree of roundaboutness of production with the increase in productivity that results. Consequently, 'waiting' and reward are positively correlated and a change in consumer's time preferences will result in an increase in saving which will lower the rate of interest and stimulate investment.

Therefore, changes in the structure of production, between the proportions of factors devoted to the production of consumer goods and producer goods respectively, will come about quite naturally as indicated by a change in relative prices, as consumers' preferences shift between present and future consumption.

In Hayek's view, the events of the trade cycle are composed wholly of real phenomena but the cycle itself is caused by monetary factors. Money is seen as a 'loose joint' in the system and consequently a source of disturbance to otherwise well-ordered and articulated real activities.

The Austrian analysis of the way in which money can produce fluctuations in output and employment is of the 'loanable funds' kind (familar from earlier chapters), derived from Wicksell and based on the relationship between the natural and market rates of interest. Though monetary changes will bring about real changes in essentially the same way under free-market or state-induced conditions, the *duration* of the consequences can be different in as much as governments may persist with disruptive monetary policies long after natural restorative measures would have brought readjustment to equilibrium in a free economy. Thus the intervention of the government may cause commensurately greater disruption and the subsequent extent of the need for readjustment.

In the Austrian view, therefore, money is not neutral; monetary change will have real effects. It does this by changing relative prices and artificially inducing a change in the structure of production (the relative length of production periods), which is not justified by consumer time preferences and which cannot, therefore, be sustained. That is, because the rate of interest determines for investors the cost of borrowing, an increase in the quantity of money will reduce the cost of loans below the level given by the quantity of voluntary saving taken in conjunction with a given investment.

The increase in the quantity of money will come about as a result, for example, of banks seeking to expand their credit following an inflow of base (reserve asset) money, via the working of the international gold standard or government open-market operations. In turn, the availability of cheap credit will induce firms to invest so that the production period is lengthened and there is a change in the structure of production as between capital goods and consumption goods.

This change requires a movement of factors, and factors are induced to move by a change in relative prices, as rewards expand in capital goods production and decline in consumption goods production. Where unemployed resources exist, due perhaps to imperfect flexibility of market prices (for example, wages), the credit-induced expansion will take up the slack, as factors, including labour, are drawn into new projects.

However, the investment-led boom cannot last because there has been no change in consumers' time preferences, so that the increased investment is not 'justified'. There is, simultaneously, a shortage of saving to finance the increased investment and an excess of consumption goods expenditure relative to the supply of consumption goods available.[1] The appearance of excess demand in the consumption goods sector will cause prices to rise and the requisite saving will be forced out of consumers' incomes.

Relative prices now change in favour of consumption goods, and factors are attracted back to meet the increased demand for output, swollen by the expansion of incomes in the longer processes. But because factors are not perfectly malleable and substitutable this cannot be accomplished immediately and projects in the longer (more roundabout) processes have to be abandoned. Therefore, as relative prices fall in the longer processes there will follow a phase of contraction and unemployment as capital losses are incurred and workers laid off.[2]

Left to itself the free-market system will enter a period of slump until the readjustment of relative prices and the movement of factors between sectors allows a return to full employment. Because the problem was caused by an artificially induced, incorrect structure of relative prices and production periods, it can only be solved by a readjustment of *relative* prices and not by a change in the *absolute* price level. Hence, any attempt by government to reduce the unemployment by discretionary monetary policy will only lead to further dislocation, inflation and unemployment.[3]

Moreover, as expectations begin to take account of inflation, monetary expansion will be required on an increasing scale as inflation must accelerate to maintain any given level of employment. It follows that any slow-down of monetary expansion, as part of an attempt to restore stability, must of necessity involve the loss of inflation-dependent jobs.

WAS KEYNES LED TO ADVOCATE INFLATIONARY POLICIES BY A CRUCIAL DEFECT IN HIS THEORY?

According to Hayek, the economic consequences of Keynesian policies over the relevant period simply reflect the above sequence of events on a massive scale. These consequences were entirely foreseeable on the basis of established pre-Keynesian analysis, and the only remaining query is why the boom lasted so long.

Hayek recognises that the 'Keynesian' policies which brought about the disastrous events of the 1970s were designed and promoted by Keynes's disciples and could perhaps be more accurately referred to as 'Kaldorian' economics.[4] Also, that Keynes himself was acutely aware of the dangers of inflation and would have been in the forefront of the efforts to contain it, for Keynes had believed that he would be able to exert a suitably moderating influence on the expansionist tendencies of his followers but was unfortunately prevented from doing so by early death.

Notwithstanding these qualifications to his argument, Hayek believes that the inspiration came from Keynes since inflationist conclusions could validly be drawn from his analysis; and it is, therefore, Keynes who must bear the ultimate responsibility for giving respectability to ideas which had previously been in discredit.[5] In fact, Hayek would see Keynes as a modern John Law, another financial genius with an excessively and dangerously optimistic belief in the wealth-creating powers of monetary policy, who has become the archetypal inflationist of liberal mythology.[6]

The reason why Keynes was led to advocate inherently inflationary policies was, in Hayek's view, because his theory contained a crucial error. This was his belief that the demand for investment is always positively correlated with and depends upon the demand for consumption goods. This belief carried the implication that because of the important role that investment played in Keynes's scheme, a deficiency of investment could always be made good by stimulating consumption demand.

This alleged defect in Keynes's argument is interesting both in its origin and its implications. It is Hayek's contention that Keynes was led into error by his ignorance of economic theory in general and Austrian capital theory in particular.[7] This caused him to overlook the possibility of investment being stimulated by other influences, including a rise in the relative price of labour (the need to substitute a cheaper factor), or a reduction in the market price of the product (the need to reduce costs). Instead he singled out consumption demand as the principal determinant. This had two implications.

First, it was this notion that was to put into the hands of government the justification for pursuing politically popular expansionary policies, which would bring short-term benefits at the expense of damaging longer-term consequences.

Second, these consequences, which are explained by the analysis outlined above, were made even more widespread and diffuse in as much as the monetary stimulus was being applied to the wide consumption goods sector rather than being confined to the more readily identifiable route through the capital market.[8]

KEYNESIAN ECONOMICS: A PRODUCT OF UNTYPICAL CIRCUMSTANCES?

Finally, Hayek has argued that the creation of Keynesian economics itself, with its rationale for state intervention, budget deficits and cheap-credit policy, was all a product of Keynes's experience of 'a very exceptional and almost unique' episode in English monetary history. This episode followed the return to the gold standard in 1925, for 'it was during this period of most extensive unemployment . . . which preceeded the world-wide economic crisis of 1929–31, that John Maynard Keynes developed his basic ideas'.[9]

The decision to return to gold at the pre-war parity involved a substantial increase in the exchange value of the pound, with a consequent rise in the real wages paid to British workers. Industry, rendered uncompetitive, was forced to contract, and unemployment resulted.

Keynes accepted that if there was to be a return to full employment the real wage would have to fall, but because of the difficulty of reducing wages directly, he convinced himself that such a policy was inefficacious and indeed harmful; and instead made unemployment a direct function of aggregate demand. It was on this basis that Keynes advocated a policy of inflationary expenditures both to make good the shortfall in demand and to reduce the real wage.

HAYEK'S CASE AGAINST KEYNES: WEAKNESSES AND A CRUCIAL OMISSION

Hayek's charge against Keynes is quickly recapitulated: (i) Keynesian ideas and the policies based upon them can produce only short-term benefits before leading inevitably to inflation and unemployment; a result wholly to be expected on the basis of established economic analysis and amply borne out by the facts of experience; (ii) Keynesian economics produces this result by its advocacy of expansionary monetary policy as a means of achieving full employment; (iii) Keynes was led to adopt this strategy by a crucial error of theory, deriving from his ignorance of Austrian capital theory, whereby investment was made to depend principally upon consumption demand; (iv) Keynes's belief in the priority of employment policy over stability of the price level stemmed from his experience of a wholly untypical and artificially induced period of heavy unemployment.

In reply, we should first notice that the evidence adduced by Hayek in support of his charge is not unassailable. There are several aspects to this. The first relates to Hayek's attempt to explain the economic history of the thirty years after 1945 in terms of Austrian trade-cycle theory. Hayek holds to his interpretation of the stagflation of the 1970s as an instance of the crisis phase of the cycle, notwithstanding that the preceding 'boom' phase was of such inordinate length that he himself refers to it as the 'Great Prosperity'.[10] Is it not, even on its own terms, a serious cause for concern, in a theory that attributes only short-run gains to monetary expansion, that the short run should have endured so well?

In addition, the Austrian indictment of Keynes relating to the 'crisis' loses much of its force when set beside the admitted beneficence of the 'boom'. If Keynesian economics got its come-uppance in the 1970s the observer can only comment that it was a long time a-coming.

Also, Hayek's case is based on evidence which is circumstantial in a curious way. Having applied Austrian (trade-cycle) theory to the diagnosis of the problems of the 1970s, Hayek then attributes the conditions necessary to produce these problems to the use of Keynesian policies. It is certainly the case that economic policy over the relevant period was avowedly Keynesian. However, despite the distinction to which he draws attention between the outlook of Keynes and his followers, Hayek nevertheless links Keynes with the 'Keynesians' by way of a very partial interpretation of his theory.

We have already seen that Hayek associates Keynes with monetary indiscipline, by accusing him of seeking to promote investment by the stimulation of consumer demand through lax budgetary and credit policy. What we have not so far explained is how and why Hayek concentrates on this relationship to the exclusion of all other aspects of Keynes's analysis.

The answer to this question must begin with the extraordinary discovery that Hayek's attack on Keynes is not based upon any substantial and detailed published criticism of the *General Theory*. This important and indeed crucial omission from Hayek's critical apparatus has been recognised by at least one sympathetic reviewer of the Hayekian case. Furthermore this same writer, although not following the line of argument pursued here, has perceived the significance for Hayek of what, on any criterion, must be regarded as Keynes's most important book. N. P. Barry writes:

> If the Keynesian argument that there is no necessity for an unhampered market economy to equilibrate at the full employment of all resources were valid then this would make Hayek's system redundant, much of conventional economics irrelevant, and would open the door to considerable state intervention.[11]

Hayek has subsequently attempted to account for his failure to provide a systematic critique of Keynes's main work.[12] For example, having spent much time and effort in the early 1930s on two articles criticising what was then thought to be Keynes's established view, Hayek was dismayed to find that Keynes soon disowned the analysis of *A Treatise on Money* (1930) and was 'working it out all over again'.[13] Subsequently, with his previous criticisms declared irrelevant, Hayek chose not to respond to the *General Theory*, believing it to be only a 'tract for the times'[14] and therefore a thesis which would in due course be superseded.

It was to be a colossal error of judgement for which Hayek was ever after to reproach himself. Keynes had made a definitive statement of his position,[15] which was then adopted as the new orthodoxy, while leaving Hayek in the wilderness.

THE HAYEK–KEYNES DEBATE OF THE EARLY 1930s

Hayek's omission also presented his admirers with an embarrassing lacuna to account for in their expositions of his anti-interventionist case. It is true that the *General Theory* is mentioned as the revolutionary book that conquered professional thought, but it is otherwise curiously absent from the reckoning. This leads in some cases to undue prominence being given to the debate of the early 1930s between Keynes and Hayek, based on the former's *A Treatise on Money* (1930) and the latter's *Prices and Production* (1931); a re-run of an old and irrelevant battle in lieu of the crucial battle which Keynes won by default.[16]

For example, in a volume of essays intended to honour Hayek in the 1970s,[17] Fritz Machlup adopts Sir John Hicks's designation of the period as 'the drama':

> When the definitive history of economic analysis during the nineteen thirties comes to be written, a leading character in the drama (it will be quite a drama) will be Professor Hayek ... there was a time when the new theories of Hayek were the principal rival of the new theories of Keynes. Which was right, Keynes or Hayek?[18]

Machlup doesn't tell us, and merely gives 'a sketch of the excitement which Hayek's theories caused in those years'. A fellow contributor is less reticent and confidently claims that:

> we are informed that historians will in due course remark that the great technical debate of the early 1930s was actually between Hayek and Keynes. One can only hope that by the time they get around to saying this, they will get around to saying that Hayek won.[19]

We are not given the grounds for this optimistic conclusion but it is a view which is surely representative of a widely held conviction among Hayek's followers, that Hayek the libertarian can defeat Keynes the interventionist on purely economic grounds.

However, the significance of this debate is put into proper perspective by Hicks himself, on the page following the passage quoted by Machlup:

> What was in common between them – all that seemed to be in common between them – was the intellectual descent which each claimed from Wicksell; but Wicksell plus Keynes said one thing, Wicksell plus Hayek said quite another. Which was right?[20]

For an answer, Hicks rightly points us forward to a consideration of the *General Theory*, in which Keynes moved fundamentally away from his position in the *Treatise*. At the same time, Hicks finds that:

> The Hayek theory is not a theory of the credit cycle ... It is an analysis ... of the adjustment of an economy to changes in the rate of genuine saving. In that direction it does make a real contribution. But it is a contribution which, when it was made, was out of due time. It does not belong to the theory of fluctuations, which was the centre of economists' attention in 1930; it is a forerunner of the growth theory of more recent years.[21]

With the theory reinterpreted in this way, the question is not whether it is Keynes or Hayek who is 'right' but rather for which set of conditions each theory is appropriate. Because, in the Hayek 'slump', prices are rising rather than falling, the theory does not help us to explain the slumps of history. It would, indeed, be more suited to the modern conditions of inflationary slump (stagflation) than it was for the deflationary slump conditions of 1931.

This can be explained as follows, bearing in mind the sequence of alternate expansion and contraction which precipitates the 'crisis' in the Hayek version of the cycle, outlined above.

In Hicks's terms, an increase in the propensity to save will reduce the (natural and we assume market) rate of interest, so that the marginal product of labour, and therefore the real wage, will rise in the more capital-intensive lines of production. In a fully employed economy, labour will be attracted away from the production of consumption goods, the supply of which will eventually fall. If the propensity to save does not (further) increase commensurately, the system of relative prices involving a low rate of interest and high real wages 'will be inconsistent with the maintenance of supply–demand equilibrium in the markets'. That is, the deficiency of saving will cause the rate of interest to rise so that the marginal product of labour in the capital-intensive processes will fall, as must the real wage.

Hicks notes that in order to produce the Hayek result of actual unemployment, the assumption of perfect price flexibility must be abandoned, for labour must be demanding a minimum real wage higher than that consistent with full employment. This will give the conditions for inflationary slump, for, as excess demand pushes up consumption-goods prices so unemployment of labour will emerge.

For this problem, the correct solution cannot be a general stimulation of demand, for this would merely exacerbate the shortages. Instead, relative prices must be allowed to adjust to restore supply–demand equilibrium.[22]

Hicks is generally sceptical about the relevance of Hayek's analysis for the problems of an advanced economy, and considers that it is only 'in the rapid development of the underdeveloped [that] it can surely be quite a serious danger'.[23]

HAYEK'S CRITICAL STRATEGY EXPLAINED

It is generally recognised that the appearance of Hayek's theory in 1931 was inopportune.[24] Hicks considered that 'in such conditions its diagnosis was wrong and its prescription could not have been worse'.[25] It was Hayek's unswerving adherence to a policy of non-intervention as the slump deepened, that reinforced the doubts of those who remained unconvinced on purely theoretical grounds and so helped Hayek's economics into obscurity.

From the vantage point of the 1970s, Hayek was to explain that with the triumph of Keynesian economics he had subsequently withdrawn from the debate; and indeed his work after the war was increasingly concerned with other questions, relating to the defence of liberty in a world dominated by interventionist governments. More recently, however, with Keynesian economics apparently discredited and libertarian doctrines in the ascendant, Hayek has sought to give a more substantial theoretical justification for his opposition to Keynes than would be evident from his scattered comments on the *General Theory*.

Realising perhaps that the reasons formerly given for his failure to return to the attack in 1936 might appear slight or even petty, Hayek has now provided a fuller and more satisfactory explanation of his strategy. It is this explanation which supplies the final link in Hayek's chain of argument and which indicates both the profundity of his thought and the limitations of his case. In the year of the centenary of Keynes's birth he wrote:

> It was not merely (as I have occasionally claimed) the inevitable disappointment of a young man when told by the famous author that his objections did not matter since Keynes no longer believed in his own arguments. Nor was it really that I became aware that an effective refutation of Keynes's conclusions would have to deal with the whole 'macroeconomic' approach. It was rather that his disregard of what seemed to me the crucial problems made me recognise that a proper critique would have to deal more with what

Keynes had not gone into than with what he had discussed, and that in consequence an elaboration of the still inadequately developed theory of capital was a prerequisite for a thorough disposal of Keynes's argument.[26]

CAPITAL THEORY: THE KEY TO HAYEK'S CRITIQUE

Hayek's work on capital theory was intended to bring to an issue the question of the *determination of investment in a monetary economy*. But what was intended as only a preliminary step in the argument, the working-out of the pure theory of capital, proved to be so formidable a task that Hayek published it as a separate book; while his analysis of the Keynesian weaknesses was itself 'indefinitely postponed'.

This book, *The Pure Theory of Capital* (1941), is the key to the Hayek–Keynes debate. In it Hayek provided a definitive statement of the Böhm-Bawerkian theory of capital, the theory upon which Hayek's economics is ultimately founded and which is of particular significance for his controversy with Keynes. Not only does it form the basis for the charge that Keynes's theory contains a 'crucial defect' but it also constitutes the core of the Austrian capital theory of which Keynes was supposedly ignorant. But in thus demonstrating, in the course of an exhaustive study, the theory's highest potential, Hayek by the same token revealed its inherent limitations and so produced the touchstone by which his attack on Keynes *on economic grounds* can be judged to succeed or fail.

The starting-point is Hayek's awareness that the treatment of capital in his previous work had been inadequate. *Prices and Production* (1931), which had analysed the destabilising effects of money on output and employment, had indeed suffered from other defects, in that it had, for example, assumed full employment of resources and had confused the rate of profit with the rate of interest.[27] These defects had to some extent been made good in *Profits, Interest and Investment* (1939), but it became clear that to sustain his non-interventionist thesis in the face of profound professional scepticism Hayek would have to set out once and for all the theoretical foundations of his case.

We saw earlier that the artificial stimulation of investment by monetary means will result in the boom–slump sequence because of the nature of capitalistic production itself. This is because the process of preparation for enhanced future output of consumption goods involves the construction of intermediate products. Production thus takes time and necessitates choice between present and future consumption. We are thus led back to the Böhm-Bawerkian theory of capital, with its promising notion of capital equipment as embodying the time-lapse in production between input of effort and output of reward and the consequent dependence of equilibrium investment on individual time preferences.

The problem that Hayek sought to resolve is as follows. An increased standard of living requires roundabout methods of production; the more roundabout the methods the greater will be the ultimate reward. That is, the greater the capital employed the greater the resulting output. But how is time-lapse in material input related to the output to which its services give rise? Here Hayek dismissed the prevailing Austrian view of myriad, disparate inputs being related to corresponding outputs in terms of an *average* period of production. Instead, he undertook the awesome task of demonstrating that the rewards to material inputs are directly related to the length of time for which they are invested, by dividing all inputs at a point of time,

> into fractions small enough to let us discriminate every different length of time-lapse which occurs between the use of such a fraction and the emergence of the consumable product which constitutes its fruit.[28]

We can relate this apparently abstruse argument to the familiar classical model of saving, investment and the rate of interest in the following way. In a fully employed economy the provision of the new capital equipment required to achieve increased production of consumables will require present sacrifice of consumption. Consumers will be motivated to undertake this saving by the prospect of earning a rate of interest, represented by the increase in the annual rate of output (income) in relation to the total amount saved (the quantity of capital).

Now, the build-up of the new equipment is envisaged as taking place by successive stages, with later stages building on the first or original stage, which by its nature is reckoned to be the most productive, in terms of capacity creation. Consequently those whose sacrifice provides the material inputs for the first stage, which is furthest in time from the realisation of output, will demand a higher return than those whose sacrifice provides for the later and therefore less-productive stages.

If the returns to each stage can be thought of in terms of notional rates of compound interest continuing through successive stages, the rewards to earlier stages will clearly be greater and the provision of a greater proportion of resources at the higher rates will enhance the productive capacity of the whole. Given the time-preferences of savers, the principle of equalisation at the margin of sacrifice and reward should dictate an optimal pattern of stages, the time intervals of which will equalise the compound rates for each stage, so that the system operates with a single rate of interest determined by the state of technology and the quantity of saving.

HAYEK'S WORK ON CAPITAL THEORY: AN ASSESSMENT

What did Hayek achieve? Did he succeed in validating Böhm-Bawerkian capital theory and, therefore, the theoretical underpinning of his attack on Keynes? The answer is equivocal.

In one sense he succeeded brilliantly, in that he produced a most rigorous and exhaustive analysis of the implications of time-lapse as the essence of capitalistic production which constituted 'as it were a final report on Böhm-Bawerk's proposal'.[29] *The Pure Theory of Capital* is, in the opinion of Professor Shackle – the scholar perhaps best able to evaluate its worth – a 'masterpiece' in which:

> Hayek has nailed his colours to the mast and has pursued to the uttermost limits the logic where it led. The result is a remarkable contribution to knowledge which could have been attained in no other way, and, I will venture to say, assuredly by no other man.[30]

But Hayek's achievement was essentially two-edged, for the conditions upon which success was attained rendered it a Pyrrhic victory in terms of his theoretical debate with Keynes. Even given the very strict assumptions from which he began his analysis and the high level of abstraction at which he conducted it, Hayek encountered such difficulties that the effort required to overcome them was of 'heroic' proportions. How are we to justify this prodigious expenditure of intellectual energy and display of moral resolution? Shackle believes the reason to be that 'Hayek very early in his scholar's life gave his allegiance to Böhm-Bawerk and to Wicksell', and became fascinated by the problems of a question of compelling importance, namely, that of the relationship between capital and time.

But can this sufficiently explain the 'huge effort ... devoted to refounding the Böhm-Bawerk–Wicksell theory of capital'? Surely the phenomenon is only explicable when set in the context of the controversy with Keynes. With Austrian economics swept aside by the Keynesian Revolution, any possibility of challenging the interventionists on theoretical grounds could only begin with the Austrian theory of capital. For, by demonstrating its validity Hayek would not only be securing his own position but also undermining that of Keynes, who had in Hayek's perception omitted it from consideration.

Such a concern would impart the necessary sense of urgency to Hayek's labours as he toiled through the years, for realisation that on this theory his case would stand or fall, was perhaps matched by a growing awareness that the original conception itself was inadequate for the task. This interpretation would seem to be supported by the following observation of Shackle:

> That such an effort was needed, that Hayek encountered numberless and daunting troubles, that so long a book was required to contain the implications of an ostensibly incisive idea ... suggests inevitably that too much was expected of a tool which had, at first sight, so brilliant a glow of promise.[31]

While, therefore, Hayek validated the theory on its own terms, those terms were so restrictive as to render it largely an exercise in pure logic and consequently of doubtful practical value. Not only does Hayek exclude money and abstract from uncertainty but he also explicitly assumes full employment. In addition, his very achievement in demonstrating the inappropriateness of the concept of an *average* period of production makes his theory unsuitable as the basis for empirical work. There are, moreover, conceptual problems of the theory itself.[32]

Defects aside, however, the main point is that the theoretical basis of Hayek's 1970s attack on Keynes became 'fixed' thirty years previously in the form of an exercise in pure logic. Hayek would, of course, reply that this purely theoretical work was a necessary, preliminary, step in his argument. But why did he not develop his theory, as an engine to demolish Keynesian economics?

The exigencies of war and the policy concerns of the post-war period provide some of the explanation. The crucial point, however, is that despite its immensity the task Hayek undertook was essentially finite. When accomplished, it was, literally speaking, *perfect* and complete in itself. Hayek, sensing perhaps its practical limitations, took the matter no further.

KEYNES ON MONEY AND CAPITAL: A REPLY

Notwithstanding some equivocation, Hayek has sought in his attack to depict Keynes as a vulgar inflationist, a modern John Law. But it should be clear from our argument in previous chapters that this charge is completely unjustified, and it is interesting to note that other commentators have independently and explicitly rejected the comparison.[33]

Laidler and Rowe do nevertheless subscribe to the view that Keynes 'undoubtedly' advocated discretionary monetary policy. But even this is true only in the sense that he would most probably not have been in favour of a monetary 'rule'. Also, that as part of his dismissal of the crude quantity theory, he examined the way in which monetary change influenced output and employment.

We have seen, moreover, that Keynes attached great importance to monetary stability and that he would not have been in favour of assigning to monetary policy a too-active and, therefore, destabilising role.

Nor did Keynes advocate a policy of fine-tuning consumer expenditures as a means of stimulating investment.[34] It has commonly been supposed that Keynes was overruled in the drafting of the 1944 White Paper, *Employment Policy*, which was decidedly unenthusiastic about the merits of the deficit budget. This myth has finally been exploded by Professor T. Wilson who has shown that the view of the White Paper was very much in tune with Keynes's own.[35]

We can now see that quite in keeping with the argument of previous chapters, Keynes advocated a continuously balanced current budget and envisaged deficits being incurred on capital account, as a means of financing investment projects managed by the state. This, of course, though it could give rise to changes in the quantity of money, is the very antithesis of discretionary monetary policy in the sense of a change in the quantity of money induced through central bank open market operations. It is much more in keeping with J. K. Galbraith's notion of 'putting money to work'.[36]

Keynes was, of course, supposedly led into the paths of monetary wantonness by his ignorance of Austrian capital theory which led him to relate investment to monetary demand. But this assertion must now be dismissed, for it is simply a convenient link between an 'Aunt Sally' caricature of Keynes's view on money and the Austrian analysis of money in the trade cycle.

We should remind ourselves that in moving towards the *General Theory* Keynes overtly rejected the major components of the neo-classical (including Austrian) theoretical apparatus, including, most appositely, the Austrian theory of capital, with an explicit rebuttal of Böhm-Bawerk's productivity theory of capital based upon the degree of roundaboutness. Keynes's own theory of investment was not a crucial error based upon ignorance but an alternative view, which posited an inverse relationship between the returns to investment and the scarcity of capital.

We should also remember that whereas the Hayek–Keynes controversy of the 1930s involved Hayek attacking an analysis from which Keynes quickly and fundamentally moved away, Keynes's criticisms of Hayek were directed at a theoretical position which Hayek's later work merely elaborated or qualified. Keynes considered *Prices and Production* (1931) to be:

> one of the most frightful muddles I have ever read, with scarcely a sound proposition in it beginning with page 45, and yet it remains a book of some interest, which is likely to leave its mark on the mind of the reader. It is an extraordinary example of how, starting with a mistake, a remorseless logician can end up in Bedlam.[37]

And yet Keynes does accept a point of criticism of his *A Treatise on Money* (1930) (concerning its inadequate treatment of the theory of capital accumulation and the determination of the natural rate of interest), which reveals Hayek's early allegiance to Böhm-Bawerk and Wicksell, and which presages concerns that were to find massive expression in *The Pure Theory of Capital* (1941) ten years later. Keynes wrote:

> It is very possible that, looking back after a satisfactory theory has been completed, we shall see that the ideas which Böhm-Bawerk was driving at, lie at the heart of the problem and that the neglect

> of him by English pre-war economists was as mistaken as their neglect of Wicksell. But there is no such theory at present, and, as Dr. Hayek would agree, a thorough treatment of it might lead one rather a long way from monetary theory.[38]

Nevertheless, though Keynes conceded the need to work out more clearly the determination of the natural rate of interest, he was to abandon the concept entirely during the next few years.

KEYNESIAN ECONOMICS AND UNTYPICAL CIRCUMSTANCES: A REPLY

The charge that the reason for the creation of Keynesian economics was Keynes's experience of a wholly untypical period of heavy unemployment following the return to gold in 1925, must now be seen as yet another manifestation of the Hayekian fixation with the pre-*General Theory* years; for the period of which Hayek speaks is *closed by* the appearance of *A Treatise on Money* (1930) and the principal ideas which Keynes developed during this period were soon to be overturned.

Keynes took a full part in the debate preceding the restoration of the gold standard and correctly predicted the effects of a return at the pre-war parity. He was also very much aware of the circumstances surrounding the Wall Street 'crash' of 1929 which precipitated the American and world slump and led eventually to Britain's departure from gold in 1931. He wrote the *General Theory* in full knowledge of these episodes and yet the analysis remains general, relating not to specific events but to a stage of evolution of industrialised society.

AUSTRIAN ECONOMICS: THE UNANSWERED QUESTIONS

Finally, there are some observations to be offered on the Austrian approach itself which will help to put Hayek's criticisms of Keynes in perspective.

First, that as an alternative to Keynesian interventionist policies Hayek offers his somewhat Panglossian notion of the *catallaxy*, which although it does not depend explicitly on a full-information model or an all-seeing auctioneer, does require freely adjusting market prices.

And this is so even where experience indicates that the prices in question are notoriously 'sticky', especially in the labour market.

Hayek has long recognised this problem, though whereas in the 1930s he advocated a sharp deflation as a means of breaking the rigidity of wages, by the 1970s he had come to accept the political unacceptability of such a course and could only suggest that 'other means' must be found of promoting wage flexibility.[39]

It is interesting, therefore, that the anti-inflation policies pursued by the Conservative government after 1979 proved to be sharply deflationary, and that the resulting unemployment brought greater 'realism' (flexibility) in wage bargaining. The question remains, however, of whether the Austrian system can work even on its own terms; of whether having experienced a sharp deflation of demand the economy will move towards full-employment equilibrium through wage flexibility alone.

A related but more general point is that although the notion of the *catallaxy* is tremendously liberating and invigorating in itself, it must face the question common to all wholly *a priori* constructions, which is, 'will it deliver the goods'? On Hayek's definitions such a question would be meaningless, in as much as any criterion to be used to judge its performance could only be available in the working of the system itself.

Nevertheless, in the real world it should be possible to obtain information concerning the ability of such a system to realise the ambitions and supply the needs of those who constitute it. Most obviously, the political system provides a necessarily limited but established means for the expression of preferences and the articulation of choice. In a free society it would always be open to the electorate to opt for socialisation of economic activity, to demand that the government treat the *catallaxy* as an *economy*. Whether the resulting intervention would ultimately bring greater economic rewards is clearly what the theoretical debate is all about.

To some extent Hayek's advocacy of *laissez-faire* must be deemed a 'fair-weather' policy and not an 'economics for all seasons', for he is prepared to countenance the use of discretionary monetary policy in two related sets of circumstances. The first of these is the prevention of a 'secondary deflation', when a recession threatens to turn into a major slump through the actual contraction of the money stock (an actual shrinkage of total demand); a circumstance which Austrians and monetarists see as the main cause of the American Great Contraction and world slump of the early 1930s. The second is when depressed economic conditions threaten to give rise to political instability.[40]

Last of all, we must mention the optimistic note struck by Hayek during the conditions of rapidly rising money supply and inflation of the 1970s, as to the extent and duration of the unemployment which would result from a monetary policy designed to control inflation. Hayek spoke of significant unemployment having to be borne for a period of several months or even more than a year, though 'this does not mean that we must expect another long period of mass unemployment comparable with the Great Depression of the 1930s if we do not commit very bad mistakes of policy'.[41]

We need only note that the persistent heavy unemployment of the 1980s, incurred during a period of monetary discipline as part of a (successful) policy to reduce the rate of inflation, must raise on empirical grounds, questions which we have asked about Austrian economics on theoretical grounds.

21 The Austrians III: Two Routes to Serfdom

INTRODUCTION

We have so far dealt with the Austrian challenge to Keynes in terms of economic theory as represented in the Hayekian theory of the trade cycle. We have concluded that this challenge cannot be shown to have succeeded. But, as noted earlier, the peculiar strength of Austrian economics, which exempts it from the tensions inherent in monetarism, lies in its successful integration of technical monetary theory into a general philosophy of society in which money is regarded as a social institution. There is, accordingly, a further challenge to Keynes based upon the broader social and political consequences of the Keynesian Revolution. It is to a consideration of these consequences that we now turn.

PANDORA'S BOX

During the years of the Keynesian hegemony, Hayek turned from the mainstream debates on the theory of money to explore instead the problems of safeguarding individual liberty in the prevailingly hostile, anti-liberal climate. In making this his central concern the Keynesian Revolution had played a role of particular importance, because for Hayek it appeared to bring into conjunction precisely the two elements which in his view would inevitably produce economic dislocation, leading to the breakdown of the market system and a consequent loss of individual freedom. These elements were, first, a theoretical justification for government intervention in the economy; and, second, the advocacy of demand management policies which, because historical evolution had given to governments the monopoly of money, would give rise to undue increases in the money supply.

In this way, Keynes had indeed, in Austrian eyes, opened a Pandora's box, and it became the major preoccupation of Hayek and the increasing number of his followers to draw attention to the precise nature of the evils which were thus let loose upon the world.

For analytical convenience we shall discuss them under two heads, which, taking inspiration from Hayekian terminology, we shall designate: *the direct route to serfdom*, which deals with the direct and necessary effect of the expansion of state activity on the freedom of choice of the individual; and, *the indirect route to serfdom*, which refers to the consequences for the system of free monetary exchange of the state's abuse of its monopoly power over money.

THE DIRECT ROUTE TO SERFDOM

By providing the justification for government intervention as a normal component of economic activity, Keynes attracted criticism from the Austrian school on a number of grounds relating to the direct diminution of individual liberty.

(a) Collective choice and individual freedom

The first is that Keynesian policies have encouraged the growth of public expenditure as a proportion of GNP, reaching a peak of 60 per cent in 1975–6. The effect of this has been to increase collective choice at the expense of individual choice so that personal liberty has been eroded. This conclusion is based upon what C. K. Rowley has called a 'realistic assessment' of the consequences of collective choice, as against the 'false paradigms' used to justify its growth.[1]

The false paradigms were initiated by Kenneth Arrow[2] as 'the paradigm of the dictatorial social decision-maker' and 'the paradigm of omniscient government'. Notwithstanding their widespread acceptance among students of collective choice Rowley rejects them as implausible. To the liberal mind the notion of a 'benevolent dictator' choosing between 'alternative collective actions after taking account of individual preferences by applying a given constitutional rule from a position of ethical neutrality', is a nonsense.

The complementary assumption, that the government is able to possess all the relevant information about individual preferences over all alternative social states and is able to use this information to maximise social welfare as defined by some constitution, is also dismissed. This notion of omniscient government derives from a philosophic approach stemming from Descartes, Hobbes and Rousseau which Hayek has called 'constructivist rationalism'. It is clear from our earlier discussion of the *catallaxy* that Hayek would reject any such assumption as fallacious, a 'synoptic delusion', on the grounds that the necessary information could not be available to any one person or authority.

Deprived of the philosophic justification which these false paradigms provided, the growth of collective choice can be seen to have pernicious effects. First, because public-sector production tends to be monopolistic in character, its growth as a proportion of total output implies a reduction of freedom of choice in consumption, a freedom to which liberals accord a high ranking. Second, because public-sector employees are paid (ultimately) out of tax revenues and not from the proceeds of voluntary exchange, liberty is threatened, both because the growth of public-sector unions takes out of the hands of taxpayers control over the level of public-sector pay and therefore the level of taxation, and because the absence of 'market' sanctions makes successful strike activity more likely.

Against the threat posed by the growth of collective choice Rowley believes that only precise constitutional safeguards will suffice. We shall deal with the political aspects of collectivisation below in Chapter 23. For the moment we might note that the plea on behalf of Keynes must be one of 'justification'; that notwithstanding the inherent dangers of providing a scientific rationale for state intervention, that rationale was valid in theory and justified in practice.

(b) Hayek's doomsday thesis

There is implied criticism of Keynes in Hayek's contention that the allowance for even a modest degree of intervention will inevitably progress to total state control and the complete loss of individual freedom in a centrally planned economy. Hayek developed his prediction of the eventual outcome of experiments in economic 'planning' in *The Road to Serfdom* (1944).[3] However, while Keynes shared Hayek's distaste for totalitarianism, he believed that his own work would itself provide the means of *avoiding* just the outcome that Hayek feared. In other words, it was only through state intervention that individual liberty could be safeguarded:

> Whilst, therefore, the enlargement of the functions of government, involved in the task of adjusting to one another the propensity to consume and the inducement to invest, would seem to a nineteenth-century publicist or to a contemporary American financier to be a terrific encroachment on individualism, I

defend it, on the contrary, both as the only practicable means of avoiding the destruction of existing economic forms in their entirety and as the condition of the successful functioning of individual initiative.[4]

(c) The prescription of Keynesian policies

Critics have sought to link Keynes with totalitarianism, by reference to remarks he made in the Preface to the German edition of the *General Theory*. The form the inference has taken ranges from the fairly mild 'Keynes, of course, was himself aware of the appeal of his policy recommendations to totalitarian regimes',[5] to Hayek's outright assertion that Keynes 'frankly recommended his policy proposals as being more easily adapted to the conditions of a totalitarian state than those in which production is guided by free competition'.[6]

It is unfortunate that indirect support for evidence of such a link has come from economists sympathetic to Keynes's cause. For example, though J. K. Galbraith stresses that the 'Nazi economic policy ... was an *ad hoc* response to what seemed over-riding circumstance', he is clear that 'by the mid-thirties there was ... in existence an advanced demonstration of the Keynesian system. This was the economic policy of Adolph Hitler and the Third Reich.'[7]

However, the suggestion of a link between Keynes and any sort of support for totalitarianism cannot be sustained. To begin with we have Keynes's own observation that 'the authoritarian state systems of today seem to solve the problem of unemployment at the expense of efficiency and freedom', whereas he himself believed that 'it may be possible by a right analysis of the problem to cure the disease whilst preserving efficiency and freedom'.[8]

Similarly, the passage in the Preface to the German edition of the *General Theory* does not yield the inference that Hayek and others claim. Keynes wrote:

> the theory of output as a whole, which is what the following book purports to provide, is much more easily adapted to the conditions of a totalitarian state, than is the theory of the production and distribution of a given output produced under conditions of free competition and a large measure of *laissez-faire*.[9]

Consider first that Keynes was writing for readers who were actually living in a totalitarian state, and that, second, he was recommending to them acceptance of a *formal theory* of economics in place of the historical approach which had been the tradition in Germany for the past century.[10] Then note that in the passage quoted above the key phrase is 'the theory ... of a *given output*', which implies that he is drawing the distinction (to which we have several times drawn attention) between the real-world monetary economy which requires the intervention of the state if full employment is to be achieved, and the purely theoretical world of the classical economics in which full employment is assumed.

Finally, we might also draw attention to the interpretation of Nazi economic policy as being corporatist rather than Keynesian, and the German economy but an aspect of the larger National Socialist political and economic system;[11] and to Professor W. Carr's comments on Keynes's attitude towards the rise of Hitler, and in particular his opinion that 'Keynes had no illusions about the Nazis from the earliest days'.[12]

THE INDIRECT ROUTE TO SERFDOM

In the previous chapter we dealt with Hayek's conception of the trade cycle as a real phenomenon caused by monetary expansion. We must now ask what will happen if monetary expansion to secure full employment is continued, as workers' expectations adjust to take account of inflation and increasing doses of inflation are required to maintain a given level of employment?

Hayek's conclusion is that continued and accelerating inflation must eventually lead to the complete breakdown of the market system.[13] It was a problem which Hayek saw as becoming increasingly acute over the period from the 1930s due to the progressive removal of the traditional constraints on government: the gold standard, the balanced budget and, latterly, the system of fixed exchange rates.

Hayek is not explicit as to the mechanism whereby inflation destroys the system of free, monetary exchange (though it is readily inferred from his general approach), but an explicit analysis of the reasons is provided by the German social philosopher and sociologist Georg Simmel. Simmel's analysis has been used as the basis for a root-and-branch attack on Keynes, which is both interesting as a complement to that of Hayek and important because of the fundamental nature of the issues raised.

The link with our previous analysis lies in the nature of money and the conditions under which money is non-neutral. Note that, in the Hayekian theory of the trade cycle, dislocation would occur following monetary expansion *even if* money were conceived of as a private durable good. This is because monetary changes have real effects by virtue of the microeconomic nature of Austrian analysis, which assigns crucial importance to the role of relative prices. It is an idea exploited by rational-expectations monetarists to explain (with difficulty) observed fluctuations in economic activity.

Now, however, we have the means whereby changes in the *absolute* price level can have real effects due to the postulated conditions which govern the extent to which voluntary exchange takes place. We recall that treating money as a private durable good has the effect of trivialising the consequences of inflation, and so poses problems for monetarists. We hinted that inflation becomes a much more serious problem if money is viewed as a social institution among a complex of social institutions. The rationale for this view is provided by Simmel's analysis.[14]

SIMMEL'S ANALYSIS

The underlying idea is that important and socially beneficial institutions can come into existence spontaneously through the actions of individuals perceiving the benefits that would follow, rather than from a conscious and deliberate act of planning policy.

In Simmel's approach to money the original notion is the phenomenon of exchange itself, which is a neutral and efficient way of increasing total welfare, by satisfying individual desires without recourse to gift or theft. Its invention is a product of experience, and is to be seen as the originator, the creator, of society rather than as an activity taking place within a previously existing society.

Because exchange increases net benefit for both participants, to maximise exchange is to maximise economic welfare. Because this in turn betokens a maximisation of individual freedom of choice, it must also maximise the extent of individual liberty.

Money, we noted in Chapter 1, is an institution created because it facilitates the process of exchange between commodities: that is, it overcomes the problems of barter. It is developed spontaneously, like a moral code or a legal system, and like them depends for its efficacy upon the trust and sanction of the whole community.

Just as the acceptance of money to perform its functions is based on trust, so there is a mutually reinforcing process whereby trust in the institution of money will in turn serve to maximise exchange and hence individual liberty. It is an apparent paradox of the monetary economy that as we maximise exchange and therefore complexity of economic life, so we become more interdependent with other participants, but at the same time more independent of particular individuals and hence less vulnerable to their arbitrary actions.

Therefore, the use of money is a liberating activity, freeing individuals from the ties of closed, moneyless societies in which all depends upon custom and convention. We see that the consequences of monetary exchange can be interpreted very differently from Marx's view of money as the alienator, breaking the (impliedly valuable) social bond created between the parties to a barter transaction under precapitalist modes of organising production. Instead its use confers a freedom which has been recognised from ancient times and of which H. G. Wells wrote:

> Instead of a worker or helper being paid in kind and in such a way that he is tied as much in his enjoyment as in his labour, money leaves him free to do as he pleases amidst a wide choice of purchasable aids, eases and indulgencies ... That is the good of money, the freedom of its universal convertibility.[15]

It follows that anything which tends to undermine trust in money will tend to reduce the extent of its use, so reducing the amount of voluntary exchange and hence individual freedom of choice and therefore liberty.

Simmel was pessimistic about the future of systems of free monetary exchange, which he thought would tend to develop pressures leading to breakdown and the substitution of an illiberal form of society. These pressures would be the product of two forms of latent weakness.

The first is that though workers are liberated by the payment of their wages in money, they become subject to uncertainty through arbitrary changes in the value of money. The second is that as the monetary economy develops and becomes more complex, it becomes more difficult to comprehend, and seems remote, heartless and alien. There will increasingly be a temptation for participants to seek comfort in the apparent certainties of the socialistic system.

Furthermore, the natural vulnerability of a free monetary economy is exploited by deliberate monetary misuse, which again can be seen as the outcome of a process of natural evolution: that is, because historical development will produce a monetary system based upon fiat money issued under a government monopoly. If, then, political pressures cause governments to over-issue money in pursuit of policy goals, the resulting instability of the price level will cause uncertainty as to its future value, so undermining trust and reducing its use. With the decline of free monetary exchange, production and distribution will increasingly be organised on a centrally planned and directed basis, and liberty will be gone.

Now we can see how, by viewing money as a social institution rather than as a private durable good, inflation will have real effects and dire consequences.[16] For, even if inflation is anticipated, we should expect there to be a movement away from market forms of trading and towards greater reliance on central direction and planning. Individuals would become more dependent on specific personalities and liberty would be diminished. If, on the other hand, inflation were unanticipated there would be increased uncertainty, which would in turn undermine trust and lead to a decline in the volume of voluntary trading.

In the face of these predicted outcomes, Simmel, as with some members of the Austrian school, saw a defence only in tying the quantity of money issued to a metal base, on the grounds that a commodity money would be the free choice of transactors in the absence of a government monopoly of money.

SIMMEL AND KEYNES

On the basis of Simmel's analysis, S. H. Frankel[17] has mounted a thorough-going attack on Keynes, both for the view of money that he is said to hold and for the policy measures derived from it that he is said to espouse. Frankel's criticism deserves to be taken seriously and not only because it raises questions of enormous interest. It is based on the work of Simmel which is now receiving enthusiastic recognition within the economics profession. Also, Frankel's view of Keynes is symptomatic, being fashionable among Austrians and libertarians in general.

Frankel draws a distinction between two alternative and incompatible views of money. One, a traditional view, sees money as a symbol of social trust. The other, a revolutionary view, sees money as a tool of state action. The first is exemplified by Simmel. The second was held by Keynes who, following the German economist, G. F. Knapp, held a cartalist view of money in which he saw money as being created by law and as depending for its validity upon the authority of the state alone.

Against a nineteenth-century background of monetary rectitude, in which the successful working of the gold standard owed more to the strength of British institutions and the high standing they enjoyed in the international financial community, than to the fact that the system was based on gold, Keynes in the twentieth century introduced the notion of the acceptability of using money as a policy tool based on the alleged superiority of public wisdom over individual choice. In so doing he began a process the continuance of which must inevitably lead to the destruction of the free monetary order.

To understand how Keynes came to adopt this view of money we must begin with the idea that Keynesian economics originated in 1919 rather than in 1936, and that the whole of Keynes's work from *The Economic Consequences of the Peace* to *The General Theory of Employment Interest and Money* was the manifestation of an essential unity of thought and purpose.

Keynes's perception of the reasons for the breakdown of the old social and economic order in Europe following the first World War made him pessimistic about the ability of the free monetary economy to achieve the goals that Keynes thought were proper for it. Before 1914 the progress of European civilisation was marked by peace, security and economic growth. But it was a fragile condition and the upheaval of the First World War exposed its dark 'night side'.

In particular, it revealed the 'unstable psychological conditions', the 'double bluff or deception' upon which economic growth depended. Through social conditioning the mass of the people were persuaded into the acceptance of a grossly unequal distribution of incomes, in which capitalists were allowed the lion's share on the tacit understanding that though they were theoretically free to consume it they would instead practise abstinence in order to accumulate and so promote the growth of future output. But the war 'disclosed the possibility of consumption to all and the vanity of abstinence to many. Thus the bluff is discovered.'

The capitalist class lost confidence. In the nineteenth century it had been sustained by a belief in itself and its value to society. Now it was characterised by a fatal weakness of spirit which allowed it to be made the scapegoat for society's ills. As the self-assurance of the capitalist class waned, the uncertainty inherent in a monetary economy left too much to chance among the forces determining the level of employment and the growth of the capital stock. Because individual choice-making behaviour under uncertainty could not produce the economic results that Keynes desired, the state had to be brought in *deus ex machina* to achieve them, by the application of 'rationality' and 'public wisdom'.

The uncertainty which Keynes saw as enfeebling economic enterprise was a consequence of the fact that we live in a monetary economy, which is to be seen as essentially different from other economies. In the face of uncertainty the characteristic stimulus to economic activity in a monetary economy, the 'money motive' or habitual appeal to the love of money, is inadequate to ensure prosperity, because it is essentially irrational. One of Keynes's most familiar criticisms of the neo-classical, neutral-money economics was that it recognised a store of value function for money; whereas Keynes himself believed money holding to be barren – a belief exemplified by his interpretation of gold-hoarding behaviour in India, in *Indian Currency and Finance* (1913), and pursued in the *General Theory*.

But, of course, money holding is but one step in the process of monetary exchange between commodities, so that if money *holding* is to be regarded as a barren activity, so is money *use*. Society would therefore benefit from the abolition of a practice which not only has no reward in itself but introduces uncertainty into economic relationships. Money use, that is, prevents the attainment of economic prosperity. But because of the difficulty in a free-market economy of preventing the use of money *in some form*, Keynes was prepared to 'see to it that there were no such assets, i.e. to go the whole hog and to destroy the free monetary order and the exchange economy, as was done in communist societies'.[18]

However, before resorting to this authoritarian, centrally planned solution, Keynes was prepared to try the alternative strategy that we have since come to know as Keynesian economics; that is, to use the monetary system itself to influence the key variables in the economic system, namely the level of real wages and the relationship between saving, investment and the rate of interest. To do this Keynes would seek to play upon the 'money motive', which he identified as the chief source of maladjustment and disco-ordination, by deliberately creating 'money illusion'.

However, Simmel's analysis has shown us that the free monetary order is based on trust, and that to undermine trust is to threaten the order, and 'the fact is that the deliberate creation of money illusion is a form of social deceit. If persisted in, it must, finally, subvert the monetary order'.[19] This comes about in two ways. The first is that as soon as 'the bluff is discovered', transactors will take account of inflation, which must accelerate for the effect to be achieved. The second is that to make use of the monetary system to influence individual decision-making, in accordance with arbitrarily chosen (from the market point of view) objectives, must inevitably destroy the moral authority of the monetary order.

Therefore, though Keynes sought by this means to escape from the problems of a monetary economy, it is 'not surprising that monetary manipulation intended to reduce uncertainty has, by destroying faith in the monetary order, actually increased it'.[20] In this way Keynes risked the destruction of freedom itself.

A REPLY TO FRANKEL

It is obvious that an interpretation of Keynes's views along these lines must excite the antagonism of those who on a variety of grounds are wedded to the ideal of individual liberty. It is also obvious that it is intended to give theoretical sustenance to the belief among Austrians and others that Keynesian economics sets us firmly on the road to serfdom.

Equally, it is clear that the attempt to discredit Keynes in the light of Simmel's analysis must involve misunderstanding and misinterpretation at significant points. Frankel's belief that Keynes's thought constitutes an essential unity, may have some justification in terms of general outlook, but it leads him to overlook the fundamental changes which took place in Keynes's economic analysis prior to the publication of the *General Theory*; and consequently to juxtapose as part of the same argument ideas which are incompatible.

We shall reply explicitly to three key points in Frankel's criticism. The first is Keynes's alleged intention to use monetary deceit to achieve full employment and growth. The second is Keynes's conception of a monetary economy as being different from a barter economy because of the presence of uncertainty. The third is Keynes's view of the nature of money, and in particular his affinity with Knapp's cartalism together with the context of his alleged assertion of the barrenness of money use.

The first point is the most important, for it is the culmination of Frankel's entire case against Keynes. For if Keynes did intend the state arbitrarily to change the value of money so as to induce an incorrect perception of the level of the real wage, he would be guilty of public deceit.[21] The other two points would then provide valuable corroborative evidence of Keynes's reasons for the pursuit of such a reprehensible course. If on the other hand he did not, then the supporting arguments would themselves become suspect.

We shall argue in the next chapter that deceitful manipulation of the real wage by way of monetary policy was *not* Keynes's strategy, and in the present chapter point out that these supporting arguments are indeed based upon misinterpretation.

THE NOBLE LIE

On the first point, however, we can for the moment draw attention to its significance in other directions, for it raises the question of Keynes's role as the 'Philosopher King' and his alleged acceptance of the Platonic belief in the validity of the 'Noble Lie'. It is obviously a question of especial importance to Keynes's Austrian critics; and even N. P. Barry, whose comments on Keynes have been more temperate and more insightful than most, has given expression to the prevailing belief that 'Keynes made lying respectable'.[22]

That Keynes in some sense surveyed the world from the Olympian height of his social and academic position is common property, but it does not accord completely with the other charge commonly levelled against Keynes, that he was primarily interested in policy and saw theory as of secondary importance. Despite his patrician standpoint his published work betrays a worldly realism in economic affairs that stands in marked contrast to the head-in-the-clouds idealism of some libertarian and socialist critics.

We shall see in Chapter 23 that there was in Keynes an element of the Philosopher King, in as much as he seemed to conceive of government in terms of rule by disinterested expert elites. But there is no counterpart to this in any intention to base policy upon the misuse of the monetary system, and hence no readiness to resort to the Noble Lie.

MONEY AND UNCERTAINTY

Before turning to the question of Keynes's conception of the nature of money, we must first deal with the charge that Keynes mistakenly believed that the monetary economy is uniquely distinguished from other economies by being subject to uncertainty.

Here Frankel's attack is vitiated by his failure to interpret correctly Keynes's distinction between a monetary economy and a barter economy. He writes:

> The confusion arises from his [Keynes's] assertion that the problems of a monetary economy are essentially different from other economies because of our ignorance of and uncertainty about the future. But why should one believe or imply that the problems of life – for that is what ignorance and uncertainty in the face of fate amount to – should be ascribed to money or be solved by the mechanics of monetary management?

Because:

> Even in the purest form of real-exchange economy there will always be transactions which do *not* cancel out. There will always be promises, obligations and expectations, and there will always be promises unkept and expectations unfulfilled – falsified by events, by ignorance or by deceit.

This means that:

> Even non-monetary 'underdeveloped' economies are subject to the same inability to secure 'full employment' due to ignorance of what to do, or fear of the risks involved, with the result that they suffer stagnation as severe, and often much more so, as that in any sophisticated money economy.[23]

It is clear (recalling the argument in Chapter 2 above) that Frankel is contrasting an uncertainty monetary economy with an uncertainty non-monetary economy, and that he believes that Keynes assumed the non-monetary economy to be free of uncertainty. We have argued at length that this is not the case; that Keynes was, rather, drawing the distinction between the uncertainty monetary economy of reality and the certainty world of pure theory. On this basis he wrote:

> Our criticism of the accepted classical theory of economics has consisted not so much in finding logical flaws in its analysis as in pointing out that its tacit assumptions are seldom or never satisfied, with the result that it cannot solve the economic problems of the actual world.[24]

MONEY HOLDING AND MONEY USE

This leads directly to one aspect of the question of Keynes's conception of the nature of money. We recall that in the full-information world of pure theory money can play no part other than that of a unit of account. Only in the uncertainty world of reality will money take substantive form.

As a necessary part of acting as a medium of exchange, money will also perform the function of a store of value. Therefore, money's attributed function of storing wealth in the presence of other stores of wealth that yield a positive return can only be explained by uncertainty as to the future value of the alternative stores.

This, of course, was the point of Keynes's criticism of the classical economics, which, because of its assumptions, could not accommodate a store of value function for money, though it paid lip-service to the concept. Frankel, however, uses this criticism in a different context, and by doing so reverses its meaning.

He begins with Keynes's analysis of the phenomenon of gold *hoarding* in India, and generalises Keynes's notion of the 'barrenness' of money *holding* – in the sense of an inefficient use of a scarce commodity – to the proposition of an alleged belief in the barrenness of money *use*. From this standpoint he then depicts Keynes as criticising (neo) classical economics for accrediting to money a store of value function for which Keynes himself can allegedly find no justification. This, of course is the opposite of the case.

Frankel then links Keynes's supposed view of the barrenness of money use with the notion of the *absurdity* of holding and therefore using money. This provides the basis of a view of uncertainty – which is depicted as a consequence of money use – as an unmitigated Bad Thing, ripe for removal through the abolition of money if it cannot be tamed by other means.

The 'other means' could be through the system contrived by men to cope with the problems of working in an uncertainty economy which is itself based upon the 'love of money' motive. Frankel associates Keynes with this strategy by way of Keynes's warning against too great a reliance on the money motive, which Frankel confuses with the barrenness-of-money-holding/use argument;[25] and, on the previous premise that the problems Keynes wished to correct arose from the fact that we live in an uncertainty-through-money-using economy, set Keynes up for the charge that he wished to tinker with the 'mechanics of monetary management' as a way of solving the 'problems of life'.

It is an ingenious argument, and provides the necessary background for a view of Keynes, the advocate of monetary deceit, in polar opposition to Simmel. But it is, as we have shown, wholly false. In addition, we saw in Chapter 12, above, that the very reason why Keynes was 'fascinated by mechanistic nostrums, like Gesell's proposal for stamped money', was because they increased the carrying-costs on money and therefore reduced the attractiveness of money-holding without the sharp fluctuations in the money supply that would increase rather than reduce uncertainty.[26]

Finally, Frankel uses Keynes's assertion that the composition of the *General Theory* had been a 'long struggle of escape', to raise the question of what it was that Keynes had been attempting to escape from? The answer he gives is that Keynes had been attempting to escape from 'the Monetary Economy itself', and so provides a neat tail-piece to the sequence of argument outlined above.

But, as with the argument itself, this interpretation is wrong. What Keynes was struggling to escape from was not the monetary economy but the futility of attempting to solve the problems of the monetary economy *by way of* the classical modes of thought in which he and his contemporaries had been raised.

CARTALISM VERSUS METALLISM

The other aspect of the question of Keynes's conception of money refers to Frankel's distinction, central to his thesis, between money as a product of trust and money as a creature of authority.

Whatever the excesses of G. F. Knapp in contending that 'money is essentially the creation of law and wholly a state affair' and that 'Money was to be regulated by the State entirely in its own interest', there seems little to quarrel with in modern eyes in the idea that 'the value of money is secondary: what is important is its validity, by which he meant its power to discharge debt'.[27]

What, however, seems surprising in the light of experience is that Frankel should regard as fallacious a conception of money in which 'the monetary unit is, according to Knapp, purely "nominal". The franc, the dollar, and the florin do not connote a fixed weight of metal. They are abstract units.'[28] For, as Goodhart has pointed out:

> The substitution of fiat, paper money, for metallic coin as the main component of currency in the last 200 years provides strong support for the Cartalist view that the monetary essence of currency can rest upon the power of the issuer and not upon the intrinsic value of the object so used.[29]

However, the real point is that Frankel finds such a development *unwelcome*; and to support his belief that cartalism provides the rationale for inflationism, of the Law–Keynes variety, he accuses Knapp of making a 'category mistake' in his formulation of the relationship between money and the state: that is, of treating the state and therefore money as something separate from society as a whole:

> For Simmel, the state is but one part of society and society is a process, not a thing. The State cannot determine the monetary process, no more than it can determine the activities of the whole society through it.[30]

Nevertheless, we recall that it was Simmel's belief that the natural evolution of money is towards a token form issued under state monopoly; hence the attraction of the gold standard as a means of keeping check on the government's monetary policy. It is to the means of forcing *governments* to maintain monetary discipline that modern Austrian and monetarist thought is directed, as we have seen.

MONEY AS A SOCIAL INSTITUTION

It would be difficult to quarrel with Simmel's thesis that stable money will help to encourage the increased use of monetary exchange in a given monetary system. Equally we must agree that money is the liberator and not the alienator claimed by Marx. But the liberating effect of money is *technical*, by producing the cash nexus. Whether money is used to fulfil this function, however, depends on its acceptability, whether through commodity content or government fiat. In either case, again, an important consideration will be its stability of value. Is it possible to reconcile this notion with the prediction concerning monetary evolution and the facts of history?

Money is said to predate the state, and, like it, to be a product of the process of exchange. It is very significant that in being based on trust the institution of money is said to arise spontaneously from the uses of experience – like the institution of *law*. But what sort of law are we to compare it with? The ancient law of England is the common law, whose origin, said the eminent seventeenth-century judge, Sir Matthew Hale, is 'as undiscoverable as the head of the Nile'; a promising, if anachronistic, start; but statute law is just as much law as common law and has obviously in modern times produced an immensely important flood of laws. Statute law is a product of government and the constitutional apparatus of the state. In a democracy the government will spring from the society of which it forms a part, but will in order to govern assume an existence of its own. Arguably, many of our troubles in recent times derive from the fact that governments have become too *weak* in relation to the rest of society, a point to which we shall return in Chapter 23.

MINDING THE GOVERNMENT

The problem, as Hayek and others have pointed out, becomes one of providing the government with the means to protect itself against political pressures which might otherwise become intolerable. Such pressures could indeed lead to the pursuit of policies which would produce the monetary breakdown envisaged.

The question therefore is one of controlling and/or protecting government. For libertarians, the strategy is one of reducing the scope of government action towards the zero involvement of *laissez-faire*. For Keynesians, who believe that *laissez-faire* will not 'deliver the goods', the problem is more complex.

22 Employment Policy

INTRODUCTION

Frankel's charge against Keynes, that he sought to use public deceit in monetary policy, by the deliberate use of money illusion in the labour market, carries with it very serious implications. Not only, it is claimed, will the discovery of the bluff lead to inflationary expectations being 'built in' to wage claims and other contracts expressed in money terms, but it will also progressively undermine the moral authority of the monetary order itself.[1]

In fact, Frankel is somewhat ambivalent in his assessment of the extent to which he believes Keynes intended to rely on monetary policy *per se*, for he admits that Keynes was sceptical as to its effectiveness as compared with state management of investment.[2]

Nevertheless, if Keynes is to be judged solely on the basis of his assessment of monetary policy as a tool for increasing employment, the charge can be met on those terms. Furthermore, when Frankel quotes [3] from passages in the *General Theory*[4] which argue for the relative merits of a 'flexible' money policy as against a 'flexible' wage policy – as an illustration of Keynes's alleged preference for the use of money illusion to give workers and employers a '*distorted* image of reality' – he is guilty of telescoping Keynes's argument and to that extent of misrepresenting it.

INVOLUNTARY UNEMPLOYMENT

The key to answering this charge lies in Keynes's notion of the *involuntary* nature of unemployment. Keynes argued that there can exist substantial levels of unemployment which are involuntary, in the sense that they are desired neither by unemployed workers nor by potential employers. However, because neither group is able unaided to bring about the changes necessary to achieve full employment (at which level remaining unemployment is *voluntary*),[5] the economy will, if left to itself, remain in a state of underemployment equilibrium.

In other words, though workers and employers are aware of the values of the variables affecting their situation, they are nevertheless powerless to influence them and so are trapped in a state of unemployment: a state from which they would wish to be released by the intervention of an outside agency.

Keynes was subsequently to revise some of his ideas on employment theory and indeed the precise nature of his employment function is still the subject of controversy; but in the *General Theory* his starting-point was with the 'postulates of the classical economics', of which he accepted the validity of the first though not the second.

KEYNES AND THE CLASSICAL POSTULATES

That is, Keynes accepted that in a competitive[6] economy the real return to the employed worker, in terms of goods and services produced (*the real wage*), would tend to equality with the increase in total product deriving from the employment of an extra unit of labour (*the marginal physical product of labour*). Therefore, because the application of extra units of labour to a given capital stock (and with a given technology) would result in a declining marginal product, an expansion of employment could only take place if there was a commensurate fall in the real wage.[7] However, because employment involves a real cost for workers, in terms of leisure time sacrificed, labour will not be supplied beyond the point at which the declining real wage (the real reward to labour) becomes equal to the *marginal disutility of labour* – that is, the value the marginal worker places on leisure time to be given up. At this point of labour market equilibrium, typical for the classical economists though a special case for Keynes, we could write

$$MPN = \frac{w}{p} = MDN$$

Where

MPN is the marginal physical product of labour (the real reward to firms)

$\frac{w}{p}$ is the real wage and is equal to the money wage divided by the average price level of goods and services entering into workers' consumption (the real reward to labour)

MDN is the marginal disutility of labour (the real cost of employment to workers)

Under classical assumptions, supply and demand in the labour market would cause the money wage to adjust (price level constant with a given money supply) until the real wage settled at a level at which all who wished to work would be employed.[8] Apart from transitional, frictional unemployment, workers without jobs would be *voluntarily* unemployed: either because they were demanding too high a real wage or because they placed a value on their leisure time that was higher than the existing real wage. Once the level of employment was determined, the resulting level of output would find a guaranteed market, because under the modern version of Say's Law the free-market interest rate would adjust to give savings–investment equilibrium at the full-employment level of output.

In Keynes's view, of course, there could be no automatic adjustment to full-employment equilibrium, so he could not accept that the marginal product of labour (and the real wage) would tend to equality with the marginal disutility of labour.[9] Rather, output and employment would be held at a level at which *the marginal product of labour and the real wage would be higher than the marginal disutility of labour.*[10] Because at this level of real wages less labour is being demanded than workers would be willing to supply, there is *involuntary* unemployment: 'when effective demand is deficient there is under-employment of labour in the sense that there are men unemployed who would be willing to work at less than the existing real wage'.[11]

THE INEFFICACY OF WAGE-CUTS

In this state of underemployment equilibrium, attempts by workers to release themselves are unavailing. Though they might be willing to accept a lower real wage than that currently being offered, there is no way in which they can bring about the necessary reduction. In particular, Keynes is insistent that reductions in money wages will not reduce real wages or act directly to increase employment.[12] If, for example, workers succeeded in bidding down money wages, so that employers, seeing their costs reduced, took on more labour, the reduction in demand in the economy would prevent the sale of the increased output at existing prices. With expectations disappointed, employers would lay off workers again, and the fall in the price level would leave the real wage unchanged at the new, lower, level of money wages.

In other words, changes in money wages cannot directly increase employment because:

> the volume of employment is uniquely correlated with the volume of effective demand measured in wage units,[13] and ... the effective demand, being the sum of the expected consumption and the expected investment, cannot change, if the propensity to consume, the schedule of the marginal efficiency of capital and the rate of interest are all unchanged. If, without any change in these factors, the entrepreneurs were to increase employment as a whole, their proceeds will necessarily fall short of their supply price.[14]

However, a reduction in money wages could increase employment *indirectly* – to the extent that it could influence the propensity to consume, the marginal efficiency of capital or the rate of interest. After reviewing the various possibilities, Keynes concludes that it is 'on the effect of a falling wage- and price-level on the demand for money that those who believe in the self-adjusting quality of the economic system must rest the weight of their argument; though I am not aware that they have done so.'[15] That is, a fall in money wages, prices and incomes relative to a given stock of money will, because of a reduced demand for money for transactions purposes, increase the effective supply and so stimulate investment via downward pressure on the interest rate.

In analytical terms, of course, a reduction in the rate of interest brought about by a fall in money wages relative to a given stock of money, is precisely equivalent to the same reduction brought about by a rise in the quantity of money with a given level of money wages.

However, as a method of securing a state of continuous full employment, falling money wages is no more reliable than an equivalent rise in the nominal money stock. In each case a moderate change may produce an inadequate fall in the long-term rate of interest; while an immoderate change could adversely affect the state of entrepreneurial confidence.

Furthermore, because of the particularly immediate and destructive effects of changes in money wages on the state of expectations through their effects on the price level, and the inequity of the manner in which the changes are likely to come about, Keynes rejects wage reductions as a method of influencing the rate of interest and argues instead for a policy of maintaining money wages constant in the short run.[16]

That is, changes in the price level and the expectations they engender can powerfully influence investment (and consumption) plans. While a flexible wage policy and monetary policy will each have an *indirect* effect on prices – via changes in the rate of interest, investment and employment – money-wage changes alone will have a *direct* effect on prices[17] because they are both a constituent of costs and a component of money incomes.

Moreover, while a substantial, swift and uniform reduction in money wages and prices, creating expectations of *rising* wages and prices in the future, could favourably influence the marginal efficiency of capital, such a reduction would be possible only in an authoritarian economic system. Where there is free wage-bargaining, reductions in money wages in response to falling employment will occur in a piecemeal and inequitable fashion, creating expectations of further falls and instability of the price level. This will adversely influence effective demand and so worsen rather than improve employment prospects.

If, on the other hand, a policy is pursued of maintaining stability in the level of money wages for the short run,

> This policy will result in a fair degree of stability in the price level;– greater stability, at least, than with a flexible wage policy. Apart from 'administered' or monopoly prices, the price level will only change in the short period in response to the extent that changes in the volume of employment affect marginal prime costs;[18]

And since, therefore, 'with a rigid wage policy the stability of prices will be bound up in the short period with the avoidance of fluctuations in employment', there is a basis also for rejecting the inaccuracies of monetary policy for 'a somewhat comprehensive socialisation of investment'.

The context in which Keynes was arguing for a 'flexible' money policy, as against a 'flexible' wage policy in the passages quoted by Frankel, is now clear. He was not promoting a plan to mislead the workforce by way of 'public deceit in monetary policy'.

THE NECESSARY RISE IN THE PRICE LEVEL

Nevertheless, it is also clear that on the analysis of the *General Theory* a policy to increase employment would necessarily involve a rise in the price level.[19] If the government were to step in to increase effective demand in the economy, the increased expenditure would, because industry operated subject to decreasing returns in the short run, cause the marginal physical product of labour and the real wage to decline *as extra workers were drawn into employment*. With a given money wage the real reward to labour must fall, by way of a reduction in the purchasing power of money. Keynes explains as follows:

> *n* men are employed, the *n*th man adds a bushel a day to the harvest, and wages have a buying power of a bushel a day. The $n + 1$th man, however, would only add .9 bushel a day, and employment cannot, therefore, rise to $n + 1$ men unless the price of corn rises relatively to wages until daily wages have a buying power of .9 bushel. Aggregate wages would then amount to 9/10 $(n + 1)$ bushels as compared with *n* bushels previously.[20]

If, therefore, an increase in the price level (or rather a series of discontinuous increases in the price level – points of 'semi-inflation' – as full employment is approached[21]) is a necessary consequence of releasing firms and individuals from a condition they did not freely choose and from which they would wish to be delivered, the charge of public deceit loses much of its force.

In any case, in moral terms there is little to choose between a situation in which output, employment and the price level all rise as a result of government-induced expansion of investment demand; and one in which the same effect is brought about by a burgeoning of entrepreneurial confidence during the expansion phase of the business cycle. In both cases the increase in employment must be accompanied by a decline in the real reward to labour.[22] In neither case do workers *initiate* the reduction in the real wage; and to the extent that the reduction is perceived, workers in both cases will or will not choose to continue in employment at the new, lower, real wage.

MONEY ILLUSION

In this regard, it must be emphasised that neither in the original nor the amended (see below) versions of Keynes's employment theory are workers assumed to suffer from 'money illusion', that is, to pursue courses of action on the basis of changes in nominal magnitudes as though they were changes in real magnitudes; nor are they assumed in any way to behave irrationally. Consequently, the use of monetary policy to stimulate employment does *not* depend upon workers being 'fooled'. Keynes argued that:

> It is fortunate that the workers, though unconsciously, are instinctively more reasonable economists than the classical school, in as much as they resist reductions in money-wages, which are seldom or never of an all-round character, even though the existing real equivalent of these wages exceeds the marginal disutility of the existing volume of employment.[23]

THE IMPORTANCE OF RELATIVE WAGES

Rather, rational individual workers and groups of workers are assumed to be aware of their relative position in the structure of real wages. They will seek to maintain their positions and to resist *cuts* in money wages which would worsen their relative position:

> Since there is imperfect mobility of labour, and wages do not tend to an exact equality of net advantage in different occupations, any individual or group of individuals, who consent to a reduction of money wages relative to others, will suffer a *relative* reduction in real wages, which is a sufficient justification for them to resist it. On the other hand it would be impracticable to resist every reduction of real wages, due to a change in the purchasing-power of money which affects all workers alike.[24]

It is this assumption, of the concern of workers and unions with their position in the pattern of wage 'differentials', that in Keynes's view accounts for the *downward* inflexibility of money wages; for no benefit would accrue to workers providing a 'lead' in money-wage reductions, and there would be no incentive for other workers to follow such a 'lead'. Conversely there would be no (incentive for) resistance to a *rise* in money wages either in absolute or relative terms. This assumed asymmetry of workers' behaviour plays a key role in maintaining the stability of a modern monetary economy – as we shall see.

Keynes faced the problem, therefore, of having to reconcile the assumed downward inflexibility of the money wage with the need for the real wage to fall as employment increased. The reconciliation, as we have seen, was to be accomplished by way of a rise in the price level. Workers' concern with relative wages meant that a rise in the price level which reduced real wages but did not disturb relativities would provoke little resistance – especially as it would accompany an expansion of employment prospects.

THE ANALOGY OF THE RELATIVE-INCOME HYPOTHESIS

This account of the supply side of Keynes's employment theory is in sympathy with the new interpretation, of Tobin and Trevithick;[25] as against the orthodox view, which saw money wages as exogenously or historically given, and workers as suffering money illusion in the face of a reduction in the real wage brought about by way of a rise in the price level. The new view brings the determination of money wages within the purview of economic analysis by explaining Keynes's relative-wage hypothesis 'in terms of labour supply functions which display a high degree of interdependence',[26] with the pattern of wage differentials maintained by 'in effect ... a labour market application of Duesenberry's (1949) relative income hypothesis'.[27]

CRITICISM OF THE RELATIVE-WAGE HYPOTHESIS: A REPLY

Criticism[28] of the new view has cast doubt on its doctrinal authenticity, though there are sufficient references in the *General Theory* to suggest strongly that this was what Keynes had in mind.[29] Also, the analogy of the relative-income hypothesis has been described as implausible, because relative-income arguments are not employed in Keynes's specification of the consumption function.[30]

However, Leijonhufvud's criticism can be seen not to present insuperable difficulties if the following two points are borne in mind. The first concerns Keynes's distinction between the determination of the *general level* of real wages, which is governed by the marginal physical product of labour, and the *distribution* of the real wage between groups of workers, which is the subject of money-wage bargaining:

> the struggle about money-wages primarily affects the *distribution* of the aggregate real wage between different labour-groups, and not its average amount per unit of employment ... The effect of combination on the part of a group of workers is to protect their *relative* real wage. The *general* level of real wages depends on the other forces of the economic system.[31]

In the short run, because money wages are inflexible downward, the fall in the marginal product of labour and the real wage as employment increases, is accommodated by the rise in the price level as costs are forced up.[32] In the long run, the *rise* in the marginal product and real wage can be accommodated by a combination either of a stable money wage with a falling price level, or a slowly rising money wage with a stable price level. Because he thought it more conducive to the attainment of continuous full employment, Keynes favoured the latter alternative.[33]

On the other hand, we can expect that the *distribution* of the aggregate real wage (relative wages) will change slowly over time with structural changes in the economy; while in the short run the pattern of wage differentials can be considered as given.

The second point concerns Keynes's consumption theory, and in particular his observation that people have established standards of life.[34] This 'long-run' view of income and consumption is at least *not incompatible* with the assumption of a given structure of real wages in the short run. While consumption will increase with real income in the long run, it will not fall commensurately with the fall in the level of real wages in the short run as employment increases:

> a man's habitual standard of life usually has the first claim on his income, and he is apt to save the difference which discovers itself between his actual income and the expense of his habitual standard; or, if he does adjust his expenditure to changes in his income, he will *over short periods* do so imperfectly. Thus a rising income will often be accompanied by increased saving, and a falling income by decreased saving, on a greater scale at first than subsequently.[35]

However, with an established structure of relative real wages it would still be necessary to allow for the case of a single firm which finds that demand for its product is declining. In Keynes's view, it would be perfectly feasible for a single firm acting alone to react by attempting to negotiate a reduction in money wages which would lead to lower costs and prices because aggregate demand is largely maintained. Workers would then face the dilemma of having to choose between unemployment and a cut in money wages that could worsen their relative-wage position. Clearly, much would depend upon workers' expectations as to their prospects for re-employment, and there may also be obstacles in the form of national wage agreements for particular kinds of labour.

The importance of 'institutional' factors should clearly not be underestimated. It has been argued, for example, that:

> the possibility of competitive bidding down of wage rates by aspiring entrants would limit ... [unions'] ability to select that combination of relative wage and size of industry that they prefer. But even in a non-unionised industry the transactions costs of dealing with each worker separately suggest that wages will tend to be held at standardised, common, fixed levels with occasional quantum-jump readjustments, rather than being perfectly flexible. In such cases workers may well not be able to find jobs, even in non-unionised occupations, despite being prepared to accept wages below the going rate.[36]

When considered in the aggregate, of course, the situation is entirely different, in as much as a cut in money wages, even if practicable, will neither reduce real wages (and may even increase them, as Keynes notes[37]) nor lead directly to increased employment. This is because the aggregate level of employment is a function not of workers' choice but of the level of effective demand – at least in the case of an *increase* in employment, though not a decrease:

> Whilst labour is always in a position to refuse to work on a scale involving a real wage which is less than the marginal disutility of that amount of employment, it is not in a position to insist on being offered work on a scale involving a real wage which is not greater than the marginal disutility of that amount of employment.[38]

THE REAL WAGE AND THE CREATION OF EMPLOYMENT

It is worth emphasising, therefore, that it is not the reduction in the real wage that brings about increased employment, but the increased effective demand, and this remains true whether the reduction in real wages comes about through a fall in money wages or a rise in the price level. It is, rather, a necessary concomitant.

This explains why it would be futile for workers to attempt to 'negotiate a collective, across the board, proportionate reduction in all (rates of increase of) money wages – thus leaving relative wages unchanged – so as to reduce the general level of real wages'.[39] Indeed the 'problem' of downward money-wage inflexibility is only relevant in the case of Keynes's equivalent of the 'Pigou Effect',[40] referred to as the 'Keynes Effect', in which a reduction in wages and prices increases the effective quantity of money and stimulates aggregate demand indirectly via a fall in the rate of interest.

It is a problem in this case for two reasons. First, money-wage stickiness prevents the activation of the only 'automatic' mechanism which could operate to counteract a demand deficiency. Second, unless the reduction in money wages were large and swift, the deleterious effect on entrepreneurial expectations of a 'sagging' wage and price level would do more harm than good. It is, rather, the case that the downward inflexibility of the money wage is a tendency to be cherished and indeed nurtured – in as much as it gives an essential element of stability to the monetary economy:

> we have a sort of asymmetry on the two sides of the critical level above which true inflation sets in . . . For whilst a deflation of effective demand below the level required for full employment will diminish employment as well as prices, an inflation of it above this level will merely affect prices . . . This result follows from the assumption that the factors of production, and in particular the workers, are disposed to resist a reduction in their money-rewards, and that there is no corresponding motive to resist an increase...If, on the contrary, money wages were to fall without limit whenever there was a tendency for less than full employment, the asymmetry would, indeed, disappear. But in that case there would be no resting-place below full employment until either the rate of interest was incapable of falling further or wages were zero. In fact we must have *some* factor, the value of which in terms of money is, if not fixed, at least sticky, to give us any stability of values in a monetary system.[41]

KEYNES'S THESIS REVISED AND STRENGTHENED

After publication of the *General Theory*, the findings of empirical studies caused Keynes to modify some of his ideas, and in particular his acceptance of the first classical postulate: that the real wage tends to equality with the marginal product of labour. Evidence suggested that firms typically adopted output and pricing policies that left the marginal product of labour at a level higher than the real wage paid. It was also found that labour's marginal product would not necessarily fall as employment increased if a firm's capital stock was initially substantially underemployed. There was no evidence that the real wage varied inversely with the demand for labour and with employment. It was not, therefore, the case that the volume of employment would be uniquely related to a given level of real wages.

In the light of the evidence, Keynes concluded [42] that because in the short period changes in real wages were typically very small in comparison with changes in other relevant variables, they could be assumed constant. Employment could now vary directly with changes in the level of effective demand – at an unchanged level of real wages *and without a necessary rise in the price level.*

Keynes's employment *theory* was thus freed from the precise calculus of the classical real-wage hypothesis, and a much clearer distinction was drawn between voluntary, classical, unemployment – associated with too high a level of the desired real wage – and involuntary, Keynesian, unemployment – associated with a deficiency of effective demand. And any suggestion that Keynes's employment *policy* depended on the classical notion of employment being increased by 'the reduction in real wages covertly effected by the rise in prices which ensued on the increase in effective demand', could no longer be entertained.

23 The Keynesian Revolution in Context

INTRODUCTION

Though the Keynesian Revolution was a revolution of theory, it was a revolution with a purpose in the real world. Its purpose was to resolve a contradiction in orthodox economics which had been exposed and brought into focus by a particular set of economic circumstances. This is *not*, however, to argue that Keynes had been misled into advocating egregiously reckless expedients by a 'very exceptional and almost unique' episode, as claimed by Hayek;[1] or that it was the 'history-bound analysis' as pictured by H. G. Johnson.[2]

Rather, it was a fundamental recasting of economic theory which was made necessary by Keynes's perception of a situation in which universal recognition of the problems posed by prolonged heavy unemployment led to a call for policies that could not be sustained on the basis of orthodox economic theory. But in recasting *theory*, Keynes intended to make clear the relevance of the particular for the general case; to demonstrate that written into the need to solve a particular economic problem were lessons that would of necessity have to guide the future conduct of economic affairs. In other words, we should not so much regard Keynes's new economics as a 'chosen way' but as an interpretation of events giving rise to a prediction and a suggested way out.

The main implication for policy was that henceforth the government would have to assume responsibility for a significant portion of economic life. This was to be a necessary condition for the establishment and maintenance of a high and stable level of employment, for the purpose of Keynes's attack had been to demonstrate the invalid theoretical basis of the predictions of *laissez-faire* 'market' economics.

But full employment was not intended to be an end in itself, though there were obvious economic and humanitarian reasons for the adoption of such an objective. It was, rather, that Keynes saw full employment as a *sine qua non* for the safeguarding of individual liberty.[3] For in the absence of correct policies unemployment would of necessity continue, and with it mounting pressure for the replacement of the political and economic system which had produced it with a system in which individual liberty might have no place.

At the same time, Keynes was well aware that by letting in the government he was providing a prime hostage to fortune; that by providing the justification for the government to enter the economy *as of right* he was opening the door to possible abuses which might destroy the very things it was intended to preserve.

Here, then, was a dilemma, a dilemma the manifestations of which are evident in events of the past half-century. For not only is the Keynesian Revolution best seen as providing a theoretical rationale for factors that were in any case forcing the pace for change in the approach to economic organisation; it was these same factors that were later to undermine the economic system set up in the name of the Keynesian Revolution and ultimately to bring about its demise.

In this chapter, therefore, we shall put the Keynesian Revolution in context, both to show the grounds upon which it justified itself in other than purely theoretical terms, and to show why, despite the problems to which it gave and must necessarily give rise, its fundamental principles remain valid today and for the future.

JUSTIFICATION IN PRACTICE

Amid a tide of influences moving in favour of a socialised economy, the Keynesian Revolution provided the theoretical basis not simply for state intervention but for state intervention of a certain kind. That is, it determined the form that socialisation should take. At a time when the only alternative solutions to the economic problem were those provided by the totalitarian systems of fascism and communism, Keynes offered an intellectually respectable justification for the maintenance of individualistic capitalism and the liberal democratic style of government that was its political counterpart. Judged on these grounds, therefore, the revolution of principles was to have immense practical significance. Robert Skidelsky has caught the point as follows:

> Before Keynes, most 'advanced' thinkers believed that some system of authoritarian planning, usually modelled on Russia, was

> the only answer to the economic problem. Keynes provided an alternative model, an alternative theory of how the economy works, and fails to work, with its in-built policy prescriptions. For the intelligentsia, inside and outside the economic[s] profession, it was essential to have such a theory. Mere inflationism would never have been accepted as a reputable alternative to centralised planning. The change in intellectual atmosphere from the 1930s to the 1950s and 1960s is striking. This was largely the work of Keynes.[4]

Thus was victory in academic debate translated into victory in policy terms.

THE DEMAND FOR SOCIALISATION

Demand for a socialised economy *of some kind* was the product of a number of identifiable influences, both general and specific.

The first is general, and relates to the aspirations of a population no longer willing to accept the rewards system represented by the working of the 'invisible hand'. Here Keynesian economics was merely recognising the inevitability of the trend, and in the circumstances of the time showed greater realism than the head-in-the-sand absolutism of the diehard classicals. For if the (neo) classical theory had once seemed appropriate for the analysis of real-world conditions, by the inter-war period the apparent correspondence had quite gone. The world had changed, or, rather, the ideas and aspirations of the peoples of European industrialised countries had changed, and there was now a lower threshold of tolerance for the perceived gap between personal goals and what was handed out by the automatic workings of a 'mechanical' system. In place of free-market capitalism and the international gold-standard, people would increasingly look to the state to intervene and realise their expectations.

The increased awareness and dissatisfaction was a function both of the spread of the franchise and of the growth of popular education. The condition was a progressive one, with the people themselves coming to demand that the state step in, *deus ex machina*, to respond to special pleading and to supply alleged deficiencies. It is a trick that once learned is never forgotten; and it is this that makes the task of those who would reverse the process one of extreme difficulty. The only remedy lies in the education of voters as to the perils involved, but it is a remedy that becomes increasingly constrained once the link between representation and taxation – between the enjoyment of benefits and the liability to sustain sacrifice – has been broken.

Is it here, perhaps, that we see the real meaning of Simmel's warning against the dangers of alienation from the 'remoteness' of the monetary economy?; when, that is, the system appears no longer to 'deliver the goods', and people cease to be willing to accept the judgements of a faceless market mechanism with regard to the level of employment and the distribution of wealth?

The latent demand for socialisation was activated and brought into focus by two historical episodes; the inter-war depression, caused by the world slump following on a decade of high unemployment in the UK; and the prosecution of 'total war' by the UK between, say, 1940 and 1945.

ECONOMISTS AND THE SLUMP

Here we need only elaborate our previous point, that interventionist policies were being advocated by a wide spectrum of economists even though such policies were inconsistent with their conclusions from theory. This point, which is often overlooked in criticisms of Keynes,[5] has been argued by D. E. Moggridge as follows:

> It was Keynes's seriousness concerning assumptions and premises that underlay much of the purpose of the *General Theory*. There Keynes attacked his 'classical' contemporaries, not because they disagreed with him on policy proposals in connection with the slump – in fact many of them wrote joint letters to *The Times* with him and sat on committees exhibiting a fair degree of unanimity in their reports – but because he believed that their policy recommendations were inconsistent with the premises of the theory they used to explain the situation. One must remember that he singled out Professor Robbins, the economist with whom he disagreed perhaps most on policy throughout the 1930s, as almost alone amongst his contemporaries as one whose 'practical recommendations belong ... to the same system as his theory'.[6]

However, the sequel to this episode is that Robbins was later explicitly to renounce as mistaken the anti-expansionary viewpoint he had adopted in the 1930s. Moreover, it was to his erstwhile acceptance of (inappropriate) orthodox economic theory that Robbins came to attribute his error. In his autobiography he wrote:

> The trouble was intellectual. I had become the slave of theoretical constructions which, if not intrinsically invalid as regards logical consistency, were inappropriate to the total situation which had then developed and which therefore misled my judgement.[7]

This recantation, taken in conjunction with Hayek's latter-day acceptance of the need to prevent a 'secondary deflation', emphasises the peculiar importance of Keynes's own position.

THE REQUIREMENTS OF WAR

It was, however, in the absolute conditions of total war that the demand for socialisation was forced to an issue. The Second World War was not a 'popular' war, and the governing classes came to see socialism in some form as the price to be paid for securing the co-operation of a disaffected generation raised in depression and privation.

Early on, there was the question of a statement of 'war aims', containing an explicit commitment to post-war socialist programmes, raised by fears concerning possible popular reaction to any peace move by Hitler. In the event, proposals by the Ministry of Information were vetoed by the Prime Minister, Winston Churchill.[8]

Nevertheless, from 1942 onward, 'fighting for a better Britain' was popularly identified with the provisions of the Beveridge Report (on social security) published in that year. Though Churchill was unsympathetic to the Report and sought to discourage discussion of its proposals, its publication 'roused embarrassing public enthusiasm'[9] which foreshadowed popular response when the matter became the subject of political choice. In 1944 there was a new Education Act, with the provision for free secondary education to the age, ultimately, of sixteen; and plans for a national health service were drawn up by the Ministry of Health. In addition, there was the White Paper *Employment Policy*,[10] with its commitment to the maintenance of 'a high and stable level of employment'. In the same year, Beveridge produced, in collaboration with the 'Keynesian' economist Nicholas Kaldor, his own 'report' on employment policy, which urged the necessity of a commitment to full employment on the premise that 'misery generates hate'.[11]

A LANDSLIDE FOR SOCIALISM

Though the war produced unprecedented commitments to future state intervention, the trend towards socialisation was reinforced and greatly extended by the 1945 landslide electoral victory of the Labour Party, pledged to the 'establishment of the Socialist Commonwealth of Great Britain', by way of a programme of nationalisation and comprehensive schemes for social welfare provision. The writing was clearly on the wall, and though Conservative governments were later to prune the programme of public ownership, the Conservative Party while in opposition in the late 1940s came to acknowledge political reality and committed itself to the welfare state and the level of government expenditure that went with it.

Despite, however, the explicitly socialist nature of the post-war Labour government's policy and the continuance of wartime direct controls, nationalisation was primarily of old basic industries which in other countries were already in public ownership; and, in general, management of the economy was Keynesian in form. For, though critical of the ability of capitalism to 'deliver the goods', Keynes was not a socialist, and by providing a philosophy of managed capitalism he satisfied the need both for freedom and plenty, and so 'buried Marxism for a generation of the mainstream British left'.[12] By the success of his system he convincingly argued against further moves in the direction of central planning.

It could, of course, be argued that the Keynesian Revolution by itself did not produce the transformation in British economic life from the pre-war decades of unemployment to the post-war decades of prosperity; that the war, victory, and the emergence of the Pax Americana were of crucial importance. But Keynesian effects flowed from American economic policy as American deficit spending sustained the economy of the Western world.

KEYNESIANISM IN DECLINE

Keynesian economics had triumphed, and there followed the years of the Great Prosperity. But ultimately prosperity was threatened by mounting inflation and unemployment, and the Keynesian era came, at least temporarily, to an end.

The causes of the decline of the system that took its inspiration from the Keynesian Revolution were both economic and political. They were economic in the sense of the actual manner in which

Keynesian ideas were put into practice and of the world economic environment in which policies had to operate. They were political in the sense that the factors that provided the context for the introduction of Keynesianism also provided the context for its demise, though these factors were now given particular emphasis by the effects of significant changes which took place in the structure of British politics during the relevant period. Economic and political causes were closely interlinked.

EXPLAINING STAGFLATION

The principal economic symptom of decaying Keynesianism was the onset of stagflation. It was a progressive condition, and for the authorities implied the need to countenance successive increases in the rate of inflation necessary to achieve any given level of employment. It also implied that demand-management measures designed to meet the government's obligation to maintain full employment were becoming increasingly less efficacious. If we can explain this problem in Keynesian terms we shall have the key to the failure of the Keynesian system.

After a long period of stability the relatively rapid decline of the system into stagflation suggests that the conditions in which it had to operate had changed significantly. This in turn leads us to suspect the influence of exogenous economic shocks, the importance of which has been widely canvassed, principally among 'Keynesian' economists. In the 1960s, for example, there were the inflationary effects of the Vietnam War and the European economic boom; while in the 1970s the obvious candidate is the spectacular increase in OPEC oil prices.

However, while many economies suffered the effects of these shocks, the inflation experienced by the UK was more severe than in comparable countries, both in the 1960s and, more pronouncedly, in the 1970s. Accordingly, it is to internal factors that we must turn to explain the discrepancy.

Both Keynesian and monetarist economists would acknowledge the role of union wage-bargaining behaviour in the inflationary process, though whereas monetarists would see unions as reacting to shocks and as transmitting inflation, Keynesians would point to the influence of autonomous union 'push' on wages and prices – usually by reference to the degree of unionisation. Inflation would follow from the upward tendency of the wage unit, as unions sought to increase the real wages of their members and left to government the responsibility for providing sufficient demand to guarantee continued full employment at the higher wage rates.

There are two points here. The first is that both monetarist and Keynesian economists could agree that in the 1970s there was an increase in what monetarists would call the 'natural rate of unemployment'; or what Keynesians would think of as the non-inflationary full-employment level of unemployment.

This formal agreement, based upon a rightward shift of the Phillips curve, involves different interpretations of the same phenomenon. To Keynesians, increased unionisation and industrial militancy means stronger push on wages with the need for a higher level of unemployment to maintain the same inflation rate. To monetarists, the same behaviour implies increased labour market rigidity and a consequent increase in the natural rate of unemployment, so that there will be inflationary consequences at a lower level of employment for any attempt to stimulate the real economy above its new equilibrium level.[13]

The second point concerns the consequences of union reaction to an inflationary shock. The autonomous increase in OPEC oil prices, which was simply the most dramatic of a series of world commodity price rises in the early 1970s, was inflationary for two reasons: first, because unions would not accept the cut in their real incomes that the transfer of resources to OPEC implied, and accordingly demanded higher money wages; second, because the government chose to stimulate demand in order to offset the unemployment consequences of the relative rise in British real wages.

In Britain, the inflationary process was reinforced by the falling exchange rate after sterling was floated in 1972 as part of the general breaking-up of the Bretton Woods system. In addition, the higher rates of inflation were validated by simultaneous changes in the financial environment, as money supply expanded rapidly following moves towards money market freedom in London.[14] Both aggregate demand and the money supply were further increased as part of the expansionist strategy of the 'Barber boom' of 1972–3.[15]

Unquestionably, the economic factors introduced above played an important part in producing stagflation and the breakdown of the Keynesian system, in whatever particular combination and upon whatever particular set of presuppositions seems congenial to the observer. But, in the context of our preceding argument, they appear *ad hoc* and lacking in a unifying theme which will allow us to explain the problems in recognisably *General Theory* terms in conjunction with political influences. Accordingly we turn next to the effects of government policy as an explanatory factor.

THE EFFECTS OF GOVERNMENT POLICY

As a preliminary, we may refer to the sharp difference of opinion that exists between monetarists and Keynesians as to the efficacy of active policies of demand management. For monetarists, active intervention is destabilising and serves only to magnify the fluctuations it seeks to smooth. In addition, use of such methods to attempt to reduce unemployment below its natural rate will lead only to cumulative instability in the price level. Finally, we should recall that Keynes himself was in favour of a continuously balanced current budget and had no conception of the use of fiscal fine-tuning.

However, governments did employ measures of active demand management – budgetary, monetary and direct – to achieve their objectives, and we shall find that the key to the economic aspect of the weakening of the Keynesian system lies in the use of these measures to attain a particular goal of policy.

From 1945, successive governments interpreted Keynes's message to mean that the achievement of full employment and prosperity would be dependent on their securing an adequate aggregate rate of investment. There was certainly justification for this view, but two questions arise. By what means was the requisite investment to be obtained; and what would be the short- and long-run consequences of adopting this strategy?

As to the first question, the general understanding was that the nationalisation of private industry was not required, but that the necessary encouragement to investment could be given both directly, through expenditure on public utilities and schemes of public works, and indirectly, through tax inducements to private firms, together with budgetary and monetary management of demand.

We might notice here that our previous discussion of this topic in Chapter 14 differs from some other accounts, in finding in Keynes's notion of 'socialisation' a greater readiness to countenance the direct organisation of investment by government, as against a general stimulation of favourable influences. It is a cruel dilemma for governments which seek both to achieve full employment and to retain maximum freedom for the market mechanism, that to increase investment by way of the general stimulation of demand is to use what is likely to be the less effective and the more inflationary method. Indeed, the choice of measures of more general application was partly responsible for the problems which emerged in the 1960s and 1970s.

The nub of the matter lies in the answer to question two, the short- and long-run consequences of investment. We begin with the commonplace idea that the effect of investment is two-fold: it not only raises the level of income and employment, but also increases capacity output. That is, in an economy in which net investment is positive, the capital stock is increasing in size and the economy is growing. Two points are relevant.

The first is that to maintain equilibrium it will be necessary for investment to increase at an increasing rate, so as to fill the widening gap between income and consumption and so sustain the rising level of full-employment income. Keynes made this point abundantly clear.[16]

The second is that as the capital stock increases the marginal efficiency of capital will fall, and this will act as a disincentive to investment unless the decline in the m.e.c. is offset by technical change, or a sufficient decline in the rate of interest. Furthermore, for technical change to be translated into innovation, prospective demand for the product must be provided, whether by way of shifts in consumption behaviour or shifts in population growth.

Consequently, a policy of continuously promoting investment might, given the appropriate conditions, produce stable growth. More likely, however, in the absence of these conditions, the economy will converge on the stationary state envisaged by Keynes.

We recall (Chapter 14, above) that Keynes extended his theory of employment to predict the long-run consequences for a mainly *laissez-faire* economy of continued capital accumulation. He showed that if the m.e.c. were to fall unimpeded to zero the economy would move into stationary state, the characteristics of which would depend on the extent to which the desire to accumulate wealth had been satisfied. If, however, the decline in the m.e.c. were to be arrested by a recalcitrant rate of interest there would be a greater likelihood that the propensity to save would still be positive, so that the economy would cycle about an underemployment equilibrium.

Dr V. Chick has applied this analysis to the events of the Keynesian era, and has argued that in their desire for growth, policy-makers had overlooked the relevance of Keynes's prediction and that inflation can be explained by their unwitting attempts to offset the consequences of an increasing capital stock:

> My thesis is that a root cause of the current inflation is a misapplication of the policy prescription of the *General Theory*; a policy designed as a short-run remedy has been turned into a long-run stimulus to growth, without examining its long-run implications.[17]

More specifically, as growth continued under the influence of government policy, factors that were present to offset the fall in the m.e.c. and so promote further investment, weakened and failed, leaving the gap between consumption and full-employment income to be filled increasingly by government expenditure. This expenditure was inflationary, both because being unselective it financed much that was 'unproductive' as compared with the incomes it generated, and because it left as residue a rising stock of money to be absorbed in an economy in which real growth was fading.

At the same time, as real growth slowed down, labour which had been displaced on an increasing scale by the move towards capital-intensive (labour-saving) techniques of production was not re-absorbed, so that unemployment increased.

The m.e.c. and therefore the incentive to invest, was sustained for a considerable time by a variety of favourable factors. For example, the period began with the need to rebuild a capital stock suitable for peacetime purposes, following the years of depression and war. There was, moreover, a high level of unsatisfied demand for consumer goods and a high level of liquidity with which to finance it. During the 1950s real incomes rose but costs and prices were kept down, as technical change, to which the war had given the customary fillip, was embodied in the production process.

However, towards the end of the decade there is evidence of a decline in the quality of technical change, while in the 1960s the overall *scale* of technical change slowed down. Furthermore, any offset to the implied decline in the m.e.c. that might have come from factors influencing demand, were either ineffectual, in the case of income redistribution, or spent, as in the case of population growth. However, inflation itself could have had a favourable influence through its reduction of the real rate of interest, but this would cease to operate as costs caught up with demand.[18]

In these conditions the maintenance of growth and full employment requires ever-greater intervention on the part of the government, and from the late 1960s, as profit rates fell, government expenditure began to rise again as a proportion of GNP from its previous peak in 1968. Because government expenditure tends to show low short-term returns in terms of output, it is likely to have added to the rate of inflation, which accelerated sharply at that time, for 'when income-creating expenditure comes long before output, it is almost a matter of arithmetic that prices will rise'.[19]

We have now explained the rise in government expenditure as a necessary consequence of the emphasis on economic growth. But we can extend the analysis by pointing out that, in fact, the two were mutually reinforcing, with economic growth itself being seen to justify rising government expenditure (and higher wage awards); and government expenditure in turn being subjected to pressure to grow through the working of the political process. It is, accordingly, to consideration of the wider political economy of the Keynesian era that we now turn.

THE POLITICAL ECONOMY OF KEYNESIANISM

Though it is true that many non-Keynesian economists would now accept the (at least temporary) importance of OPEC-style economic shocks for the inflationary process, the main emphasis of monetarists and Austrians has been on monetary mismanagement as the primary cause of inflation and unemployment and, more broadly, on the political economy of Keynesianism as the framework within which monetary mismanagement would be endemic.

This point has hitherto emerged most strongly in our discussion of Hayek's critique, with its emphasis, on the one hand, on Keynes's justification of inflationist policies and, on the other, the decline of traditional restraints on the behaviour of politicians. However, in a volume published in 1977 to mark what was then identified as the terminal phase of the Keynesian age, writers of various persuasions drew attention to what they regarded as Keynes's failure to allow adequately for the political environment in which his economic system might have to operate. It was as a consequence of this that the Keynesian Revolution was doomed to be a transitional stage rather than a permanent state, rendered unstable by changed political conditions as compared with the period in which the *General Theory* was written.

There had, of course, been a great extension in the economic and social activities of government, in the creation of the welfare state and the mixed economy; but, paradoxically, as the range and extent of the government's responsibilities increased, there was a concomitant decline in its powers of control. This was an outcome unforeseen by both Keynes and his critics.

Forty years ago, in *The Road to Serfdom*, Hayek attacked the vision of the mixed economy as a dangerously misleading chimera. He argued that the ideal of the Middle Way, which was intended to combine the benefits of capitalist enterprise and individual liberty with the need for overall state direction and social justice, would prove to be the thin end of the statist wedge and would lead ultimately to totalitarian rule.

Keynes, on the other hand, though professing himself in perfect sympathy with Hayek's fears and sentiments, did not accept his premise that any move in the direction of state intervention would inevitably lead to disaster. Rather, he believed that in a politically mature, right-thinking society it would be possible to obtain with relative impunity the benefits from acts which in other contexts would have to be judged foolhardy and dangerous.

In the event, neither prediction was to prove correct. On the one hand, no erstwhile mixed economy has yet followed Hayek's road to serfdom. On the other hand, economists from both sides of the monetarist–Keynesian divide have argued that Keynes's vision of government 'by a small group of the educated bourgeoisie, who were inspired by a disinterested concern for the public good',[20] was overtaken by the realities of the political market place, for:

> once economic life became a matter of continuous political decision, economic rationality (however defined) ... [became] subordinated to political demands through the auction for votes of a competitive political system.[21]

The 'economics of politics' argument would then envisage a *weakening* of rational direction from the centre, as rival political parties competed for the electoral support of pressure groups seeking to increase their share of government expenditure; while the level of that expenditure would itself tend to grow as a result of their activities.

This will have the effect of 'overloading' governments with commitments which will in turn constrain their conduct of economic policy. It will, in addition, draw governments ineluctably into the regulation of the micro-economy, an area which it was intended should be left to private enterprise. And with the extension of state activity into areas not envisaged by Keynes, the ossification of the market mechanism will produce a cumulative movement in the direction of further state control.

The result of all this will be a mutual weakening of the government and the governed, with a decline in individual freedom and endeavour as increasing numbers become dependent on the state; together with an emasculation of policy as governments attempt to serve the multitude of interests upon whose support they are forced to rely. As government expenditure increases, so too will the economic burdens to be borne, in the form of taxation and the public debt, together with the inflation that represents a worsening of the terms upon which low rates of unemployment can be obtained.

In other words, the Achilles heel of Keynesianism lay in the conjunction of its two most characteristic features: the government intervention which distinguished it from classical economics; and the working of the democracy which such intervention was intended to save.

But was it *inevitable* that Keynes's vision of rational government should have been overtaken by this trading of interests through the political process? S. Brittan has reminded us that Keynes's contemporary, Joseph Schumpeter,

> put forward three main preconditions for the insulation of liberal representative democracy against the internally generated economic forces that would tend to destroy it. It is interesting that these conditions were also part of Keynes's implicit view of the political world. But because of the latter's underlying optimism about the political process, he did not bother to spell them out himself or consider the circumstances in which they might be endangered.[22]

The first condition is that the obtrusion of purely political considerations upon the exercise of rational decision-making must be strictly limited. Brittan suggests that Keynes may have envisaged that the government would operate in the manner of one of Britain's traditionally non-political institutions such as the pre-1914 Bank of England.

The second condition is that there must be a well-trained bureaucracy of independent character, able and willing to convince politicians of the need to pursue 'expertly' determined policies. Keynes, argues Brittan, would have seen evidence of this in the inter-war period when, for example, the government accepted advice to return to the gold-standard on terms that would lead to unemployment at home. In addition, in an age in which both civil servants and ministers were men of independent means, able to disdain popular clamourings of which they disapproved, the fulfilment of this condition would have been a reasonable assumption.

Schumpeter's third condition calls for the exercise of political restraint, of democratic self-control, on the part of the electorate. That the masses were slow to realise their power Brittan attributes to traditional virtues, derived from the lingering moral heritage of the feudal system, which succumbed only gradually to the new awareness that the capitalist system itself engendered.

Inevitably, however, with the demise of the old beliefs and loyalties, political restraint evaporated. With it went the system in which the first two conditions could be satisfied, and we are back with our theme of the demand for socialisation.

Political restraint is, therefore, the key to the problem. Without self-control on the part of the participants in the democratic process the socialised economy will be rendered unworkable. When, in Britain, cultural changes broke down a tradition of self-control, the pressures exerted through the political process subjected the Keynesian system to strains it could not endure.

THE POLITICS OF THE ECONOMICS

The pattern established in economic relationships during the Keynesian era, of a long period of stability followed by rapid decline, is faithfully mirrored by changes in the structure of British politics. The reason that stability persisted for so long is partly due to the influence of the economic factors dealt with earlier, but also because of favourable political conditions. The political economy of Keynes's day, which was conducive to the exercise of 'rational' government, was succeeded by the equivalent conditions appropriate to a collectivist society. That is, government by 'expert' elites in a largely *laissez-faire* economy gave way to a model system for the effective exercise of public choice in a largely socialised economy.

Professor Beer[23] has referred to this model system as the 'collectivist polity'. Its achievement excited the envy of the Western world and secured for Britain an unprecedented period of political stability combined with economic prosperity. But political stability and economic performance were mutually dependent, and when the collectivist polity crumbled, economic prosperity was forfeit.

The model system failed because of internal pressures generated by its inherent contradictions in conjunction with the impact of the cultural revolution which swept Britain in the 1960s and 1970s. The result was the paralysis of public choice, with consequent drift and the loss of control over public expenditure. With the passing of the collectivist polity, the conditions necessary for the exercise of rational government in a socialised economy were removed, and the consequent lapse of policy into short-term expediency manifested itself in rising inflation.

The collectivist polity comprised a choice mechanism in which political parties and pressure groups together fashioned policies relating to the managed economy and the welfare state; but in which those policies in turn influenced interests and created pressure groups. The two-way, interactive, nature of the process is important for our main thesis, which sees the demand for socialisation in a democratic society as giving rise to a system which itself generates pressures that render the political economy unstable.

In substantive terms the collectivist polity becomes 'a moving equilibrium between two [political] parties in basic agreement, but accommodating policy to the demands of groups of consumers and producers'.[24] There are three distinct but related elements here, developments in which, together with the changes that their interaction produced, caused the abrupt demise of the collectivist polity.

We begin with the party system of government and the marked differences of outlook and policy of the two main parties at the 1945 election. Victory for the Labour Party set the tone for post-war politics, and it was the Conservatives who had to shift their ground substantially in favour of socialisation to meet the challenge at future elections.

By the 1950s the picture is one of strong rivalry between parties of roughly equal strength, each of which had been forced to broaden its appeal in order to win votes. Despite the absence of the marked ideological disparities of the 1940s, the parties continued to provide for the exercise of public choice by competitively adjusting their programmes to meet changes in public preference. Thus it was that changes in public policy in Britain came to take place *between* elections, as:

> the two main rivals for power sought to anticipate the drift of public favour. With awkward leads and lags, the two parties wheeled in unison to Left and to Right.[25]

The outcome of this interaction within the party system was the emergence in the late 1950s of the *consensus*, in which despite obvious differences of emphasis and detail, party programmes came to assume a common view on the social and political order and the approach to economic management. In this way the political parties were fulfilling their traditional functions of choice, aggregation and consensus, for through their mutual adjustments of policy towards a consensus they allowed for the voluntary adjustment of public preferences to a position of general assent.

The second element of the collectivist polity was the 'new group politics', a term which refers to pressure groups intimately connected with the activities of government in a socialised society.[26]

That is, the intervention of the state in social and economic affairs will itself create new interests and give rise to groups organised to defend and extend them. Moreover, because such intervention will itself derive from acceptance of the need to achieve particular public goals, pressure on a government to achieve those goals will require it to seek the co-operation of the interest groups involved. Because the consequences of intervention by the government are likely to affect the interests of many groups, effective public choice will only be possible if the government is able to mobilise consent on a sufficiently large scale. In other words, the implementation of policies designed to produce public benefits will require the co-operation of the intended beneficiaries.

It was, of course, the function of the party system to provide the programmes which could accommodate the demands of the new group politics, and within the framework of the party philosophy to produce coherent policies on the basis of the necessary consent.

However, the ability of the party system to provide for effective public choice was seriously impaired by the achievement of consensus. The decline of ideological distinctiveness meant that voters were denied the opportunity to choose between broad social and economic viewpoints, and attention instead focused on group interests. This had the effect of dissolving traditional party loyalties as groups freely entered the political market place to seek the best return. By the same token, parties were forced to compile policy programmes designed to secure maximum group support in the short term and with less regard to the mutual consistency of individual pledges or their longer-term economic and social effects.

Nevertheless, these would have remained weakening tendencies rather than a death blow to the collectivist polity had it not been for the fundamental change in Britain's political culture in the 1960s. The 'civic culture', with its notions of authority and deference, was swept away, to be replaced by a new populism. By removing traditional inhibitions and restraints this cultural revolution led to fundamental changes in political attitudes. These in turn increased the group pressures acting within the collectivist polity to levels that made the exercise of rational government impossible.

In other words, the mechanism of public choice broke down as the collectivist polity degenerated into 'a swamp of pluralistic stagnation'.[27] The result was an immobilising drift in public affairs that helps to explain an apparent loss of control in economic policy during a period of importance for present purposes. That is, it provides an explanation from the political side for the sharp rise in public expenditure which took place during the 1960s and, as such, a complement to the economic influences, discussed earlier, arising from the need to sustain full-employment growth.

From the political side the problems of the 1960s had their roots in tendencies developed during the 1950s. The record levels of economic growth achieved under Keynesianism engendered a mood of optimism among politicians, and were seen to justify acceptance of the high levels of public expenditure required for economic management and the welfare state. This was the age of 'growthmanship', or what Beer has called 'Hubristic Keynesianism',[28] when political parties formulated ambitious programmes of economic and social betterment and encouraged public expectations of a rising standard of living, all on the optimistic expectation that through Keynesian techniques of management the economy could be made to grow at the appropriate (high) rate.

These tendencies were to be accentuated during the 1960s, when competition for support between the parties, in the context of pressure from the new group politics, created a self-reinforcing spiral of rising voter expectations and party commitments, with irresistible consequences for public expenditure.

POLITICAL AND ECONOMIC FACTORS EXPLAIN INFLATION IN THE SOCIALISED ECONOMY

Taking political and economic factors together gives us a nicely circular argument to explain the longer-term inflationary influences at work in the socialised economy.

The argument begins with the demand for socialisation, which made the state responsible for the attainment of democratically determined public goals. Through the working of the political process the commitments increased, as did the public expenditure implications of the resulting programmes. These, nevertheless, were seen as being justified if economic growth could be sustained at the high rates which seemed possible in a Keynesian economy. Hence the strategy for growth through the management of demand.

However, as investment proceeded and the economy grew, the ever-widening gap between income and consumption had to be filled with increased investment or government expenditure if full employment was to be sustained. Because investment was inadequate, government expenditure had to grow.

Consequently, we have a curious sequence of events, in which government expenditure was being incurred in order to promote economic growth, which was itself intended to justify the increases in government expenditure taking place for political reasons. Finally, the maintenance of full-employment income as growth proceeded, itself required government expenditure to grow.

This last tendency was particularly strong from the late 1960s, and followed on a decade through which government expenditure had grown under the influence of purely political pressures. In the 1970s, the various influences, economic and political, combined to produce stagflation as real growth slowed and public expenditure grew out of control amid the pressures of political drift.

THE END OF THE KEYNESIAN CONSENSUS

In reaction to the pluralistic stagnation which paralysed public choice from the late 1960s, the 1970s saw a polarisation of political and economic ideas and attempts by the Conservative and Labour governments to break out – right and left – from the consensus. Each initiative failed, being followed in due course by the familiar 'U-turn'. But if economic failure, as represented by stagflation, was partly a consequence of political failure, represented by drift, how was the situation to be redeemed given that the demand for socialisation had, through the democratic process, led ineluctably to consensus?

One answer was through the imposition of restraint from without, and here we could instance the monetary discipline required by the IMF in return for a substantial loan in 1976. Of course, Austrian economists in particular have argued the need for restraint imposed by some autonomous institution such as the gold-standard, as a means of protecting politicians against the consequences of their own inclinations, but it is unlikely that the reimposition of such a restraint in modern conditions would be practicable.[29]

Nevertheless, the strictures of the IMF hinted at what was necessary, but for a government to embark on a policy which had at its centre the need for monetary restraint – as a means, in the context of the present argument, of escaping from consensus and drift – there would first have to be a change of mind on the part of the electorate. There had, of course, been the 'new style of government' of Edward Heath, but despite its neo-liberal intentions the Heath administration had lacked an unequivocal doctrine and a mode of discipline to protect it against the political pressures which arise from the consequences of short-run economic fluctuations. Consequently, when unemployment began to rise, counter-cyclical policy action caused public expenditure to follow.

In the late 1970s, commentators representing a variety of viewpoints attempted to forecast what kind of political economy would succeed Keynesianism.[30] A majority, arguing on the basis of the prevailing trend, envisaged some system involving a further extension of state activity. This in turn might be on a variety of bases, ranging from Marxist-inspired state socialism to the sort of command-economy model familiar under National Socialism, in which the state controls an economy left largely in private ownership. On the other hand, a minority, arguing on the basis of monetarist/Austrian principles, saw a way out only through a *reversal* of the prevailing trend. None, however, could forsee that the triumph of Keynes's critics, as embodied in the formation of government policy, was just round the corner.

A NEW DEPARTURE?

The 1979 government of Margaret Thatcher possessed two strengths which augured for its success where others had failed. One was the benefit of Mr Heath's experience, which illustrated the danger of the U-turn; the other was an overt and unqualified commitment to the monetarist/Austrian position. This in turn provided a clear social and economic doctrine, against the previous trend, which if accepted by the voters would impose an implied commitment upon them as well as upon the government.

In addition, the main policy prescription of monetarism committed the government to a publicly announced target rate of growth for the money supply, and this provided not only an indicator for economic policy-making but also a visible means of self-discipline and protection against the pressures of group politics.

With the election of the Conservative government in 1979, the dilemma of the 1970s was apparently resolved by a change in political conditions as the electorate drew back in fear of further drift and voted for discipline.

There are two aspects to this. First, it was a victory for that perennially attractive notion – the cool, healthy *douche* of the slump phase of the classical trade cycle, which implied acceptance of the need for the judicious weeding, the invigorating winnowing, of moribund areas of economic life hitherto perpetuated by public patronage. Second, it was a victory not so much for the technical correctness of monetarist doctrine, but for acceptance of the need to reassert traditional values, of which the commitment to monetary control and the defeat of inflation as the main objective of policy was but the visible expression.

So the conditions which produced the need for the Keynesian Revolution passed away. Not because Keynes's theory was wrong or inappropriate or indeed because unemployment was no longer a problem; but because of a change of attitude on the part of the public, symbolised by and focused in their acceptance of the supreme importance of the need to conquer inflation at the possible expense of (further) unemployment.

An assessment of the success or failure of Mrs Thatcher's bold initiative is not yet possible, but two comments are in order. The first is that the government have encountered severe problems in seeking to achieve their money-supply targets,[31] and, given their emphasis on money-supply control through the regulation of government borrowing, this indicates the difficulties involved in seeking to moderate the rate of growth of public expenditure. This in turn will reflect the entrenched strength of 'new group' interests.

The second point is that in successfully controlling inflation the government is seen to be achieving the principal objective of its economic policy. It was expected, of course, that there would be a cost, possibly heavy, in the form of short-term unemployment, but that the economy would then adjust to equilibrium at the natural rate.

However, the actual levels of unemployment experienced have been very heavy – and probably far heavier than anticipated, even allowing for the effects of the world recession. Moreover, with adult unemployment standing at 3.21 million (January 1986) the underlying trend is still upward, or at least, has no more than stabilised, and as ministers continue to express 'disappointment' at the failure of the economy to readjust in the prescribed manner, the question arises as to what has gone wrong. To the monetarist the point would be answered by the inference that the natural rate of unemployment had risen, but it seems implausible to expect this to explain the full extent of the problem.

There is, of course, another explanation; one that could not be countenanced on monetarist or Austrian premises but which follows directly from Keynes's analysis. That is, that there is a deficiency of demand; that whereas excessive *increases* in public expenditure may create inflationary pressures, cuts in expenditure will fall disproportionately on output rather than prices. Moreover, once income has fallen to the new lower level there will exist no automatic tendency for the economy to return to full-employment equilibrium.

Therefore, there is a further, insistent, question: if unemployment continues to increase from the present high level, will the demand for socialisation reassert itself, either through the electoral system or directly through social unrest? For though an underemployed economy can be held to be 'stronger', in relation, for example, to foreign trade competitors, because of the higher productivity and efficiency and moderation of pay awards that heavy unemployment implies, can those who are unemployed be expected to wait passively until 'the market turns up'? Because whereas for a monetarist/Austrian economist unemployment is but a transitional phase during which the economy adapts to and indeed creates new patterns of demand, on Keynes's analysis it is likely to become a semi-permanent state.

24 In Conclusion

Much recent criticism of the Keynesian Revolution results from confusion in the minds of the critics between the difficulties that have arisen in the application of Keynes's ideas, and the core of his theory. The residual problem of application is largely political, in the sense that Keynesian economics is inherently vulnerable to pressures which arise through the political process in a democratic society. But the question remains of whether these problems are more intractable than those which stem from the alternative *laissez-faire* approach.

If the Keynesian Revolution was important in that it provided the principles upon which capitalist democracy could be saved from destruction during a particular historical episode, does anything remain from the wreck of the Keynesian political economy?

The principles remain. The Keynesian Revolution was a revolution of principles, which involved the repudiation of theories based on Say's Law, and the derivation of a new theory from the first principles of a monetary economy that has at its centre the principle of effective demand. If the nature of the political process rendered the mixed economy of the post-1945 era ultimately unworkable, this does not invalidate Keynes's revolution of theory. It does not somehow make Keynes's critics 'right', in terms of economic theory, and Keynes 'wrong'. A reversion to a *laissez-faire* economy will not make Say's Law valid and so ensure that the economy will automatically adjust to a unique, full-employment, equilibrium.

Keynes showed the way, if full employment was to be attained. Keynes was *also* of the opinion that full employment should be the main objective of policy. But this was a conclusion of the 1930s, when unemployment was heavy and the threat from the consequences of unemployment seemed the overriding concern. In later years Keynes would, no doubt, as Hayek has argued, have been in the forefront of the fight against inflation, and would have advocated appropriate policies with suitable theoretical justification to accompany them. This, again, does not imply that Keynes would have abandoned the principles of the *General Theory* and so proved his critics right.

Therefore, if full employment is considered to be the main priority, the state will have to intervene in the absence of that conjunction of favourable influences which would produce full employment in a *laissez-faire* economy, and the necessary political, social and constitutional arrangements will have to be made to ensure that the system is made workable. If full employment is not considered the main priority, a strategy will still have to be worked out within a Keynesian framework – even if this only means being aware of the consequences for employment of an anti-inflation policy based on expenditure cuts.

A revolution of principles was clearly not intended to dictate the details of policy, the formation of which would be a largely pragmatic process adapted to changing circumstances. It would not be ideologically bounded, except as regards the fundamental commitment to the maintenance of democratic government and individual liberty. So long as effective demand was maintained at the required level, Keynesian policy would be consistent with the privatisation of individual industries or the nationalisation of individual utilities. Employment policy would not, moreover, be pursued to the point at which inflationary pressures threatened economic stability. Rather, it would have to be formed in the light of (for example) international financial arrangements and a particular country's political culture, the degree of social cohesion it enjoyed and the state of its industrial relations.

One of Keynes's most disturbing conclusions, which is similarly not in vogue, concerns his thesis of secular stagnation. This thesis was made to seem implausible through the effects of war and socialisation; but we have argued that the consequences of failure to recognise the relevance of the analysis was a contributory factor in the onset of stagflation and the decline of the Keynesian system. Its implications, moreover, are of profound significance for the future of all industrialised societies and deserve to be more widely discussed. Professor A. J. Brown has surmised that 'if and when we stop worrying about stagflation, the stagnation hypothesis will be well up among our candidates for the next thing to worry about'.[1]

Above all, we must beware of regarding Keynesianism as simply a preferred style of economic organisation, which was defeated by the Pandora's box that it opened up, and which can *by the choice of economists* be discarded in favour of some new system of economic organisation which is considered to be more resistant to political pressures. For the movement in favour of socialisation was a product of social, political and historical forces, and Keynesianism could only be replaced by an alternative system as a consequence of changes in these same forces.

In the light of the Conservative election victories of 1979 and 1983, those changes may now have taken place, but if unemployment at present or higher levels proves to be intractable, the resulting clamour for the socialisation of economic life may become politically irresistible. If socialisation is to be tolerable it will have to be ordered on Keynesian principles. The principles themselves hold good, but unless they are applied with that increased awareness of the possibilities and limitations of Keynesian economics that past experience has revealed, then the Keynesian hope, of prosperity in a free society, must almost inevitably be a hope betrayed. For Keynesian economics did not so much open up the Pandora's box of state intervention – that was due to broader influences; rather it gave substance to the hope that remained.

Notes and References

Note References to the following three volumes of the *Collected Writings of John Maynard Keynes* (Macmillan for the Royal Economic Society) are given in abbreviated form, as indicated in parentheses:

Vol XIII (1973) *The General Theory and After: Preparation* (Keynes, *CW*, XIII)

Vol XIV (1973) *The General Theory and After: Defence and Development* (Keynes, *CW*, XIV)

Vol XXIX (1979) *The General Theory and After: A Supplement* (Keynes, *CW*, XXIX)

Reference to John Maynard Keynes, *The General Theory of Employment, Interest and Money* (Macmillan, 1936) is also given in an abbreviated form, as: Keynes, *General Theory*.

Introduction

1. Published by Macmillan in February 1936.
2. All published in *The Collected Writings of John Maynard Keynes* (Macmillan for the RES), Volumes VII, XIV, XXIX; also Vol XIII.

1. The Institution of Money: An Introduction

1. The sequence described here is not intended to be representative of some actual historical development, though some historical parallels will be apparent. Rather, the intention is to examine the nature, characteristics and functions of money – by tracing the process by which a barter economy might develop into a money-using economy.
2. For a fuller account of the considerations involved in the calculation, see R. W. Clower (ed.), *Readings in Monetary Theory* (London: Penguin, 1969) pp. 8–11.
3. This is because allowance must be made for commodity 1 to be separately traded for commodities 2, 3 . . . 10; commodity 2 for commodities 3, 4 . . . 10; and so on. The number of posts required is given by the formula $\frac{1}{2}n(n-1)$.
4. Clower, *Readings in Monetary Theory*, pp. 11–12. The effect of this innovation is to reduce the number of posts and the number of price ratios to nine ($=n-1$ commodities).
5. R. W. Clower, 'Theoretical Foundations of Monetary Policy', in *Monetary Theory and Monetary Policy in the 1970s*, ed. G. Clayton, J. C.

Gilbert, R. Sedgwick (Oxford University Press, 1971) p. 20; plus the references given.

6. K. Brunner and A. H. Meltzer have suggested that it is the uneven distribution of information, rather than an undifferentiated uncertainty, that motivates transactors to seek alternatives to barter. In attempting to economise on resources devoted to the process of exchange, transactors will be motivated to choose sequences of transactions – transactions chains – which involve assets with low marginal costs of information: i.e. commodities which are most widely used and best known. As the most efficient transactions sequences emerge, individuals' chains will converge to a common pattern and one or more assets will be used with dominant frequency in transactions. See K. Brunner and A. H. Meltzer, 'The Uses of Money: Money in the Theory of an Exchange Economy', *American Economic Review* (December 1971) pp. 784–805.
7. The use of organised markets implies the observance of trading rules; in this case that commodities exchange for money and money for commodities.
8. This quality has a broader significance in that the outstanding stock of a highly durable monetary commodity is likely to be large in relation to the volume of current production, so that changes in the latter will not seriously affect the stability of the commodity's value.
9. More accurately, perhaps, 'having utility', thus encompassing any object to which a society attributes value – for whatever reason. While, for example, in ancient Babylon, 'exchangeable goods' (as legally distinguished from 'non-exchangeable goods') consisted of commodities in common use, 'in other parts of the world, the earliest means of payment seems to have been ornaments or objects with a ceremonial or religious significance, including "models" of tools and implements'. See E. V. Morgan, *A History of Money* (Harmondsworth: Penguin, 1965) pp. 11–12.
10. Pellets of electrum (a natural alloy of gold and silver), each marked by weight, were in use among merchants from Lydia, in Asia Minor, in the eighth century BC.
11. From the seventh century BC, kings of Lydia issued coins of electrum of recognisably modern shape; but it was Croesus, king of Lydia in the sixth century BC who moved away from the use of electrum and established issues of gold and silver coins minted separately. For an account of early money and coinage, see N. Angell, *The Story of Money* (London: Cassell, 1930) ch. 4.
12. In a democratic society this development would be aided by, for example, the incidence of national crises, during which individuals tend more readily to concede increased powers and activities to the state in return for the central direction and co-ordination thought necessary for the effective resolution of the problem – for example, war or national economic crisis. It is reasonable to assume, therefore, that correspondingly it would be found increasingly acceptable for the intrinsic value money to be replaced in effect by the promises of the state, and for the quantity of state money to be regulated, at least nominally, by the same, issuing, authority.

13. That is, removing metal from coins by shearing off slivers from the edge or by shaking them together in a bag.
14. The value of the coinage in terms of the precious metal would be self-regulating if citizens possessed the right to melt (or export) and mint coin. For example, as trade fell away in a recession the excess supply of coin would cause its value to fall relative to its commodity value. The volume of coin in circulation would then fall as citizens exercised their right to melt or export. Conversely, as trade expanded the relative scarcity of coin would cause its value to rise relative to its commodity value so that citizens would take metal to the mint. See R. F. Harrod, *Money* (London: Macmillan, 1969) pp. 9–13.
15. See C. A. E. Goodhart, *Money, Information and Uncertainty* (London: Macmillan, 1975) pp. 9–13, on the various state abuses of the coinage and the checks that operated to restrain them.
16. A process begun in the earliest days of banking, when receipts were issued against deposits of precious metal. In time, the receipts became the circulating medium and accepted in settlement of debts.
17. While this economised on real resources it was essentially an historical development, forced at the behest of governments faced with the need to make international payments in time of war and economic stress (for example, 1797, 1914, 1947). Notice that, by the same token, inconvertibility removed an important restraint on government expenditure and hence the scale of state activity.
18. The proceeds of the sale will in turn provide the means for traders to settle outstanding debts of their own.
19. In addition, the establishment of a standardised monetary asset with well-known properties will encourage transactors to enter into contracts in which *payment is deferred*. This will stimulate the development of finance and the growth of credit and influence the intertemporal allocation of resources. See Brunner and Meltzer, '*The Uses of Money*', p. 800.
20. Using this term in the sense in which it is used by G. L. S. Shackle in G. Clayton *et al.*, *Monetary Theory and Monetary Policy in the 1970s* (London: Oxford University Press, 1971) p. 32; and by Goodhart, *Money, Information and Uncertainty*, pp. 2–3. The further qualification, *generalised* means of payment, might be added, so as to exclude certain specialised means of payment (peppercorn rents, royal tributes or, in primitive societies, the bride price) which do not function as general media of exchange. See C. A. E. Goodhart, 'The Role, Functions and Definition of Money', in G. C. Harcourt (ed.), *The Microeconomic Foundations of Macroeconomics* (London: Macmillan, 1977) p. 206.

2. The Monetary Economy

1. Or, as is frequently the case, in small closed communities: 'institutions' of various kinds, in which life is arranged along communal lines.
2. Goodhart, in Harcourt (ed.), *Microeconomic Foundations of Macroeconomics*, pp. 223–4.
3. Goodhart, ibid, pp. 225–6.

4. Goodhart, ibid, p. 224.
5. Goodhart, ibid, p. 223, n. 3. Italics in original.
6. For a note on money as a unit of account and the distinction between accounting prices, money prices and relative prices, see D. Patinkin, *Money, Interest and Prices*, 2nd edn (New York: Harper & Row, 1965) pp. 15–16.
7. The 'auctioneer' was employed in Walrasian value theory, but other theoretical means have been suggested for solving the essential problem of providing the requisite information to transactors and for co-ordinating behaviour based on that information. F. Y. Edgeworth, for example, allowed traders to 'recontract'; but the best-known device, and certainly the most intuitively persuasive in modern political economy, is Adam Smith's 'invisible hand'. For an assessment of the invisible hand as an imperfect approximation of actual market mechanisms, together with implications for policy, see F. H. Hahn, 'Reflections on the Invisible Hand', *Lloyds Bank Review* (April 1982) pp. 1–21.
8. This exposition is based on the account in M. Blaug, *Economic Theory in Retrospect*, 2nd edn (London: Heinemann, 1968) ch. 5.
9. Because commodities are produced for exchange, to *supply* a commodity (offer it in exchange) is by the same action to *demand* other commodities in exchange.
10. Singling out money because of the functions and attributes discussed earlier.
11. With the general price level determined in the money market and relative prices determined in the commodity market, the economy is effectively 'dichotomised' into monetary and real sectors. For a rigorous examination of this dichotomy, the homogeneity postulate and the meaning of the neutrality of money, see Patinkin, *Money, Interest and Prices*, pp. 174–86.

3. Money, Investment and Saving

1. J. M. Keynes, 'The General Theory of Employment', *The Quarterly Journal of Economics* (Feb. 1937) p. 213.
2. Ibid, p. 214.
3. Ibid, p. 215.
4. Keynes, *General Theory*, p. 18.
5. Ibid, p. 19.
6. Goodhart, in Harcourt (ed.) *Microeconomic Foundations of Macroeconomics*, p. 226. Italics added.
7. Keynes, *General Theory*, p. 83.
8. These conditions are in accord with what in Chapter 2 we referred to as Say's Identity.
9. Keynes, *General Theory*, pp. 179–80.
10. Keynes, *General Theory*, pp. 182–3.

4. Keynes's Revolution

1. See, for example, A. Leijonhufvud, *On Keynesian Economics and the Economics of Keynes* (New York: OUP, 1968) pp. 10, 16; D. E. Moggridge, *Keynes*, 2nd edn (London: Macmillan, 1980) pp. 94, 95; S. E. Harris in A. Hansen, *A Guide to Keynes* (New York: McGraw-Hill, 1953) p. ix; J. C. Gilbert, *Keynes's Impact on Monetary Economics* (London: Butterworth, 1982) pp. 25, 26.
2. Keynes, *General Theory*, p. viii.
3. See Moggridge, *Keynes*, ch. 5; D. Patinkin, 'The Process of Writing *The General Theory*: A Critical Survey'; and D. Moggridge, 'Cambridge Discussion and Criticism Surrounding the Writing of *The General Theory*: A Chronicler's View', in D. Patinkin and J. C. Leith (eds), *Keynes, Cambridge and the General Theory* (London: Macmillan, 1977) pp. 3–24; 64–71.
4. See Keynes, *CW*, XIV and XXIX.
5. Published in 1937 and reprinted in *CW*, XIV, pp. 109–23.
6. In a letter to R. G. Hawtrey, in Keynes, *CW*, XIV, p. 47.
7. Keynes, *CW*, XIV, pp. 133–4.
8. Ibid, pp. 179–83.
9. Keynes, *CW*, XIII, pp. 492–3.
10. Keynes, *CW*, XIV, p. 122.
11. Keynes, *General Theory*, p. vi.
12. Ibid.
13. Keynes, *CW*, XIV, p. 88.
14. Keynes, *CW*, XIII, pp. 469–70.
15. Keynes, *General Theory*, p. viii.
16. Ibid, p. v.
17. Keynes, *CW*, XIV, pp. 100–1.
18. Ibid, p. 85. This view is reproduced in a later letter to D. H. Robertson and in his notes for the Stockholm lecture. He had previously written to H. O. Meredith in similar vein. See Keynes, *CW*, XXIX, p. 213.
19. Notes for Stockholm lecture, referred to earlier. One of the main targets for Keynes's anti-classical controversial style had been A. C. Pigou with whose review of the *General Theory* Keynes was plainly disappointed. In Keynes's view Pigou's 'predominant emotion' was 'that of a sixth form boy who had been cheeked'. See Keynes, *CW*, XIV, p. 87.
20. Letter to D. H. Robertson, in Keynes, *CW*, XIV, p. 87.
21. Published in *Econometrica*, April 1937.
22. Keynes, *CW*, XIV, p. 79.
23. In B. Ohlin, D. H. Robertson, R. G. Hawtrey, 'Alternative Theories of the Rate of Interest: Three Rejoinders', *Economic Journal*, Sept. 1937; see also, Keynes, *CW*, XIV, p. 215, and *CW*, XXIX, pp. 267, 269, n. 61.
24. Keynes, *General Theory*, p. 3.
25. See also, letter to R. G. Hawtrey, *CW*, XIV, p. 24. Notice that as both Marshall and Edgeworth were dead, it was inevitable that Pigou would bear the brunt of Keynes's attack, as the principal living English exponent of 'classical economics'.
26. Letter to G. Haberler, in Keynes, *CW*, XXIX, p. 270.

27. Letter to R. G. Hawtrey, in Keynes, *CW*, XIV, p. 26.
28. Letter to R. F. Harrod, in Keynes, *CW*, XIV, p. 85.
29. See Chapter 23 of present volume.
30. See: letter to A. P. Lerner, in Keynes, *CW*, XXIX, p. 215; Keynes, 'The General Theory of Employment', in *CW*, XIV, p. 123; letter from J. R. Hicks, in *CW*, XIV, p. 81.
31. Keynes, *General Theory*, p. 183.
32. The letters to G. Haberler, in *CW*, XXIX, p. 270; and to R. G. Hawtrey, in *CW*, XIV, p. 24.
33. In Chapter 20; where we shall explain that following his disappointment over his review of Keynes's *A Treatise on Money* (1930), Hayek failed to respond to the Keynesian Revolution for almost forty years.
34. For comment on the breach between Keynes and Robertson, see, for example: Gilbert, *Keynes's Impact on Monetary Economics*, pp. 8–11; Moggridge, *Keynes*, pp. 159–60.
35. T. Wilson, 'Professor Robertson on Effective Demand and the Trade Cycle', *Economic Journal* (Sept. 1953) p. 520.
36. In a letter to Wilson in October 1953. Quoted in J. R. Presley, *Robertsonian Economics* (London: Macmillan, 1979) p. 84, n. 80.
37. Keynes, 'Alternative Theories of the Rate of Interest', *Economic Journal* (June 1937), in *CW*, XIV, pp. 202–3, n. 2.
38. Presley, *Robertsonian Economics*, p. 83.
39. Keynes, 'General Theory of Employment', in *CW*, XIV, p. 109.
40. Letter to Robertson, Dec. 1936, in Keynes, *CW*, XIV, p. 94.
41. Robertson to Keynes, in Keynes, *CW*, XIV, p. 95.
42. D. H. Robertson, *Banking Policy and the Price Level* (London: P. S. King & Son Ltd., 1926).
43. See the letter to Robertson, Dec. 1936, in Keynes, *CW*, XIV, p. 94.
44. Letter to Keynes 1925, in Keynes, *CW*, XIII, p. 29.
45. See Keynes's comment that, though Robertson was not a classical economist but a pioneer in 'the other lines of approach', he 'seems constantly trying to make out that he does still hold the classical theory as well as one of the newer versions'. The letter to Haberler 1938, in Keynes, *CW*, XXIX, p. 270.
46. Letter to Robertson Dec. 1937, in Keynes, *CW*, XXIX, p. 165. For the literary allusion, see A. C. Swinburne's 'The Garden of Proserpine':

    That even the weariest river
    Winds somewhere safe to sea.

47. Recall the lines from the 'Triumph of Time':

    I will go back to the great sweet mother
    Mother and lover of men, the sea.
    I will go down to her, I and no other,
    Close with her, kiss her and mix her with me

48. Ian Fletcher, *Swinburne*, Writers and their Work No. 228 (London: Longman, for the British Council (n.d.)) pp. 7, 23.
49. Keynes, *General Theory*, p. 183.
50. Of the many studies of Ibsen, John Northam's *Ibsen: A Critical Study* (CUP, 1973) is particularly helpful here.

51. See the survey of views in Gilbert, *Keynes's Impact on Monetary Economics*, pp. 63–4.
52. Presley, *Robertsonian Economics*, p. 82.
53. The meaning of this innovation was, however, misinterpreted by Robertson and his followers and regarded as an indication that Keynes was shifting his ground.
54. Keynes, 'Mr. Keynes on "Finance"', *Economic Journal* (June 1938), in *CW*, XIV, pp. 232–3.
55. Presley, *Robertsonian Economics*, p. 182, n. 18.

5. The Robertsonian Critique

1. In the interpretation of Robertson's economics and his attack on Keynes, I am greatly indebted in what follows to Dr Presley's *Robertsonian Economics*, introduced in the previous chapter. This does not, however, apply to criticisms of Robertson, which are made in the light of my interpretation of Keynes's position.
2. We should also mention imaginary capital, which is the public's holding of government debt.
3. The various kinds of lacking and their relationship to the different kinds of capital are discussed in Robertson, *Banking Policy and the Price Level*, ch. 5.
4. See Chapter 20. For Robertson this phenomenon had repercussions for his account of the trade cycle.
5. It is in the criticism of Robertson and the rebuttal of his attack on Keynes that we depart from Dr Presley.
6. See Presley, *Robertsonian Economics*, pp. 110–11. The paper in question is one read by Keynes to the Political Economy Club and reproduced in *CW*, XIII, pp. 2–14.
7. See Chapter 7 of present volume.
8. Though, here, we should notice that Robertson differs from the classical 'straw man' of the textbooks in that there is no automatic tendency for S and I to be equated through movements in the rate of interest.

6. The Principle of Effective Demand

1. See J. A. Kregel, 'Economic Methodology in the Face of Uncertainty: The Modelling Methods of Keynes and the Post-Keynesians', *Economic Journal* (June 1976) p. 213, n. 1.
2. Ibid.
3. Keynes, *General Theory*, p. 25.
4. Where the 'aggregate supply price of the output of a given amount of employment is the expectation of proceeds which will just make it worth the while of the entrepreneurs to give that employment'. Keynes, *General Theory*, p. 24.
5. Keynes, *General Theory*, p. 55.

6. Ibid, p. 29.
7. Ibid, pp. 27–8.
8. Ibid, p. 165.
9. Ibid, p. 135.
10. Ibid, p. 136.
11. Ibid, p. 248.
12. Ibid, p. 28.
13. Ibid, p. 26.
14. Ibid, p. 30.
15. Kregel, 'Economic Methodology', p. 211.
16. Ibid. A point Keynes made in his lectures to students in 1933.
17. Kregel, 'Economic Methodogy', p. 217.
18. See Chapter 8 in present volume.
19. See Kregel, 'Economic Methology', p. 214.

7. Keynes's Theory of Investment and Saving

1. It has been a marked feature of economic development that innovation in financial arrangements has been at the initiative of deficit spenders.
2. Keynes, *General Theory*, pp. 183–4.
3. Ibid, p. 65.
4. Ibid, p. 63. Keynes later stressed in a letter to G. Haberler that 'Aggregate saving and aggregate investment are equal in the same sense that the aggregate quantity of sales in the market is equal to the aggregate quantity of purchases. It does not follow from this that sales and purchases have identically the same meaning or that one term can be substituted for the other.' Keynes, *CW*, XXIX, p. 253.
5. With a given marginal propensity to consume.
6. Keynes, *General Theory*, p. 117.
7. Because 'real income, in terms of product, may be incapable of precise numerical measurement, it is often convenient to regard income in terms of wage units... as an adequate working index of changes in real incomes'. Keynes, *General Theory*, p. 114.
8. Keynes, *General Theory*, p. 115.
9. Ibid, pp. 122–3.
10. Ibid, p. 84.
11. J. Robinson, *Introduction to the Theory of Employment* (London: Macmillan, 1937, repr. 1960) pp. 9, 10.
12. Keynes, *General Theory*, p. 117.
13. Robinson, *Introduction to the Theory of Employment*, p. 11.
14. Ibid, p. 13.
15. Keynes, *General Theory*, p. 210.
16. See Keynes, *General Theory*, p. 211.
17. See Chapter 22 in present volume.
18. Keynes, *General Theory*, p. 64.
19. Ibid, p. 82.

8. Robertson and Keynes on Investment and Saving

1. J. C. Gilbert, *Keynes's Impact on Monetary Economics* (London: Butterworth, 1982) p. 78.
2. See A. Hansen, *A Guide to Keynes* (London: McGraw-Hill, 1953) pp. 59–60.
3. Presley, *Robertsonian Economics*, pp. 85–6, 165–6.
4. See ibid, pp. 112, 119, 166–7, 172–3, etc.
5. J. M. Keynes 'Alternative Theories of the Rate of Interest', *Economic Journal*, (June 1937) in *CW*, XIV, p. 211.
6. J. M. Keynes, 'The Process of Capital Formation', *Economic Journal* (Sept. 1939) pp. 571–2.
7. Presley, *Robertsonian Economics*, p. 165.
8. Ibid, pp. 97–8.
9. Hansen, *Guide to Keynes*, pp. 62–3.
10. In the price level rather than output, which was given at the full-employment level.
11. Keynes, *General Theory*, p. 78.
12. Keynes, *CW*, XIV, p. 120.
13. See Keynes, *General Theory*, pp. 64–5; and *CW*, XXIX, p. 215.
14. Indicating the level of aggregate output which will be supplied at each of a range of price levels, with the money wage rate and the schedule of the marginal productivity of labour assumed to be given. The exposition of the analysis followed here is in L. Shapiro, *Macroeconomics*, 3rd edn (New York: Harcourt Brace Jovanovich, 1974) pp. 245–9.
15. '[T]he rise of prices during a boom is due partly to the rise in the wage unit and partly to the non-homogeneity of resources.' Keynes, *CW*, XXIX, p. 223; plus many references in the *General Theory*.
16. Keynes, *CW*, XXIX, p. 280.
17. Keynes, *CW*, XIV, p. 184.
18. Ibid, p. 185.
19. A. Leijonhufvud, *On Keynesian Economics and the Economics of Keynes* (New York: OUP, 1968) pp. 62–3, n. 8.
20. Ibid, p. 62.
21. See Keynes, *CW*, XIV, p. 216. The point is that when investors are investing, savers will be blissfully unaware that they are going to be saving and consuming out of the income generated by the investment.
22. See Keynes, *CW*, XIV, pp. 119–20, 181; *General Theory*, pp. 95–6.
23. See Keynes, *General Theory*, pp. 93–4, 95–6, 110–12, 178–9.
24. Keynes, *General Theory*, pp. 110–11.
25. Leijonhufvud, *On Keynesian Economics*, p. 62, n. 8.
26. Keynes, *CW*, XIV, p. 183.
27. Keynes, *CW*, XXIX, p. 280.
28. Keynes, *CW*, XIV, p. 323.
29. Ibid, pp. 213, n. 2; and 322.
30. Ibid, pp. 207, 216, 218.
31. See Keynes, *CW*, XIV, p. 219, for an example of Keynes's use of this terminology.
32. Keynes, *General Theory*, p. 122.

33. Ibid, pp. 123–4.
34. Ibid, p. 124. At the same time, the replenishment of stocks will increase aggregate investment to compensate for the previous reduction due to the depletion of stock levels.
35. See, for example, the statement in the *General Theory*, p. 300.
36. Keynes, *CW*, XIV, p. 58.
37. Ibid, p. 71.
38. Ibid. Italics in original.
39. Keynes, *General Theory*, p. 328. This point is dealt with at greater length in Chapter 22 of present volume.
40. See Keynes, 'The Process of Capital Formation', *Economic Journal* (Sept. 1939) p. 572.
41. Keynes, *General Theory*, p. 83.
42. Keynes, *CW*, XIV, p. 71, para. 2.

9. The Finance of Investment

1. J. C. Gilbert, *Keynes's Impact on Monetary Economis* (London: Butterworth, 1982) p. 78; also stated on p. 29. There are other references on, for example, pp. 69 and 76 which indicate that Gilbert did not see any problem with the idea of saving financing investment.
2. G. Horwich, *Money, Capital and Prices* (Homewood: Irwin, 1964) ch. 10.
3. The distinction between a medium of exchange and a means of payment is not relevant here.
4. Keynes, *General Theory*, p. 195.
5. Ibid.
6. Ibid.
7. Keynes, *General Theory*, p. 168.
8. Ibid.
9. Keynes, *General Theory*, p. 196. Italics added.
10. Keynes, *General Theory*, p. 170.
11. Ibid, p. 196.
12. Ibid, p. 170.
13. Ibid, pp. 170–1.
14. For example, in the simplest case, the 'running yield' on a bond which pays £5 for every £100 nominal will be 5 per cent. If the market rate of interest rises to 10 per cent the market price must fall to £50 to keep the yield in line with the market rate.
15. Keynes, *General Theory*, p. 203.
16. Ibid, p. 172.
17. Ibid, p. 201.
18. See J. R. Presley, *Robertsonian Economics* (London: Macmillan, 1979) pp. 87, 178, 179, 213.
19. Keynes, *General Theory*, p. 194.
20. Ibid.
21. Ibid.

22. Keynes, *General Theory*, p. 209.
23. Keynes, *General Theory*, p. 166.
24. See Keynes, *General Theory*, p. 174.
25. J. Robinson, 'The Concept of Hoarding', *Economic Journal* (June 1938) p. 233.
26. Keynes, *General Theory*, p. 299. In addition, Shackle has drawn attention to the positive advantages of dealing in stock terms. See G.L.S. Shackle, *The Years of High Theory* (Cambridge University Press, 1967) p. 145.
27. D. H. Robertson, 'Alternative Theories of the Rate of Interest', *Economic Journal* (1937) p. 428.
28. Presley, *Robertsonian Economics*, p. 213.
29. C. N. Henning, W. Pigott and R. H. Scott, *Financial Markets and the Economy*, 2nd edn (New Jersey: Prentice-Hall, 1978) p. 365.
30. Keynes, *CW*, XIV, pp. 207, 218.
31. Keynes, *CW*, XXIX, p. 282. See also *CW*, XIV, pp. 220, 230.
32. The sequence of argument in the last two paragraphs can be followed in: Keynes, 'The Process of Capital Formation', *Economic Journal* (Sept. 1939) p. 573; *CW*, XIV, pp. 220, 207, 218, 209, 216.
33. The same principles apply to the handling of money balances by firms in the active and inactive circulation.
34. Keynes, *CW*, XIV, p. 220.
35. Ibid, pp. 208–9.
36. Ibid, p. 219.
37. Ibid.
38. See Keynes, *CW*, XIV, pp. 219–20.
39. Keynes, *CW*, XIV, pp. 209, 210.
40. Ibid, pp. 222, 223.
41. Ibid, p. 217. For an exposition of the 'active' demand for money as determined by the lags between receipts and payments, see Keynes, 'Mr. Keynes' "Finance"', *Economic Journal* (June 1938), in *CW*, XIV, p. 230.
42. Keynes, *CW*, XXIX, pp. 282, 281, respectively.
43. Keynes, *CW*, XIV, pp. 224, 230.
44. See, for example, Keynes, *CW*, XIV, pp. 220, 221; XXIX, p. 282.
45. Keynes, *CW*, XIV, p. 110.
46. Ibid, pp. 225, 232.
47. See Keynes, *CW*, XIV, pp. 209, 216–17, 218–19, 220, 231–2.
48. Keynes, *CW*, XIV, p. 222.
49. Ibid, pp. 221, 222, 233; Keynes, 'The Process of Capital Formation', *Economic Journal* (1939) pp. 572–3.
50. Keynes, *CW*, XIV, p. 222. Italics added to 'latter' to emphasise that money is released by *ex post* investment rather than saving.
51. Keynes, 'Process of Capital Formation', p. 574.
52. Keynes, *CW*, XIV, pp. 232–3.
53. See A. H. Meltzer, 'Keynes's *General Theory*: A Different Perspective', *Journal of Economic Literature* (March 1981) pp. 34–64; Keynes, *General Theory*, pp. 47–8; *CW*, XIV, pp. 80–1, 120–1.
54. Keynes, *CW*, XIV, p. 222; see also p. 232.

10. The Rate of Interest

1. See, for example, W. T. Newlyn and R. Bootle, *Theory of Money*, 3rd edn (Oxford: Clarendon Press, 1978) ch. 5.
2. Keynes, *CW*, XXIX, p. 280.
3. D. H. Robertson, 'Mr. Keynes and the Rate of Interest', in J. R. Hicks (ed.), *Essays in Money and Interest* (London: Fontana, 1966) p. 165. See also, J. R. Presley, *Robertsonian Economics*, (London: Macmillan, 1978) pp. 98, 195–6, 211.
4. See Keynes, *General Theory*, pp. 93–4, 95–6, 110; *CW*, XIV, pp. 119, 181, 268–9. See also references in Chapter 8 of present volume.
5. Keynes, *General Theory*, pp. 110–12. The inverse relationship between the rate of interest and aggregate saving is to be seen as a shibboleth for true believers. See *CW*, XIV, p. 269.
6. Keynes, *General Theory*, pp. 168, 196.
7. Ibid, p. 196.
8. Monetary factors influence the long-term rate through their influence on thrift.
9. See Keynes, *General Theory*, p. 207.
10. The best example is A. D. Crockett, *Money*, 2nd edn (London: Nelson, 1979) ch. 3.
11. Robertson, 'Mr. Keynes and the Rate of Interest', in Hicks, *Essays in Money and Interest*, p. 174.
12. Robertson, 1947. Reference given in Presley, *Robertsonian Economics*, p. 303.
13. A. Leijonhufvud, *On Keynesian Economics and the Economics of Keynes* (New York: OUP, 1968) p. 213.
14. See Keynes, *CW*, XXIX, p. 222.
15. See Keynes, *CW*, XIV, pp. 109–10.
16. Keynes made the point explicitly by quoting from Joan Robinson's *Introduction to the Theory of Employment* (London: Macmillan, 1937, repr. 1960) pp. 82, 83. See *CW*, XXIX, p. 184.
17. See Keynes, *CW*, XIV, p. 225.
18. Keynes, *CW*, XXIX, p. 168.
19. Ibid.
20. See, for example, *CW*, XIV, pp. 223, 224, 230.
21. *CW*, XIV, p. 224.
22. See A. Hansen, *A Guide to Keynes* (London: McGraw-Hill, 1953) pp. 140–1, 146–7.
23. *CW*, XIV, p. 80.
24. The necessary composition of the income was explained in Chapter 7 of present volume.
25. Keynes, *CW*, XIV, pp. 202, 205–7.
26. Hansen, *Guide to Keynes*, p. 63. The article in question is, Keynes, 'The Process of Capital Formation', *Economic Journal* (Sept. 1939) p. 573.
27. Keynes, *CW*, XXIX, p. 169.

11. A Monetary Theory of the Rate of Interest

1. Keynes, in a letter to R. G. Hawtrey, March 1936, in Keynes, *CW*, XIV, p. 11.
2. J. M. Keynes, 'Alternative Theories of the Rate of Interest', *Economic Journal* (June 1937), in Keynes, *CW*, XIV, p. 212.
3. From a draft of the *General Theory*, in Keynes, *CW*, XIV, p. 476.
4. See Keynes, *CW*, XIV, p. 212; and a letter to R. F. Harrod, in *CW*, XIV, p. 85.
5. Keynes, *CW*, XIV, p. 212.
6. See Keynes, *General Theory*, pp. 137–9.
7. Keynes, *General Theory*, pp. 140–1; and 'The Theory of the Rate of Interest', in *CW*, XIV, p. 101, n. 2.
8. Keynes, *General Theory*, pp. 145–6.
9. Keynes, *General Theory*, pp. 137, 140, 184; see also, Keynes, 'The General Theory of Employment', *Quarterly Journal of Economics* (1937), in *CW*, XIV, pp. 122–3.
10. Keynes, *General Theory*, pp. 140, 184; plus previous draft of *General Theory*, in *CW*, XIV, p. 477.
11. Keynes, *General Theory*, pp. 139–40.
12. For example, as the rate of interest falls, the present value – the demand price of capital assets – rises. New investment is stimulated and income will rise. Production of capital assets will continue until the m.e.c. falls to equality with the rate of interest.
13. Keynes, 'General Theory of Employment', in *CW*, XIV, pp. 117–18, 122–3.
14. Keynes, 'Alternative Theories of the Rate of Interest', in *CW*, XIV, p. 213.
15. Keynes, *General Theory*, pp. 137, n. 1, 167 n. 2, 205.
16. Ibid, p. 210.
17. Ibid, p. 211.
18. Ibid, p. 212.
19. Keynes's reference is to A. Marshall, *Principles of Economics*, 6th edn, (London: Macmillan & Co., 1910) p. 583, n. 1, but the page reference is identical in the 8th edn. The references there given are to E. von Böhm-Bawerk, *Positive Theory of Capital* (1889), bk. V, ch. 4, p. 261, and bk. II, ch. 2, p. 84, respectively.
20. Keynes, *General Theory*, p. 214.
21. With a given state of technique and endowments of natural resources.
22. Keynes, *General Theory*, p. 217.
23. The phrase is Marshall's, though we do not follow his productivity argument.
24. Keynes, *General Theory*, p. 215.
25. Ibid, p. 213.
26. Ibid, p. 214.
27. Ibid, p. 216.
28. Ibid, p. 217.
29. Ibid, p. 167. For a variant of this in terms of a contract for forward delivery, see also p. 222.

30. Keynes, 'Alternative Theories of the Rate of Interest', *CW*, XIV, p. 215. For other references to 'books on arithmetic', see 'The Theory of the Rate of Interest' and 'The General Theory of Employment', *CW*, XIV, pp. 101, 116.
31. Keynes, 'Alternative Theories of the Rate of Interest', *CW*, XIV, p. 206.
32. Keynes, letter to R. F. Harrod, *CW*, XIV, p. 85.
33. Keynes, 'Alternative Theories of the Rate of Interest', *CW*, XIV, p. 210.
34. Keynes, 'The Theory of the Rate of Interest', *CW*, XIV, p. 101.
35. Keynes, *General Theory*, p. 222.
36. No problem arises through a change in the relative values of the standards themselves, so long as the change in the value of the standard and the marginal efficiencies of the capital assets are measured in the same terms; and the same standard is applied to every capital asset.
37. Keynes, *General Theory*, p. 227.
38. Ibid, p. 228.
39. Ibid, p. 229.
40. Ibid.
41. Keynes, *General Theory*, pp. 230–1.
42. See, for example, R. F. Harrod, *Money* (London: Macmillan, 1969) p. 149. Current output is small in relation to the existing stock.
43. Keynes, *General Theory*, p. 230.
44. The same could not apply to unique works of art, the economic effects of the demand for which would be specific and not general. Also, in addition to cases in which a purchaser intends to acquire an artefact literally 'regardless of price', there are cases (for example, a picture sought by a gallery that will form part of a (secret) acquisitions list) in which the result of being outbid on one item will be to divert available funds to demand for items in the same class.

    A better example would be the effects, shown in spiralling interest rates, of the need of institutions to balance their books in a money market not directly supported by official smoothing operations; for instance, the London interbank market in sterling funds.
45. Keynes, *General Theory*, p. 233. Italics added.
46. One such reformer whose insights into the working of a monetary economy had greatly impressed Keynes was Silvio Gesell (1862–1930). Gesell had distinguished between the rate of interest on money and the marginal efficiency of capital and had argued that it is the former which sets a limit to the rate of growth of real capital. He had also seen that the significance of the money rate of interest stems from money's role as a means of storing wealth. He suggested that currency should only retain its legal-tender status if stamped periodically at a rate determined by the authorities. In Keynes's terms the rate would be 'roughly equal to the excess of the money rate of interest . . . over the marginal efficiency of capital corresponding to a rate of new investment compatible with full employment' (Keynes, *General Theory*, p. 357). Gesell, however, failed to provide a complete theory of interest in as much as he did not explain why the rate of interest is not governed by the yield on productive capital and did not show that the existence of a positive rate is due to liquidity preference.

12. The Conditions for Money as the Standard

1. Keynes, *General Theory*, pp. 223–4, 229.
2. Ibid, pp. 237, 239.
3. Ibid, pp. 240–1. Recall the calculation of an asset's total return, in Chapter 11 of present volume.
4. Keynes, *General Theory*, p. 241, n. 1.
5. In addition to the discussion and references given in Chapter 1 of the present volume, Milton Friedman's and Anna Schwartz's critique of alternative approaches to the definition of money, in 'The Definition of Money: Net Wealth and Neutrality as Criteria', *Journal of Money, Credit and Banking* (February 1969) pp. 1–14, is required reading.
6. Keynes, *General Theory*, p. 167, n. 1. In this respect it is helpful to think in terms of primary (legal-tender) money and secondary (bank-deposit) money components of the quantity of directly spendable resources. In the British context the distinction between current (demand) and deposit-account (time) deposits is insignificant. The most successful *a priori* demonstration that money should be defined as co-extensive with (clearing bank) deposits is provided by W. T. Newlyn, *Theory of Money* (Oxford: Clarendon Press, 1962). Though Friedman dismisses this approach, he reaches the same conclusion by an entirely different route: see Friedman and Schwartz, 'Definition of Money'.
7. Keynes, *General Theory*, p. 238.
8. Ibid, p. 237.
9. Ibid, pp. 236, 238.
10. Ibid, p. 239.
11. Keynes was subsequently able to modify his view in the light of empirical evidence that short-term changes in employment do not involve countercyclical movements in the real wage (see Chapter 22 of present volume). This modification would not, however, compromise his conclusions concerning the need for stability of the money wage.
12. Ibid, p. 239.

13. The Market Rate of Interest and its Economic Significance

1. Keynes, *General Theory*, p. 217.
2. J. R. Hicks, 'Mr. Keynes and the Classics', *Econometrica* (1937) reprinted in M. G. Mueller, *Readings in Macroeconomics*, 2nd edn (London: Holt, Rinehart & Winston, 1971) p. 143.
3. Keynes, *General Theory*, p. 218.
4. Ibid, p. 202.
5. Ibid, p. 207.
6. Ibid, pp. 202–3.
7. The Dalton experiment is of interest in a number of contexts, and is referred to again, in Chapter 16 of present volume.
8. Keynes, *General Theory*, p. 203.
9. Ibid, p. 356.
10. Ibid, p. 148.

11. Ibid, p. 144.
12. Ibid, pp. 208, 219.
13. Ibid, pp. 144–5.
14. See Keynes, *General Theory*, pp. 217–20.
15. Ibid, p. 219.
16. Ibid.
17. Ibid, p. 220.

14. The Keynesian Economic Problem and Its Solution

1. Keynes, *General Theory*, p. 249. See also p. 254.
2. Ibid, p. 250.
3. The full argument is in Keynes, *General Theory*, pp. 250–4.
4. Keynes, *General Theory*, p. 204.
5. Ibid.
6. Ibid, p. 253.
7. Ibid, p. 318.
8. Ibid, p. 314.
9. See ibid, pp. 315–17.
10. Ibid, p. 154.
11. Ibid, p. 156.
12. See, for example, B. S. Yamey, 'Commodity Futures Markets, Hedging and Speculation', in E. Victor Morgan *et al.*, *City Lights* (London: IEA, 1979) pp. 46–50.
13. Keynes, *General Theory*, p. 157.
14. Ibid, p. 151.
15. Ibid, p. 164.
16. Ibid, p. 316.
17. Ibid. Italics in original.
18. Due, that is, to the prevalence of factors influencing the prospective yield.
19. Keynes, *General Theory*, p. 164.
20. Ibid, p. 317.
21. Ibid, p. 320.
22. Ibid, p. 164.
23. See ibid, pp. 320–2.
24. Ibid, pp. 348–9, 382–3.
25. Ibid, p. 382.
26. Ibid, p. 383.
27. Ibid, p. 241.
28. Ibid, p. 352.
29. These influences were: 'the growth of population and invention, the opening up of new lands, the state of confidence and the frequency of war over the average of (say) each decade . . . taken in conjunction with the propensity to consume'. Keynes, *General Theory*, p. 307.
30. Keynes, *General Theory*, pp. 308–9.
31. He called this the 'most stable and least easily shifted element in our contemporary economy'. Ibid.

32. To get the importance of monetary policy in perspective we must bear in mind that: (a) monetary policy works via a change in the rate of interest; (b) the effectiveness of monetary policy in reducing the rate of interest is limited; (c) the rate of interest, as we have seen, takes second place to the marginal efficiency of capital in the determination of investment.
33. Keynes quotes (*General Theory*, p. 309) the nineteenth-century saying, quoted by Walter Bagehot, that 'John Bull cannot stand 2 per cent'. Nor, perhaps, we should add, in the light of the Dalton experiment, can he stand 2.5 per cent.
34. See the references in the *General Theory* to the state 'fixing' the rate (p. 378); and of 'steps being taken to ensure' etc. (p. 220). Note also the approval with which he speaks of 'wise' governments seeking to curb rates which tend to rise too high for the maximum social advantage 'by statute and custom and even by invoking the sanctions of the moral law' (p. 351).
35. Keynes, *General Theory*, p. 164. Italics added.
36. Ibid, p. 378.
37. Ibid.
38. Ibid, p. 164.
39. Ibid, p. 325.
40. Ibid, p. 377. Italics added.
41. See Keynes's note on the relationship between the two rates, in *CW*, XIV, pp. 156, 157.
42. Keynes, *General Theory*, pp. 220, 377.
43. Ibid, p. 325.
44. Ibid, p. 373. Keynes also refers to this point on pages 106, 219, 375, 377, 378, 379, 380.
45. Ibid, pp. 220, 377.
46. Ibid, p. 378.
47. Ibid, p. 375.
48. Ibid, p. 221.
49. Ibid, p. 375.
50. Ibid, p. 376; also p. 221.
51. Ibid, pp. 220–1.
52. Ibid, pp. 378–9.
53. Ibid.

15. The Consequences of Mr Keynes?

1. A claim made, for example, by H. G. Johnson in his *Further Essays in Monetary Economics* (London: Allen & Unwin, 1972) pp. 53–4.
2. J. M. Keynes, *A Treatise on Money* (London: Macmillan, 1930).
3. See C. H. Feinstein, *National Income, Expenditure and Output of the United Kingdom 1855–1965* (CUP, 1972) table 57. See also, J. Tomlinson, 'Unemployment Policy in the 1930s and 1980s', *The Three Banks Review* (September 1982) pp. 17–33.
4. W. Beveridge, *Full Employment in a Free Society* (London: Allen & Unwin, 1944) pp. 127–8.

5. See T. Wilson, 'Policy in War and Peace: the Recommendations of J. M. Keynes', in A. P. Thirlwall, *Keynes as a Policy Adviser*, (London: Macmillan, 1982) p. 59.
6. See M. Peston, *The British Economy: An Elementary Macroeconomic Perspective* (Deddington, Oxford: Philip Allan, 1982) pp. 53–5.
7. Ibid, pp. 59–60.
8. In particular, the quadrupling of the posted price of oil by the Organisation of Petroleum Exporting Countries (OPEC) at the end of 1973.
9. An empirical relationship employed as a tool of analysis and as a basis for policy formation, developed from the work of A. W. Phillips and predecessors. See A. W. Phillips, 'The Relation between Unemployment and the Rate of Change of Money Wage Rates in the United Kingdom, 1861–1957', *Economica* (November 1958) pp. 283–99.

16. Monetarism. I: The Counter-Revolution

1. These are: that the demand for money is a stable function of a few measurable variables; that changes in the quantity of money are the principal determinant of changes in the level of money income; that the division of the change in nominal income between output and prices can be analysed by means of the expectations-augmented Phillips curve; that the balance of payments and the exchange rate can best be analysed in monetary terms; that monetary policy should specify a growth rate for the money stock and avoid discretionary changes. A corollary of these propositions is the prior assumption that the economy is inherently stable and will if left to itself tend towards a long-run full-employment equilibrium.
2. See the useful survey by J. Burton, 'The Varieties of Monetarism and Their Policy Implications', *The Three Banks Review* (June 1982) pp. 14–31. Also of interest is J. E. Meade's demonstration of the difficulty of trying to assign a particular view to a particular school of thought. See J. E. Meade, 'Comment on the Papers by Professors Laidler and Tobin', *Economic Journal* (March 1981) pp. 49–55.
3. For an account of this methodology by which theories are assessed on their empirical performance rather than by the degree of realism of their assumptions, see M. Friedman, *Essays in Positive Economics* (Chicago: Chicago University Press, 1952) pp. 3–43.
4. M. Friedman, 'Comments on The Critics', *Journal of Political Economy* (Chicago, 1972) p. 908.
5. H. G. Johnson, *Further Essays in Monetary Economics* (London: Allen & Unwin, 1972) p. 57.
6. Ibid, p. 58.
7. M. Friedman, *The Counter Revolution in Monetary Theory*, Wincott Foundation Lecture 1970 (London: IEA, 1970) p. 10.
8. Ibid, p. 13.
9. Ibid, p. 17.
10. At least the quantity theory specified by Friedman, though a tradition of monetary effects being transmitted *indirectly*, via the rate of interest, stretches back to Henry Thornton's *Paper Credit* of 1802.

11. Friedman, 'Comments on The Critics', p. 923.
12. Ibid, p. 928.
13. Ibid, p. 942.
14. Ibid.
15. M. Friedman, *A Theoretical Framework for Monetary Analysis*, Occasional Paper 112 (New York: National Bureau of Economic Research, 1971) p. 27.
16. Friedman, 'Comments on The Critics', p. 910.
17. Ibid, p. 944.
18. Ibid, p. 918.
19. Ibid.
20. Ibid, p. 948.
21. Ibid, p. 944.
22. Ibid, p. 948.
23. Ibid, pp. 925–6.
24. Ibid, pp. 941–2.
25. Keynes, *General Theory*, p. 236: quoted in Friedman, 'Comments on The Critics', p. 925.
26. Friedman, 'Comments on The Critics', p. 944.
27. M. Friedman, 'The Quantity Theory of Money: A Restatement', in M. Friedman (ed.), *Studies in the Quantity Theory of Money* (Chicago: UCP, 1956) pp. 3–21.

    Patinkin's criticism was contained in D. Patinkin, 'The Chicago Tradition, The Quantity Theory and Friedman', *The Journal of Money, Credit and Banking* (1969) pp. 46–70.
28. Friedman, 'Comments on The Critics', pp. 944–5.
29. Ibid, p. 925. Italics added.
30. That this is a generally accepted monetarist view, see D. Laidler, 'Monetarism: An Interpretation and An Assessment', *Economic Journal* (March 1981) p. 8.
31. Versions of the classical quantity theory envisage changes in the quantity of money as taking effect either *directly*, in the goods market, or *indirectly*, via a movement in the market rate of interest relative to the return on investment.
32. That Friedman has come to acknowledge that 'monetarism ... has benefited much from Keynes's work' and, for example, that his transmission mechanism incorporates 'the liquidity effect stressed by Keynes', goes some way to meet Patinkin's assertion that his framework is Keynesian; but on the question of the relationship of Friedman's work to particular classical theories and to the 'oral tradition' in monetary economics at Chicago, the reader is referred to Patkinkin, 'The Chicago Tradition'; and the papers by Patinkin and Friedman in *Journal of Political Economy* (1972).
33. Friedman, 'Comments on The Critics', p. 919.
34. Ibid, pp. 942–3.
35. Keynes, *General Theory*, pp. 200–1.
36. Johnson, *Further Essays in Monetary Economics*, p. 63. Italics added.
37. D. Laidler, *The Demand for Money* 2nd edn (New York: Dun-Donnelley, 1977) p. 68.

38. That is, the *LM* curve tends increasingly to the horizontal and wealth is increasingly held in liquid form. If monetary policy attempts to *raise* the market rate beyond the upper limit, the *LM* curves tends increasingly to the vertical and liquidity preference falls towards zero in anticipation of certain capital gains.
39. See Keynes, *General Theory*, pp. 202–4, esp. 204.
40. See G. A. Fletcher, *The Discount Houses in London: Principles, Operations and Change* (London: Macmillan, 1976) p. 67; J. C. R. Dow, *The Management of the British Economy 1945–60* (Cambridge: Cambridge University Press, 1968) pp. 223–7.
41. Friedman, *The Counter Revolution in Monetary Theory*, p. 11. Italics added.
42. Ibid.
43. See, for example, Keynes, *General Theory*, p. 173, para. 1.

17. Monetarism. II: Monetarism, Keynes and the 'Keynesians'

1. D. Laidler, 'Monetarism: An Interpretation and an Assessment', *Economic Journal* (March 1981) p. 3. and references cited.
2. Laidler, *The Demand for Money*, pp. 68–9.
3. See D. Patinkin, 'Friedman on the Quantity Theory and Keynesian Economics', *Journal of Political Economy* (Sept.–Oct. 1972) p. 886; also *Anticipations of the General Theory*? (Oxford: Blackwell, 1982).
4. M. Friedman, 'Comments on The Critics, *Journal of Political Economy* (Chicago, 1972).
5. M. Friedman, *The Counter Revolution in Monetary Theory* (London: IEA, 1970) p. 24.
6. 'Since we regarded prices as flexible, though not "perfectly" flexible, it was natural for us to interpret the transmission mechanism in terms of relative price adjustments over a broad area rather than in terms of narrowly defined interest rates'. M. Friedman, *A Theoretical Framework for Monetary Analysis*, Occasional Paper 112 (New York: NBER, 1971) pp. 27–9.
7. Laidler, 'Monetarism', p. 5.
8. Friedman, 'Comments on The Critics', pp. 923–4.
9. Ibid, p. 925.
10. Also, as an illustration of the gulf between the presuppositions of Keynesians and neo-classicists, we have Friedman's criticism of P. Davidson that, 'He appears to *start* from the proposition that there does not exist a long-run equilibrium position characterised by full employment.' To Friedman this is to stand theory on its head. Friedman, 'Comments on The Critics', p. 929.
11. Laidler, 'Monetarism', p. 2.
12. Friedman, 'Comments on The Critics', p. 910.
13. Laidler, 'Monetarism', p. 2, plus references he cites.
14. Ibid, p. 3.
15. Friedman, 'Comments on The Critics', p. 944. The reference is to J. M. Keynes, *A Tract on Monetary Reform* (London: Macmillan, 1923) p. 51.
16. See Friedman, 'Comments on the Critics', pp. 916–18.

17. James Tobin, 'The Monetarist Counter-Revolution Today – An Appraisal' *Economic Journal* (March 1981) p. 34.
18. See Friedman, 'Comments on The Critics', pp. 916–17.
19. Keynes, *General Theory*, p. 200.
20. Laidler, 'Monetarism', p. 25.
21. Ibid, p. 7.
22. N. Kaldor, *The Scourge of Monetarism* (Oxford: Oxford University Press, 1982). See the penetrating review by R. L. Harrington: 'Monetarisms': Real and Imaginary – A Review Article', *Manchester School* (March 1983) pp. 63–71.
23. Laidler, 'Monetarism', p. 9.

18. Monetarism. III: Rational Expectations

1. H. G. Johnson, *Further Essays in Monetary Economics* (London: Allen & Unwin, 1972) pp. 66–7.
2. D. Laidler, 'Monetarism: An Interpretation and an Assessment', *Economic Journal* (March 1981) p. 8. The following paragraphs lean heavily on Laidler's authoritative survey and interpretation.
3. An approach the origins of which go back to J. F. Muth, 'Rational Expectations and the Theory of Price Movements', *Econometrica* (July 1961) pp. 315–35. However, its modern application in macroeconomics theory and policy derives from the work especially of R. E. Lucas in the 1970s. B. Kantor, 'Rational Expectations and Economic Thought', *Journal of Economic Literature* (Dec. 1979) has the principal references.
4. J. Burton, 'The Varieties of Monetarism and Their Policy Implications', *Three Banks Review* (June 1982) p. 20.
5. L. M. Lachmann, *Capital and its Structure*, 2nd edn (Kansas City: Sheed Andrews & McMeel Inc., 1978) p. 68.
6. Kantor, 'Rational Expectations', p. 1431.
7. Ibid. Italics added.
8. G. L. S. Shackle, 'Keynes and Today's Establishment in Economic Theory: A View', *Journal of Economic Literature* (June 1973) p. 516. 'ERNIE' is the Electronic Random Number Indicating Equipment which chooses winning Premium Bond numbers.
9. Keynes, 'The General Theory of Employment', *Quarterly Journal of Economics* (Feb. 1937), in *CW*, XIV, p. 114.
10. Ibid.
11. Reported in Kantor, 'Rational Expectations', p. 1430.
12. R. E. Lucas, 'Understanding Business Cycles', *Journal of Monetary Economics* (Supplement 1977) p. 15.
13. G. L. S. Shackle, 'F. A. Hayek, 1899–', in D. P. O'Brien and J. R. Presley (eds), *Pioneers of Modern Economics in Britain* (London: Macmillan, 1981) p. 240.
14. Lucas, 'Understanding Business Cycles', p. 15. Italics added.
15. See, for example, Laidler, 'Monetarism', pp. 11–15; James Tobin, 'The Monetarist Counter-Revolution Today – An Appraisal', *Economic Journal* (March 1981) pp. 36–38; Kantor, 'Rational Expectations', pp. 1433–6.

16. See Chapter 22 of present volume.
17. Laidler, 'Monetarism', p. 13.
18. Tobin, 'Monetarist Counter-Revolution', p. 35.
19. See R. Bootle, 'How Important Is It To Defeat Inflation – The Evidence', *The Three Banks Review* (Dec. 1981).
20. F. H. Hahn, *Money and Inflation* (Oxford: Blackwell, 1982) pp. 73–4.
21. D. Higham and J. Tomlinson, 'Why Do Governments Worry About Inflation?', *National Westminster Bank Quarterly Review* (May 1982) pp. 4–7.
22. M. Friedman, 'Inflation and Unemployment', *Journal of Political Economy*, Vol. 85, no. 3 (Chicago: Chicago University Press, 1977) pp. 466–7.
23. Ibid.
24. Higham and Tomlinson, 'Why Do Governments Worry About Inflation?', p. 6.
25. D. Laidler and N. Rowe, 'Georg Simmel's Philosophy of Money: A Review Article for Economists', *Journal of Economic Literature* (March 1980) p. 101.
26. Ibid, p. 102.

19. The Austrians. I: Tenets of the Faith

1. The Austrian position was recently confirmed by Hayek, in 'The Keynes Centenary: The Austrian Critique', *The Economist* (11–17 June 1983) p. 46. For a curious example of a lapse from this position, see F. A. Hayek, *New Studies in Philosophy, Politics, Economics and the History of Ideas* (London: Routledge & Kegan Paul, 1978) p. 213, para. 1.
2. The *catallaxy* is the market order as *catallactics* refers to the theory of the market order. Both words are derived from 'the Greek verb *Katallatein* (or *Katallassein*) which significantly means not only "to exchange" but also "to receive into the community" and "to turn from enemy into friend"'. See Hayek, *New Studies*, p. 90.
3. Again, however, Hayek does allow the state to breach this apparent absolutism by payments to individuals who cannot survive under the market system. See Hayek, *New Studies*, p. 92.
4. Even to the extent of not seeking to impose rules to discourage practices in restraint of trade ('anti-trust' legislation and the like), on the grounds that the costs in terms of market efficiency of government intervention are likely to be greater than the benefits. A qualification with regard to monetary policy is, however, introduced later in this present volume.

20. The Austrians. II: Hayek and the Trade Cycle

1. For the correct working of the process by means of movements in relative prices we must assume that *initially* the supply is maintained, being based upon work done in the past, but eventually it will fall off as factors are drawn away and consumption goods prices will rise. See J. R.

Hicks, 'The Hayek Story', in *Critical Essays in Monetary Theory* (Oxford: Clarendon Press, 1967) pp. 211–12.
2. It is, therefore, because capital goods are imperfectly mobile that the outcome can be said to be marked by 'capital scarcity'.
3. To attempt to reduce unemployment by stimulating consumption demand can only exacerbate the problem given the existing shortfall in consumption goods output.
4. See F. A. Hayek, *New Studies in Philosophy, Politics, Economics and the History of Ideas* (London: Routledge & Kegan Paul, 1978) p. 230; after (Sir) Nicholas Kaldor, formerly Keynes's junior colleague at Cambridge. Kaldor's influence on the formation of post-war employment policy through, for example, his work with Sir William (Lord) Beveridge, will be mentioned again, in Chapter 23 of present volume.
5. F. A. Hayek, 'The Austrian Critique', *The Economist* (June 1983) p. 45.
6. 'It was against the sort of view represented by Law that Richard Cantillon and David Hume began the development of modern monetary theory.' See Hayek, *New Studies*, pp. 229–31.
7. See, for example, Hayek, *New Studies*, pp. 218, 230–1; and 'The Austrian Critique', pp. 45–6.
8. See Hayek, *New Studies*, p. 212.
9. Ibid, p. 199.
10. Ibid, p. 197.
11. N. P. Barry, *Hayek's Social and Economic Philosophy* (London: Macmillan, 1979) p. 168. The references to Hayek's crucial omission are on pages 155, 167, 170.
12. Hayek, *New Studies*, pp. 219, 283–4; 'The Austrian Critique', p. 47.
13. Letter to Hawtrey, June 1932, in Keynes, *CW*, XIII, p. 172.
14. Hayek, *New Studies*, p. 284.
15. Recall Chapter 4 of present volume; and see again the letter to Lloyd George of 1935, in Keynes, *CW*, XIII, pp. 492–3.
16. This is *not* a defect of Barry, who recognises that the controversy is of historical interest only, and who attempts to isolate some key areas for discussion between Hayek and Keynes (of the *General Theory*). See Barry, *Hayek's Social and Economic Philosophy* pp. 155, 167–74.
17. F. Machlup (ed.), *Essays on Hayek* (London: Routledge & Kegan Paul, 1977).
18. Hicks, 'The Hayek Story', p. 203, quoted in Machlup, *Essays on Hayek*, p. 18.
19. W. F. Buckley, Jr, in Machlup, *Essays on Hayek*, p. 96.
20. Hicks, 'The Hayek Story', in *Critical Essays in Monetary Theory*, p. 204.
21. Ibid, pp. 210–11. Hicks comes to this conclusion because of the lack of justification given by Hayek for the question he is asking, which is, 'what happens to quantities in a Wicksellian cumulative process?' On strict assumptions the answer should be nothing, and it is his failure to discover satisfactory lags sufficient to sustain the process postulated by Hayek that leads Hicks to his reinterpretation. See Hicks, pp. 205–10.
22. The sequence of the argument is in Hicks, 'The Hayek Story', pp. 211–15.
23. Ibid, p. 213.

24. See, for example, Machlup, *Essays on Hayek*, p. 26; Barry, *Hayek's Social and Economic Philosophy*, pp. 154–5, 164ff; Hicks, 'The Hayek Story', p. 210.
25. Hicks, 'The Hayek Story', p. 214.
26. Hayek, 'The Austrian Critique', p. 48.
27. In his use of Austrian capital theory as a basis for his trade cycle, Hayek also overlooks the influence of the *durability* of existing capital as a constraint on investment. He also omits the role of *expectations* in the relationship between investment and saving. Finally, he treats the economic system as *hydraulic*, with the flow of money stimulating the system to activity and abstracting from the psychology of economic behaviour. See G.L.S. Shackle, 'F.A. Hayek, 1899–', in D. P. O'Brien and J. R. Presley (eds), *Pioneers of Modern Economics in Britain* (London: Macmillan, 1981) pp. 239–42.
28. Shackle, in *Pioneers of Modern Economics in Britain*, p. 243.
29. Ibid, p. 242.
30. Ibid, p. 250.
31. Ibid, p. 249.
32. For example, though the central concern is to demonstrate the relationship between particular elements of input and output, Hayek does not answer the prior question of the *principle* upon which the relationship is to be established. Also, Hayek's stages-of-production, linear, approach whereby inputs are added sequentially to the production process, ignores the universal interdependence of economic activity which is exemplified by the input-output table.
33. D. Laidler and N. Rowe, 'Georg Simmel's Philosophy of Money: A Review Article for Economists', *Journal of Economic Literature* (March 1980) pp. 102, 103. See also Chapter 22 in present volume.
34. Though Keynes does make the entirely reasonable observation that the only valid object of economic activity is consumption. See Keynes, *General Theory*, pp. 104, 211.
35. T. Wilson, 'Policy in War and Peace: The Recommendations of J. M. Keynes', in A. P. Thirlwall (ed.), *Keynes as a Policy Adviser* (London: Macmillan, 1982) p. 48.
36. J. K. Galbraith, *Money* (London: Penguin, 1976) p. 229.
37. J. M. Keynes, 'The Pure Theory of Money. A Reply to Dr. Hayek', *Economica* (Nov. 1931), in *CW*, XIII, p. 252.
38. Ibid, p. 253.
39. F. A. Hayek, *New Studies in Philosophy, Politics, Economics and the History of Ideas* (London: Routledge & Kegan Paul , 1978) p. 211.
40. See Hayek, *New Studies*, pp. 193, 206, 210, 211.
41. Hayek, *New Studies*, p. 205.

21. The Austrians. III: Two Routes to Serfdom

1. The most accessible account is in C. K. Rowley, 'Liberalism and Collective Choice', *National Westminister Bank Quarterly Review*, (May 1979) pp. 11–22.

2. K. J. Arrow, *Social Choice and Individual Values*, 2nd edn (Yale University Press) 1970.
3. F. A. Hayek, *The Road to Serfdom* (London: Routledge & Kegan Paul 1944).
4. Keynes, *General Theory*, p. 380.
5. W. Breit and R. L. Ransom, *The Academic Scribblers*, revd edn (Chicago: Dryden Press, 1982) p. 209.
6. F. A. Hayek, 'The Austrian Critique', *The Economist* (June 1983) p. 48.
7. J. K. Galbraith, *Money* (London: Pelican, 1976) pp. 237, 238. See also Galbraith's reference to remarks by Joan Robinson.
8. Keynes, *General Theory*, p. 381.
9. Keynes, *General Theory*, in *CW*, VII, p. xxvi.
10. Ibid.
11. For an explicit denial that Nazi economic policy was Keynesian, see R. J. Overy, *The Nazi Economic Recovery 1932–1938* (London: Macmillan for the Economic History Society, 1982).
12. W. Carr, 'Keynes and the Treaty of Versailles', in A. P. Thirlwall (ed.), *Keynes as a Policy Adviser* (London: Macmillan, 1982) p. 100.
13. F. A. Hayek, *New Studies, in Philosophy, Politics, Economics and the History of Ideas* (London: Routledge & Kegan Paul, 1978) pp. 193, 196, 197–8, 203, 205.
14. G. Simmel, *The Philosophy of Money* (1900); English trans. (London: Routledge & Kegan Paul, 1978).
15. H. G. Wells, *Outline of History* (London: Cassell, 1920) p. 233.
16. See D. Laidler and N. Rowe, 'Georg Simmel's Philosophy of Money: A Review Article for Economists', *Journal of Economic Literature* (March 1980) p. 102.
17. S. H. Frankel, *Money: Two Philosophies* (Oxford: Blackwell, 1977).
18. Ibid, p. 75.
19. Ibid, p. 77.
20. Ibid, p. 92.
21. Frankel does mention Keynes's own conception of monetary policy, as operating via changes in the rate of interest, but curiously does not pursue this most important point.
22. N. P. Barry, 'Austrian Economics on Money and Society', *National Westminster Bank Quarterly Review* (May 1981) p. 27.
23. Frankel, *Money: Two Philosophies*, pp. 81, 82.
24. Keynes, *General Theory*, p. 378.
25. Frankel, *Money: Two Philosophies*, p. 77.
26. Ibid, p. 75.
27. All quotations, Frankel, *Money: Two Philosophies*, p. 48.
28. Ibid.
29. C. A. E. Goodhart, *Money, Information and Uncertainty* (London: Macmillan, 1975) pp. 9–10.
30. Frankel, *Money: Two Philosophies*, p. 51.

22. Employment Policy

1. S. H. Frankel, *Money: Two Philosophies* (Oxford: Blackwell, 1977) p. 77.
2. Ibid, p. 72.
3. Ibid, pp. 71–2.
4. Keynes, *General Theory*, pp. 267–9.
5. This definition of full employment will be assumed throughout.
6. If competition is imperfect, the argument must be revised to take account of the downward-sloping demand curve for the product, though fundamental principles are not affected.
7. See Keynes, *General Theory*, ch. 2; especially pp. 17–18: 'the marginal product in the wage-good industries (which governs real wages) necessarily diminishes as employment is increased [so that] . . . *any* means of increasing employment must lead at the same time to a diminution of the marginal product and hence of the rate of wages measured in terms of this product'.
8. Keynes, *General Theory*, pp. 15–16.
9. Ibid, p. 28.
10. See ibid, p. 30.
11. Ibid, p. 289.
12. Ibid, pp. 260–2, 269.
13. A measure of the quantity of employment. The wage unit is equal to the money wage payable to a labour unit, which represents an hour's employment of ordinary labour.
14. Keynes, *General Theory*, pp. 260–1.
15. Ibid, p. 266. To concentrate attention on the monetary effects of a fall in money wages Keynes assumes a closed economy; but notes that in an open economy a fall in money wages relative to wages abroad will stimulate investment via an increase in the balance of trade. Keynes, *General Theory*, pp. 262–3.
16. Retaining sufficient flexibility to facilitate labour mobility and so increase efficiency.
17. Keynes refers explicity to collateral (money) wage-price reductions in the *General Theory*, pp. 262, 263, 264, 266; and to money wage stability as a condition for price stability on pages 268, 270 and 271.
18. Keynes, *General Theory*, pp. 270–1.
19. Or at least in the price level of 'wage goods': A. C. Pigou's term, borrowed by Keynes, for the 'goods upon the price of which the utility of the money-wage depends'. See Keynes, *General Theory*, p. 7.
20. Keynes, *General Theory*, p. 17, n. 1.
21. Ibid, p. 301.
22. Ibid, p. 81.
23. Ibid, pp. 14–15.
24. Ibid.
25. See, for example, J. Tobin, 'Inflation and Unemployment', *American Economic Review* (March 1972) pp. 1–8; J. Trevithick, 'Money Wage Inflexibility and the Keynesian Labour Supply Function', *Economic Journal* (June 1976) pp. 327–32.

26. J. Trevithick, 'Money Wage Inflexibility', p. 328.
27. J. T. Addison and J. Burton, 'Keynes's Analysis of Wages and Unemployment Revisited', *The Manchester School* (March, 1982) p. 9.
28. Ibid, pp. 12–13.
29. See, for example, Keynes, *General Theory*, pp. 9, 13–15, 264, 301, 303.
30. A. Leijonhufvud, *On Keynesian Economics and the Economics of Keynes* (New York: OUP, 1968) p. 97. It is interesting to note that Leijonhufvud's criticism by way of comparison with the consumption function is reversed in the later criticism by H. Grossman of Leijonhufvud's own acceptance of R. W. Clower's reinterpretation of the consumption function. See H. Grossman, 'Was Keynes a "Keynesian", A Review Article', *Journal of Economic Literature* (1972) pp. 26–30.
31. Keynes, *General Theory*, p. 14. Italics in original.
32. Ibid, p. 17.
33. Ibid, p. 271.
34. See p. 91 of present volume.
35. Keynes, *General Theory*, p. 97. Italics added.
36. C. A. E. Goodhart, 'The Role, Functions and Definition of Money', in *Microeconomic Foundations of Macroeconomics*, p. 222. Labour mobility and wage flexibility will also be reduced by the reluctance of employers to replace established work-teams with untrained entrants and by the cost to workers of moving their families to a new locality.
37. Keynes, *General Theory*, p. 269.
38. Ibid, p. 291.
39. The question raised by Addison and Burton, 'Keynes's Analysis', p. 18. Furthermore, to epitomise as 'transactions costs', as they suggest (pp. 18–19), the difficulties of bringing about a universal reduction of money wages for what *in effect* would be its sole useful purpose – that is to reduce the rate of interest to the level consistent with full employment without at the same time destabilising entrepreneurial expectations – seems barely adequate.
40. By the Pigou Effect an increase in real money balances brought about by a general price deflation leads directly to increased consumption expenditures.
41. This is a composite quotation taken from passages on pages 291, 303–4 of the *General Theory* that make the same point.
42. J. M. Keynes, 'Relative Movements of Real Wages and Output', *Economic Journal* (March 1939) pp. 34–51.

23. The Keynesian Revolution in Context

1. F. A. Hayek, *New Studies in Philosophy, Politics, Economics and the History of Ideas* (London: Routledge & Kegan Paul, 1978) pp. 199, 200.
2. H. G. Johnson, *Further Essays in Monetary Economics* (London: Allen & Unwin, 1972) p. 57. Generally dismissive, Johnson has described Keynes's vision of the stationary-state role of the entrepreneur as a 'Victorian *fin-de-siècle* intellectual period piece'. See H. G. Johnson, 'Keynes and the Developing World', in R. Skidelsky (ed.) *The End of the*

Keynesian Era: Essays on the Disintegration of the Keynesian Political Economy (London: Macmillan, 1977) pp. 93–4.
3. Keynes, *General Theory*, pp. 380, 381.
4. Skidelsky, *End of the Keynesian Era*, pp. viii–ix.
5. It answers, for example, S. H. Frankel's charge that the economy was to be made to pursue goals that *Keynes* thought were appropriate for it. See Frankel, *Money: Two Philosophies* (Oxford: Blackwell, 1977) pp. 6, 84.
6. D. E. Moggridge, *Keynes* 2nd edn (London: Macmillan, 1980) p. 32. The reference is to Keynes, *General Theory*, p. 20n. See also the reference to Keynes, *CW*, XIV, p. 259.
7. Lord Robbins, *Autobiography of an Economist* (London: Macmillan, 1971) p. 153. See also pages 133 and, in particular, 152–5.
8. The proposals were drawn up by (Sir) Harold Nicolson. His chagrin on hearing of Churchill's decision is recorded in his diary: 'all those days of work have led to nothing'. See N. Nicolson (ed.), *Harold Nicolson: Diaries and Letters 1939–1945* (London: Collins, 1967) p. 139. See also pages 101, 102, 130, 143–4, which refer to the purpose and content of the proposals.
9. Sir George Clark, *English History: A Survey* (Oxford: Clarendon Press, 1971) p. 533.
10. *Employment Policy*, Cmd 6520 (London: HMSO, May 1944).
11. W. Beveridge, *Full Employment in a Free Society* (London: Allen & Unwin, 1944). It is interesting that this very 'moral' document made the achievement of full employment in a free society conditional on the maintenance of a proper attitude of restraint on the part of wage negotiators and price setters.
12. Stuart Holland, 'Keynes and the Socialists', in Skidelsky, *The End of the Keynesian Era*, p. 67.
13. Argued by M. Peston, *The British Economy: An Elementary Macroeconomic Perspective* (Deddington, Oxford: Philip Allan, 1982) pp. 67–8. Peston points out that the rise in the natural rate may also be associated with structural changes that were taking place.
14. Under the reforms of Competition & Credit Control, 1971. For an account, see G. A. Fletcher, *The Discount Houses in London: Principles, Operations and Change* (London: Macmillan, 1976) chapters 13, 14.
15. The policy of (Lord) Anthony Barber, Chancellor of the Exchequer 1970–4.
16. For example, Keynes, *General Theory*, pp. 29–30; also 104–5.
17. V. Chick, *Macroeconomics After Keynes: A Reconsideration of the General Theory* (Oxford: Philip Allan, 1983) p. 338.
18. Chick hazards a guess at 1972 as the year in which inflation ceased to be helpful. Chick, *Macroeconomics After Keynes*, p. 348.
19. Chick, *Macroeconomics after Keynes*, p. 343.
20. S. Brittan, 'Can Democracy Manage an Economy', in Skidelsky, *End of the Keynesian Era*, p. 41.
21. R. Skidelsky, 'The Political Meaning of the Keynesian Revolution', in Skidelsky, *End of the Keynesian Era*, p. 38.
22. Brittan, in Skidelsky, *End of the Keynesian Era*, p. 46.

23. Samuel H. Beer, *Britain Against Itself: The Political Contradictions of Collectivism* (London: Faber & Faber, 1982).
24. Ibid, p. 15.
25. Ibid, p. 8.
26. It is to be distinguished from the 'old group politics' which refers to the economic groups produced by industrialisation, which came to exert political power, for example, in the formation of the Labour Party.
27. Beer, *Britain Against Itself*, p. 17.
28. Ibid, p. 39.
29. A generally held conclusion, recently given support in Michael D. Bordo and Anna J. Schwartz (eds), *A Retrospective on the Classical Gold Standard, 1821–1931* (Chicago & London: The University of Chicago Press, 1984) pp. 16–20. As an alternative, Hayek has argued for free choice in currencies for transactors: *New Studies*, pp. 223–9.
30. In Skidelsky (ed.), *The End of the Keynesian Era*.
31. Abandonment of a target for the broad, sterling M3, measure of the money stock was formally announced in November 1985.

24. In Conclusion

1. A. J. Brown, in A. P. Thirlwall, *Keynes as a Policy Adviser*, p. 69.

Index

In general, subjects included in the Index are those that are discussed in the main text. Other references to sources can be found in the Notes and References (pp. 307–307–35).

MIX
Papier aus verantwortungsvollen Quellen
Paper from responsible sources
FSC® C105338

FSC
www.fsc.org

If you have any concerns about our products,
you can contact us on
ProductSafety@springernature.com

In case Publisher is established outside the EU,
the EU authorized representative is:
Springer Nature Customer Service Center GmbH
Europaplatz 3, 69115 Heidelberg, Germany

Printed by Libri Plureos GmbH
in Hamburg, Germany